DAVID HUME'S
POLITICAL ESSAYS

The Library of Liberal Arts
OSKAR PIEST, FOUNDER

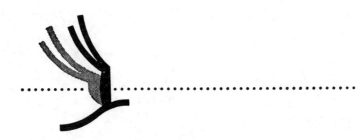

DAVID HUME'S
POLITICAL ESSAYS

Edited, with an Introduction, by
CHARLES W. HENDEL

The Library of Liberal Arts
published by
THE BOBBS-MERRILL COMPANY, INC.
INDIANAPOLIS · NEW YORK

David Hume: 1711-1776

COPYRIGHT © 1953

THE LIBERAL ARTS PRESS, INC.

A DIVISION OF THE BOBBS-MERRILL COMPANY, INC.

Printed in the United States of America

Library of Congress Catalog Card Number 54-6

ISBN 0-672-51014-6
ISBN 0-672-60198-2 (pbk)
Sixth Printing

CONTENTS
. . . .

THE POLITICAL ESSAYS

INTRODUCTION

I. IMPORTANCE OF THE POLITICAL ESSAYS

In *My Own Life,* one of the briefest of autobiographies, told in less than eight pages, David Hume speaks of his *Political Discourses* (1752) as "the only work of mine that was successful on the first publication. It was well received abroad and at home." That book was a second volume of *Essays Moral and Political,* the first of which had appeared ten years earlier in 1742, at which time also Hume says, "the work was favorably received and soon made me entirely forget my former disappointment." The "disappointment" had been over his first philosophical work, a large book in three volumes, *The Treatise of Human Nature,* "which fell dead born from the press." The favor shown the *Essays* during the years immediately after that failure revived Hume's spirits, however, and he kept writing more essays, adding them as successive editions were published. He also attempted to make the first volume of the ill-fated *Treatise* more palatable by presenting it likewise in the briefer essay form under the title *Philosophical Essays Concerning the Human Understanding* (1748)—advertising it, too, as written "by the author of the *Essays Moral and Political.*" The advertisement evidently had some of its intended effect, since a second edition was necessary in 1751. It was clear to Hume himself that his moral and political essays were "carrying," so to speak, his philosophical writings, and he proceeded to write the whole new series, which came out in 1752 under the title *Political Discourses* and was an instant success.

Hume was grateful for that recognition, and apparently he was inspired by it. *My Own Life* goes on to tell how he at once began work in an entirely new field, as a sequel to those political writings. For the year 1752 he obtained the post of librarian of the Faculty of Advocates in Edinburgh, where he had a large library at his disposal and began work upon a *History of*

England. There is a close and important connection between the *History* and the political essays.

But the story of the *History* was not one of success, though Hume could not complain of not being noticed, as had been the case of his *Treatise* years before. In 1754 the first volume of the *History* appeared, dealing with the reigns of James I and Charles I; the second volume came out in 1756, treating of the period up to the Revolution of 1688. Then Hume worked backward, doing the history of the House of Tudor in 1759 and finishing in 1761 with the early beginnings of England. There had been much "clamor" about the history of the Stuarts (for he "had presumed to shed a generous tear for the fate of Charles I and the Earl of Strafford"), a little less clamor about that of the Tudors, and the story of the remoter period alone met with "tolerable, and but tolerable success." This was the reception of the *History* in Britain.

Abroad Hume's name had already been made as a political thinker, so that the Earl of Hertford in Paris, whom Hume did not know in the least, suddenly asked in 1763 that he come and serve as secretary to the Embassy. At first Hume had shied away from "the great" and from the "gay company of Paris," but eventually he accepted, and there he spent three years of "real satisfaction" in that society of "sensible, knowing, and polite" people. He enjoyed fame at last. He was even tempted to make Paris his home, but finally returned to Edinburgh in the hope of "enjoying long my ease, and of seeing the increase of my reputation."

Hume had seven years in which to indulge this hope. His "ease" was the leisure a philosopher would enjoy. "I possess the same ardor as ever in study, and the same gaiety in company," he writes in *My Own Life,* which he humorously calls "this funeral oration of myself," lapsing purposely into the past tense in speaking of himself, for he knew then that he had but a short time to live. He confesses his "love of literary fame" and tells that he has had some gratification in spite of the "disappointments." And "I see many symptoms of my literary reputation's breaking out at last with additional lustre." But Hume was not destined to see the full measure of his glory, for he died in a few months, on August 25, 1776, at the age of sixty-five. His "dearest friend," Adam Smith, supplements the autobiography with a letter telling how cheerful and Socratic David Hume had been in those last days.

The picture Hume gives of himself is quite unfamiliar to present-day students of philosophy. We commonly regard him as having been the most important sceptic in modern philosophy and find it hard to believe that such a reputation as he enjoyed in his lifetime came almost exclusively through his *Essays,* and particularly the political essays. If that was actually his only title to renown, then we begin to understand why Hume continually hoped for more attention to his writings. This was not an inordinate craving for fame unbecoming to the philosopher. Indeed, it was the proper desert of the philosopher that his "discoveries" in thought should be recognized and evaluated. Hume sought a response from others to the challenge of the essential questions which he had raised about reasoning in terms of cause and effect, and which he confessed he could not satisfactorily solve, so that he had honestly to avow himself a philosophical sceptic. It was enough for most of his contemporaries to read that confession of scepticism—they were little interested in the reason for it. As Hume said in letters on this subject: "The arguments have been laid before the world, and by some philosophical minds have been attended to"; [1] but the answer, it seemed, would have to be given eventually by distant "posterity." [2] We know these to have been prophetic words, since Immanuel Kant in far off Königsgerg, in East Prussia, perceived at last the ground as well as the significance of Hume's problems and thereupon focused all philosophy on the task of meeting Hume's scepticism. Since then we have honored Hume as a great philosopher in the realm of knowledge.

It is worth noting, incidentally, that Hume himself tried in more than one way to bring his essential question concerning reason and knowledge to the notice of the philosophical world

---

[1] See J. H. Burton, *Life and Correspondence of David Hume,* 2 vols. (Edinburgh, William Tait, 1846), Vol. I, Ch. I, p. 98.

[2] See J. Y. T. Greig, editor, *The Letters of David Hume* (Oxford, Clarendon Press, 1932), Vol. II, pp. 252, 322.

and that he did not simply trust to posterity to rediscover it. At the very time that he was writing the *Political Discourses,* he began work (1751) on an entirely new piece called *Dialogues Concerning Natural Religion.* For ten years, while he was working on the *History of England,* he kept improving and correcting his argument in that work. He thought so much of it that he made provision in his will for its publication posthumously and was especially concerned that either Adam Smith or his friend, the publisher William Strahan, should bring it out after his death.[3] But there was risk involved in such a publication. Aside from the danger of public odium in view of the book's critical examination of religion, there was the consideration mentioned in his *History,* where Hume commented on the attempts of James I and the Puritans to reason speculatively about religion at a time of great excitement over the religious issues:

The Puritans were here so unreasonable as to complain of a partial and unfair management of the dispute, as if the search after truth were in any degree the object of such conferences, and a candid indifference, so rare even among private inquirers in *philosophical* questions, could ever be expected among princes and prelates in a theological controversy.[4]

It is possible that this observation came from his reflection on his own problem about the *Dialogues* rather than from his study of history. However that may be, it seems that, notwithstanding the literary perfection of the *Dialogues,* Hume was not depending upon them after all to enlighten the world about the meaning of his scepticism. And the only hope of an appreciation of his philosophy by "the intellectual world" lay, therefore, in some reflex working of the essays upon the mind of his own generation. This was one reason why the political and moral essays were so important for Hume himself.

We should be making a great mistake, however, if we were to underestimate the intrinsic value of the political writings by

[3] See C. W. Hendel, *Studies in the Philosophy of David Hume* (Princeton, N. J., Princeton University Press, 1925), pp. 13–19, 305 ff.

[4] *History of England* (New York, Harper and Brothers), Vol. IV, Ch. XLV, p. 387.

thinking of them only as useful external aids to effect the recognition of Hume's "real" philosophical achievement. For they were an essential part of Hume's achievement in philosophy. When honor was paid him on their account, he did not brush it aside deprecatingly as something undeserved and unworthy of himself. It is necessary to remember that his unhappy *Treatise of Human Nature* had a subtitle, viz., *Being an Attempt to Apply the Experimental Method of Reasoning to Moral Subjects*. In the very Introduction he had affiliated himself with a number of writers "who have begun to put the science of man on a new footing, and have engaged the attention and excited the curiosity of the public." [5] Those named were "John Locke, My Lord Shaftesbury, Dr. Mandeville, Mr. Hutchinson, Dr. Butler, etc.," the representatives of the British tradition of moral philosophy which was at its prime in that century, the age of man, preoccupied with human nature, human understanding, morals, government, art, criticism, and natural religion. All these interests in what concerned man had somehow to be gathered under one rubric. The term "natural philosophy" had been used for the whole of the study of physical nature, the signal example of which was Newton's *Principles of Natural Knowledge*. By contrast, then, "moral philosophy" was used to designate a similarly comprehensive knowledge of all the things relative to man, the things where man himself is implicated in the facts, where his opinions, tastes, judgment, reason, and will are in some way involved. Here was a field of experience where man's knowledge of himself could be of use for the improvement of his life, through education and political reform. Moral philosophy then comprised all that is the subject matter of psychology, aesthetics and criticism, ethics, political and economic science, and the rudiments of sociology, and made a consummate moral knowledge available for the general welfare and happiness of mankind. [6]

[5] *Treatise of Human Nature*, edited by T. H. Green and T. H. Grose (London, Longmans, Green and Company, 1898), Vol. I, p. 308 and footnote.

[6] This description is taken from an account by the editor of "The Character of Philosophy in Canada," in *Journal of Philosophy and Phenomenology* (March, 1952), Vol. XII, No. 3, pp. 365–376.

Moral philosophy included, then, the "science of politics," and this in turn included political economy. Thus Adam Smith, the friend of Hume's last years, and in some respects his pupil, was a professor of moral philosophy and the author of both *The Wealth of Nations* and *The Moral Sentiments*. Hume had at the very outset envisaged all these "moral subjects" as the subject of his book on *Human Nature,* and he devoted a large part of the third volume to "Justice and Injustice" and many particular questions concerning the origin of justice and property, the origin of government, the nature of moral obligation in general and of political allegiance in particular, and the law of nations. That material was what he salvaged in his political essays and discourses and in his *Enquiry Concerning the Principles of Morals* (1751), which Hume called "incomparably the best" of his writings. All of this taken together constituted "moral philosophy," and Hume regarded himself as a moral philosopher —that being the role and achievement to which he aspired.

Recent studies have emphasized this point, notably *The Philosophy of Hume* by Norman Kemp Smith.[7] But our habit of studying Hume only in the history of the theory of knowledge is very strong, so that we find it hard to see any importance in his moral and political philosophy. Hume's contemporaries saw value only in that quarter, while we tend to focus exclusively on the scepticism in regard to knowledge. The first step to an adequate knowledge of Hume today is a due understanding of his writings on politics and their significance.

II. THEMES AND ARGUMENTS OF THE POLITICAL ESSAYS

However sceptical Hume may have been regarding "speculative tenets" and all vast pretensions of the human mind in metaphysics, he had definite convictions in politics as well as in morals. These were not simply dogmatic assertions; they were "inferences and conclusions" from "experience and history." He

[7] London, Macmillan and Company, Ltd., 1941.

presented them as hypotheses which needed verification. He adduced the facts relevant to each theme discussed, weighed the evidence, and then delivered his opinion as something sustained by both reason and experience.

Hume's political essays present not only themes but arguments. They constitute a philosophy of politics, but the concept of politics is here broader than that with which we are familiar. For instance, the topics treated in the second series as *political* discourses we would today classify as *economic*. Moreover, Hume's discussions of politics cannot be separated entirely from the larger context of his thinking, namely, the new "science of man," which he had forecast in his youth—a science that took manifold forms, including the sciences of government, of political economy, of society, of morals, and even, to employ an expression of today, the science of culture. It is necessary, if we are to grasp the argument adequately, to make reference to these cognate matters in our introductory survey and analysis of the political essays, especially since the economic essays have not been included here for lack of space.

There is an essay on the theme "That Politics May Be Reduced to a Science," namely, political science. Such a science is important because it is not at all a matter of indifference under what form of government we live. The "differences" between the forms are "essential"; indeed:

So great is the force of laws and of particular forms of government, and so little dependence have they on the humors and tempers of men, that consequences almost as general and certain may sometimes be deduced from them as any which the mathematical sciences afford us.[1]

There is a connection, therefore, between the political forms and the kind of life a nation has under them. This thought was implicit in the words from Pericles' funeral oration, as recorded by Thucydides in his history of the Greek wars: "What was the road by which we reached our position, what the form of government under which our greatness grew, what the national

[1] Page 13.

habits out of which it sprang. . . . "[2] And Polybius, in another epoch, wrote of his own history of Rome:

The best and most valuable result I aim at is that readers of my work may gain a knowledge how it was and by virtue of what peculiar political institutions that in less than fifty-three years the whole world was overcome and fell under the single dominion of Rome.[3]

Hume was interested in precisely such regular connections of things in the modern as well as the ancient world. He pointed out, for example, what had happened in the later Roman Republic, where the constitution "gave the whole legislative power to the people, without allowing a negative voice either to the nobility or the consuls." In due time, "the whole government fell into anarchy, and the greatest happiness which the Romans could look for was the despotic power of the Caesars. Such are the effects of democracy without a representative."[4]

This interpretation of ancient history was made in the light of English experience. Hume actually laid it down as a "universal axiom in politics *that a hereditary prince, a nobility without vassals, and a people voting by their representatives form the best monarchy, aristocracy, and democracy.*"[5] This was the first example Hume chose of a political science, a most striking and pertinent one for his own day. Others, however, were also presented: "free governments have been commonly the most happy for those who partake of their freedom, yet are they the most ruinous and oppressive to their provinces,"[6] a proposition particularly applicable to the treatment of Ireland and the British colonies of North America. A strange proposition is then offered that "the ages of greatest public spirit are not always most eminent for private virtue,"[7] the point being that, while laws may

[2] *The Peloponnesian War*, translated by Richard Crowley (London, J. M. Dent and Sons, Ltd.), Bk. V, Ch. XVI, p. 21.

[3] Polybius, *Histories*, Vol. III, Bk. VI, Preface 2. Translated by W. R. Paton, Loeb Classical Library (Harvard University Press, 1923).

[4] Page 13.
[5] Page 15.
[6] Page 15.
[7] Page 19.

be good for instilling order and moderation into the conduct of public affairs, the actual "manners and customs" prevailing in society at large may have bred "little humanity or justice into the tempers of men."[8] Here Hume dwells on the case of a disparity between "custom" and "law," and suggests a view contrary both to that of Thucydides in the passage we have quoted and to Aristotle in his *Politics*.[9] The moral was that those who are members of political parties should govern themselves better in their "zeal" and cultivate a personal "moderation," in order that they may not wreck the constitution and the "good laws" of the country. The same lesson is taught in several later essays treating of the British government and parties.[10] However, Hume is here advancing other propositions of quite general character. He urges his basic view that "it is . . . on opinion only that government is founded." This "opinion" is forthwith analyzed into two kinds. One is opinion as to "the sense of the general advantage which is reaped from government"; and when this opinion obtains, the government has "great security." The other kind is opinion as to the "right," which, in turn, is of two kinds: one, the right to power; the other, that to property. All government in any society actually rests, then, on the state of opinion in these three respects: the public interest, lawful power, and property. It follows that the most enduring government is that in which the three types of opinion are all properly satisfied and in balance.

The essay "Of Civil Liberty" characterizes some great advances made in modern times over the ancient world, notably in that "the civilized monarchies . . . are a government of laws, not of man."[11] There is a connection asserted, too, between the rise and progress of arts and sciences and such civil liberty under a constitution —a theme pursued further in two separate essays on the arts

[8] Page 19.

[9] See Aristotle's *Politics* 1269a.

[10] "Whether the British Government Inclines More to Absolute Monarchy or to a Republic," pp. 72 ff.; "Of the Parties of Great Britain," pp. 85 ff.; and "Of the Independence of Parliament," pp. 68 ff.

[11] Page 106.

and sciences.[12] A further thought, based on a general observation of Europe, is that civilization is much enhanced by the coexistence of "a number of neighboring and independent states, connected together by commerce and policy." [13] This remark forecasts the subsequent essay, "Of the Balance of Power," and likewise several economic essays that treat of the mutual benefits of active, unimpeded trade. In "Of Civil Liberty," however, the point is made that this condition of the close neighborhood of independent states constitutes a desirable check on "power and authority" in every one of the societies, and thus is favorable to liberty.

The theme of liberty is developed in a very original way in another context, namely, the economic system of modern society. Hume's essays on political economy show the important consequences of the politics of a free society for the whole life of the people: the well-being of individuals, the wealth of nations, the health and progress of their culture. There is an adumbration in these essays of a science of society or sociology and of a philosophy of culture. The themes of the distinctively economic essays must be mentioned here because, as we have said, they are part of Hume's argument and reveal its significance.

The essay "Of Commerce" demonstrates the value of freedom in trade and industry. The conditions of the modern world are such that sovereigns who may only be concerned with their own interests of power are nonetheless obliged to consult the public interest. For their power rests upon the wealth of their respective peoples, which is determined by free commerce; and that in turn depends upon giving scope to men's personal desire for goods and enjoyment.

Everything in the world is purchased by labor, and our passions are the only causes of labor. . . . The more labor, therefore, that is employed beyond mere necessaries, the more powerful is any state. . . . Thus the greatness of the sovereign and the happiness of the state are in a great measure united with regard to trade and manufactures.[14]

[12] "Of the Rise and Progress of the Arts and Sciences" pp. 111 ff.; and "Of Refinement in the Arts" p. 123 ff.

[13] Page 116.

[14] Pages 135–136.

Another essay, "Of Money," is a study of price and value, with emphasis again on "good policy" in government with respect to keeping "alive a spirit of industry in the nation" and thereby increasing "the stock of labor in which consist all real power and riches." Here speaks the teacher of Adam Smith. Many other *aperçus* may be seen, such as the following:

It seems a maxim almost self-evident that the prices of everything depend on the proportion between commodities and money, and that any considerable alteration on either has the same effect either of heightening or lowering the price. . . .

It is also evident that the prices do not so much depend on the absolute quantity of commodities and that of money which are in a nation, as on that of the commodities which come or may come into market, and of the money which circulates. . . . It is only the overplus, compared to the demand, that determines the value.[15]

And as to the wealth of a nation, "men and commodities are the real strength of any community." [15]

It is worthy of notice in passing that Karl Marx studied the essays of Hume on the subject of the cause of surplus value and connected the above assertion about surplus value with Hume's previous one that labor is the source of value. Marx could not fail to note, moreover, the statement in the essay "Of Interest":

In all these transactions, it is necessary and reasonable that a considerable part of the commodities and labor should belong to the men to whom in a great measure they are owing. . . . Merchants . . . beget industry, by serving as canals to convey it through every corner of the state: and at the same time by their frugality, they acquire great power over that industry and collect a large property in the labor and commodities, which they are the chief instruments in producing. . . .[16]

Hume was not concerned here with ownership but with the whole operation of the economy, disregarding the question of justice in the enjoyment of the fruits of the economy:

[15] *Essays, Moral, Political, and Literary,* edited by T. H. Green and T. H. Grose (London, Longmans, Green and Company, 1898), pp. 316, 319.

[16] *Ibid.,* pp. 325, 326. See extracts from Marx's unpublished material in the volume of selections translated by G. A. Bonner and Emile Burns, entitled *Theories of Surplus Value* (London, Lawrence and Wishart, 1951), pp. 34–40.

And thus if we consider the whole connection of causes and effects, interest is the barometer of the state, and its lowness is a sign, almost infallible, of the flourishing condition of a people. It proves the increase of industry, and its prompt circulation through the whole state, little inferior to a demonstration. . . .[17]

The argument is extended beyond the state, in the essay "Of the Balance of Trade."

How is the balance kept in the provinces of every kingdom among themselves, but by the force of this principle, which makes it impossible for money to lose its level and either to rise or sink beyond the proportion of the labor and commodities which are in each province? . . .
What happens in small portions of mankind must take place in greater.[18]

It is the balance that is important. In this respect states or governments have a power and a responsibility. They have the power to take "artificial measures both to raise money beyond its material level in any kingdom" and to lower it.

Hume examines first the policy of depreciation. A lowering of the value of money can be effected by authorizing paper money or credit, which will "raise proportionately the price of labor and commodities." Internally this makes no difference to the actual wealth of any particular individual as compared with any other, yet it does have a general result of giving further "encouragement to industry." Externally, however, this device is of doubtful value, since it cannot change the governing principle of a balance in respect of labor and commodities, "the only thing valuable in commerce." Such "questions of trade and money are extremely complicated," Hume adds; and he cautions against too ready a condemnation of the disadvantages of inflationary measures, for these may well "admit of a compensation, and even an over-balance from the increase of industry and of credit, which may be promoted by the right use of paper money."[19] Similarly the practice of discounting bills is a useful institution facilitated by credit: "Merchants . . . acquire a great facility in supporting each other's

[17] *Ibid.*, p. 327.
[18] *Ibid.*, pp. 334, 335.
[19] *Ibid.*, pp. 337–339.

credit, which is a considerable security against bankruptcies.[20] And, likewise, companies or associations are another "invention" which can be of general advantage to industry and commerce.

On the other side of the ledger, however, such devices to raise the value of money artificially as by hoarding bullion and withdrawing it from circulation must be scrutinized. The state possessing the hoard is likely then to use such "wealth" in "dangerous and ill-concerted projects," and thereby "probably destroy with it what is much more valuable: the industry, morals, and numbers of its people." Essentially it is the enterprise of the people and the free circulation of the products of their industry that are important for the wealth of the nation.

From these principles we may learn what judgment we ought to form of these numberless bars, obstructions, and imposts, which all nations of Europe, and none more than England, have put upon trade, from an exorbitant desire of amassing money. . . . [And the] general ill effect . . . results from them, that they deprive neighboring nations of that free communication and exchange which the Author of the world has intended, by giving them soils, climates, and geniuses so different from each other.[21]

The nations heedlessly adopt a hundred "impolitic contrivances, which serve no other purpose but to check industry, and rob ourselves and our neighbors of the common benefits of art and nature."[22]

Hume interjects at this point a warning not to regard all taxes whatsoever as "prejudicial or useless," but only those which are motivated by the "jealousy above mentioned," where people see loss to themselves in a neighbor's prosperity. He concludes his observations with regard to operations of the state for the regulation of its commerce as follows:

In short, a government has great reason to preserve with care its people and its manufactures. Its money, it may safely trust to the course of human affairs, without fear or jealousy.[23]

[20] *Ibid.*, pp. 339–340.
[21] *Ibid.*, pp. 341–343.
[22] *Ibid.*, p. 343.
[23] *Ibid.*, pp. 343–345.

The theme of the mutual benefits of commerce is pursued further in the essay, "Of the Jealousy of Trade," where Hume avows in conclusion that "not only as a man, but as a British subject, I pray for the flourishing commerce of Germany, Spain, Italy, and even France itself." [24]

The essay "Of Taxes" continues the subject introduced in the previous essay and affirms, contrary to the usual opinions, that taxation as such can be quite salutary and stimulating to industry. Some taxes are of course detrimental; the most pernicious of all taxes are arbitrary taxes which are intended primarily as "punishments on industry."

"Of Public Credit" likewise follows up suggestions given in the prior essay "Of the Balance of Trade." In describing an aspect of political economy that relates to the position of the state with respect to war and preparedness for war, Hume, the frugal Scot, becomes sarcastic:

. . . our modern expedient, which has become very general, is to mortgage the public revenues and to trust that posterity will pay off the incumbrances contracted by their ancestors; and they, having before their eyes so good an example of their wise fathers, have the same prudent reliance on *their* posterity; who at last, from necessity more than choice, are obliged to place the same confidence in a new posterity. . . .[25]

The temptations to this policy are very great for the modern statesmen in time of war because modern war is "attended with every destructive circumstance: loss of men, increase of taxes, decay of commerce, dissipation of money, devastation by sea and land." [26] And yet, much as such recourse to public debt may be condemned, there is "the new paradox that public encumbrances are of themselves advantageous, independently of the necessity of contracting them." [27] For, the argument runs, "Public securities are with us become a kind of money, and pass as readily at the current price as gold or silver," [28] and this means "promoting cir-

[24] *Ibid.*, p. 348.
[25] *Ibid.*, p. 361.
[26] *Ibid.*, p. 362.
[27] *Loc. cit.*
[28] *Ibid.*, p. 363.

culation and encouraging industry." But "in the interior economy of the state" there are nevertheless many weightier disadvantages. First is the flocking of the population of the country to cities, the consequent overweening importance of a capital city over other towns, and the permanent interest of the capital in always supporting the policies of the government in whose solvency it has such a stake. Second, the public securities drive out private financing, which tends to "render all provisions and labor dearer than otherwise they would be." [29] Third, the taxes for the interest payment cause an increase in the cost of labor, and besides they also weigh heavily on the poorer people. Fourth, large holdings of bonds by foreigners make the public of the nation "tributary" to them, and in time even the home industry may come to be transferred to them. Fifth, the greater part of the securities will be held by "idle people who live on their income" and this means "our funds, in that view, give great encouragement to a useless and inactive life." [30] But these drawbacks are far less important than the

. . . prejudice that results to a state considered as a body politic which must support itself in the society of nations and have various transactions with other states in wars and negotiations. The ill there is pure and unmixed, without any favorable circumstance to atone for it; and it is an ill too of a nature the highest and most important.[31]

For "self-preservation" is of paramount value.

The policy Hume develops in this argument is that bounds should be set to national debts. "I must confess when I see princes and states fighting and quarreling, amidst their debts, funds, and public mortgages, it always brings to my mind a match of cudgel playing fought in a china shop." [32] Individuals and states alike will be ruined by unlimited use of public credit.

These seem to be the events which are not very remote, and which reason foresees as clearly almost as she can do anything that lies in the womb of time. And though the ancients main-

[29] *Ibid.*, pp. 364–365.
[30] *Ibid.*, pp. 365-366.
[31] *Ibid.*, p. 366.
[32] *Ibid.*, p. 396.

tained that in order to reach the gift of prophecy a certain divine
fury or madness was requisite, one may safely affirm that in order
to deliver such prophecies as these no more is necessary than
merely to be in one's senses, free from the influence of popular
madness and delusion.[33]

Hume saw the need of balance and limitation of power everywhere—balance in opinion, balance between interest and right,
balance of labor and commodities, and balance of commerce. This
principle has been "demonstrated" by experience and is one by
which all governments ought to be governed if they attend
strictly to their duty of preserving the state and the individual
whose labor, industry, and genius secure their own safety and
welfare. Throughout, too, Hume has been aware of international
relations and the actual need of a balance of power for the sake
of the liberty and independence of each nation and state. He
wrote an essay "Of the Balance of Power" and referred to the idea
many times, and in the essay "Of Public Credit" he again speaks
a dire prophecy, this time even with genuine fervor:

The balance of power in Europe our grandfathers, our fathers,
and we have all deemed too unequal to be preserved without our
attention and assistance. But our children, weary of the struggle, and fettered with encumbrances, may sit down secure and
see their neighbors oppressed and conquered till at last they
themselves and their creditors lie both at the mercy of the
conqueror. . . .[34]

The political import of this whole argument is that any power
in the state must always be limited if there is to be, not only liberty for men, but also safety and well-being for the nation. A constitutional system is the indispensable means to these ends. Thus,
writing in "Of Some Remarkable Customs," Hume says:

. . . a power, however great, when granted by law to an eminent
magistrate is not so dangerous to liberty as an authority, however
inconsiderable, which he acquires from violence and usurpation.
For besides that the law always limits every power which it bestows, the very receiving it as a concession establishes the author-

[33] *Ibid.*, p. 374.
[34] *Ibid.*, p. 374.

ity whence it is derived and preserves the harmony of the constitution. . . .[35]

But the limitation of power is effected not only by the laws of the constitution, but also through the co-existence (exactly as in the case of neighboring nations limiting each other) of other bodies vested likewise with authority, as in different branches of government. Furthermore, the strength of these several competing authorities is derived from the opinion of the nation as to right and interest. Thus the best political system is a constitutional system, where laws rule and not men, and where the powers are distributed and the authority or credit attaching to each part of the government depends upon its standing in the opinon of the people. Sometimes the loyalty of the nation is given to the monarch or executive; sometimes it is given to the parliament or legislative body, who are the representatives of the people; and sometimes it may be given to that body which interprets the law under which all the bodies and individuals carry on their business, private and public.

To demonstrate these general truths, Hume wrote a number of political essays that dealt particularly with the English constitution and the ways in which the government of the land was conducted. He began with "Of the Liberty of the Press," the keynote of the system since the Revolution of 1688.[36] He then developed his ideas in "Of the Independence of Parliament," "Whether the British Government Inclines More to Absolute Monarchy or to a Republic," and several studies of the party system: "Of Parties in General," "The Parties of Great Britain," and "The Coalition of Parties." The respective tenets of the monarchical and republican parties were discussed in "Of the Original Contract" and "Of Passive Obedience," as well as the commonly accepted theory of government since the Revolution of 1688 in "Of the Protestant Succession." These essays are illustrative of the themes argued generally in the other essays. They also teach the lessons learned from English history, and the values and

[35] *Ibid.*, pp. 379–380.
[36] Page 3.

principles to which the present generation should hold fast in the perils of the time. Here was Hume's constructive moral philosophy.

It may not seem so strange, then, to discover that Hume closed his *Essays and Treatises* with an essay on the "Idea of a Perfect Commonwealth." One might expect him to be scornful of any suggestion of ideal perfection. He does say, indeed, that "All plans of government which suppose great reformation in the manners of mankind are plainly imaginary. Of this nature are the *Republic* of Plato and the *Utopia* of Sir Thomas More." [37] Hume declares that it is foolish to "try experiments merely upon the credit of supposed argument and philosophy," [38] for "The bulk of mankind" are "governed by authority, not reason," [39] But what is the authority that Hume has in mind? It is the authority of whatever is founded in the settled opinion and custom of the people. Thus the English people had valued liberty and struggled for it for centuries. They had formed a constitution through the experience of their wars of rebellion and their conflicts of parties. This constitution was not constructed and recorded in a document; it was no mere philosophical concept, but a product of history and experience which the British people had come to cherish with conviction. But Hume had no aversion to a discussion of the best form of government for any given nation. He actually says that Harrington's *Oceana* is "the only valuable model of a commonwealth that has yet been offered to the public." [40] This plan of government did not violate his canon that the statesman in such business should "adjust his innovations as much as possible to the ancient fabric and preserve entire the chief pillars and supports of the constitution." [41] But the *Oceana* was defective in several particulars, the prime one being that it "provides not a sufficient security for liberty, or the redress of grievances." [42]

Hume goes on to remedy the design of the system. He discusses the senate and the people, and the advantage of having the veto

[37] Page 146.
[38] Page 145.
[39] *Ibid.*
[40] Page 146.
[41] Page 145.
[42] Page 146.

power vested in the executive and not lodged in the senate, which could thereby prevent matters from ever reaching the floor for discussion. And he cites Machiavelli: "A government . . . must often be brought back to its original principles,"[43] which means in this context the principle of liberty of discussion, the right to meet and present grievances, and thus to secure a balance among the powers of government. Hume takes up a number of other details, providing carefully for representative government at every level: local, county, national. "Every county," he writes, "is a kind of republic within itself."[44] Then as to the army, which had been such a troublesome problem in the Civil War: "The militia is established in imitation of that of Switzerland,"[45] and the appointment of its officers shall be made by the civil authority, which must always be superior to the army authority.

The national government, however, wherein all such authority is lodged is the locus of the most serious problems. The "higher offices of the republic" must be distributed so as not to fall into the same hands. The English struggle for liberty had been conducted through Parliament, originally a mere council for the king and consisting of two houses, the Lords and Commons, and this pattern is retained. "All free governments must consist of two councils, a lesser and a greater, or, in other words, of a senate and a people."[46]

But how will the people discuss in an assembly?

Divide the people into many separate bodies, and then they may debate with safety. . . . Separate this great body; and though every member be only of middling sense, it is not probable that anything but reason can prevail over the whole.[47]

The deliverance of the "good sense" of the people in the voice of their representative, the House of Commons, presupposes their own local meetings for discussion of the issues. Hume recom-

[43] Page 147.
[44] Page 150.
[45] Page 151.
[46] Page 152.
[47] Page 153.

mends this modified Harrington plan because it "seems to have all the advantages both of a great and a little commonwealth." [48]

The plan is recommended as sound in theory and practicable. A semblance of a federal system had been in effect in the United Provinces for some years.[49] Its principle could readily be brought into working accord with the present British constitution, especially if Cromwell's plan for Parliament were revived, "making the representation [in Commons] equal," and steps were taken to secure responsibility in the members of that body. But Hume confessed that the present established "limited monarchy" in Britain, even if reformed as proposed, would still suffer from "three great inconveniences," namely, the persistence of two factions divided according to the interest of "Court" and "Country," which subordinated the public interest; the excessive importance of the king's personal character in the working of the government under such conditions; and the matter of the executive's having sole power over the standing army.[50]

What, then, is to be done? Hume leaves that an open question. He has endorsed a conservative plan for the reform of the constitution, adjusted "as much as possible to the ancient fabric." If adopted, the result, however, would still be unsatisfactory. The parties needed to be emancipated from their ancient slogans and factious character. The present issue should be debated and determined by the discussions of the people in their local assemblies, and the debates in Parliament would then represent the opinion, the "good sense," the reason of the people so elicited. Can anything more be done in Great Britain? Hume does not answer.

Can it nowhere be done, and is the *Oceana* plan therefore a Utopia? Hume does not reject it as such. It remains within the realm of possibility, even in a large state or nation. He concludes by saying that it is quite false to suppose, as was commonly done,

that no large state such as France or Great Britain could ever be modeled into a commonwealth, but that such a form of government can only take place in a city or small territory. The contrary

[48] Page 155.
[49] *Ibid.*
[50] Page 157.

seems probable. Though it is more difficult to form a republican government in an extensive country than in a city, there is more facility, when once it is formed, of preserving it steady and uniform without tumult and faction.[51]

Such a republic may not endure forever, but then nothing of this sort is ever immortal. The thing to guard against is the danger arising from its very strength and success, for "republics have ambition as well as individuals, and present interest makes men forgetful of their posterity."[52] No law of the constitution can safeguard a state against the folly of conquest if the people are not mindful of these truths.

On this sober note Hume concludes his political essays. We shall see in a later section how people of British stock in North America cast themselves for the very part that Hume had here described. The first Americans, toward the end of the century, learned at first hand how great was the difficulty of founding a "republican government." They relied upon their town meetings and upon local militia, and above all they were mindful of the faults of human nature and the ruin they can work. There was a difference, of course, in the overtones of the play as it was composed and as it was acted. Hume's final remark was:

It is a sufficient incitement to human endeavors that such a government would flourish for many ages, without pretending to bestow on any work of man that immortality which the Almighty seems to have refused to his own productions.[53]

But as we shall see, Americans spoke another language and were impelled by other convictions.

III. THE ARGUMENT AND ILLUSTRATIONS IN THE *HISTORY OF ENGLAND*

As we have already noted, Hume set about the writing of his *History of England* the very year of his success with the *Political*

[51] Page 157.
[52] Page 158.
[53] Page 158.
[53] *Ibid.*

Discourses, the second series of his *Essays.* The *History* was a sequel to them in the development of his political thought.

We should note here Hume's view of history in general. He conceived of history as an adjunct of moral philosophy. It is a means of exhibiting some general truths about man, politics, and society. For there is the same sort of causal relationship in human affairs and society as in the events of nature. The purpose of writing history is to search out the facts and connections of fact in the past in order to draw useful conclusions for the present. Hume is thus in the tradition of the first scientific historian, Thucydides, whom he often cites, and Polybius, and even Machiavelli, though his reaction to the latter was mixed, as when he commented on a penetrating observation made by Machiavelli: "I think [it] may be regarded as one of those eternal truths which no time nor accidents can vary," but "I wish he had not mixed falsehood with truth." [1] Speaking for himself Hume wrote: "The chief use of history is that it affords materials for disquisitions of this nature" —that is, general observations on manners, finance, commerce, arms, arts, and sciences—"and it seems the duty of an historian to point out the proper inferences and conclusions on all these matters." [2] Besides the moral intent, the range of interest indicated aligned Hume with his brilliant contemporary, Voltaire. Here was a new sort of history being written—not history limited to political and military events, and to the reigns of kings, but social, intellectual, and cultural history. Thus Hume's *History* constitutes a *supplement* to many of the political essays. The same themes are pursued, and their philosophic argument is illustrated and confirmed in the particular details of English history.

Hume began his work with the accession of James I, after the death of Elizabeth, and carried it through a distinct period, namely, to the end of the Stuart line with the Revolution of 1688. During that series of reigns came the rebellion against Charles I and his execution, the short duration of the Commonwealth, the restoration of Charles II, and the succeeding short

---

[1] Pages 17, 18.

[2] *History of England,* Vol. VI, Ch. LXII, conclusion to "The Commonwealth" (1660). See also Appendix to the Reign of James I, Vol. IV.

reign of James II from 1685 until the Revolution. This was the period of primary interest to Hume. The English constitution took its characteristic form during this turbulent century of political and religious conflict. The major lessons were then learned which the settlement at the time of the Revolution affirmed: the supremacy of the constitution; the balance between executive and legislative powers; the guarantee of personal, civil, and political liberty; the moral strength of the national character and the public spirit that pulled the people through the bitterest controversies; the importance of the practice of discussion and debate in the formation of public opinion; and the intellectual vitality of the British genius throughout the years of tribulation of the three nations, Ireland, Scotland, and England. Hume had here the historical evidence to support his theses in the *Essays.*

It is very interesting, too, that long after the *History* was published, when Hume, in retirement at Edinburgh, was engaged in correcting and improving his work for a new edition, he bethought himself of an additional essay for his *Essays,* a short piece entitled "Of the Origin of Government." [3] In this essay he speaks of a dual necessity of mankind, the need of both "peace and order" and "liberty." Both needs must always be provided for in government, and neither can be neglected save with peril. Then Hume offers a very significant historical reflection:

In all governments there is a perpetual intestine struggle, open or secret, between Authority and Liberty, and neither of them can absolutely prevail in the contest. . . . In this sense it must be owned that liberty is the perfection of civil society, but still authority must be acknowledged essential to its very existence. . . . [4]

In this statement Hume has made very explicit the great guiding theme of his story of England during that ill-starred Stuart regime. The *History* is a demonstration of the truth that neither *authority* nor *liberty* must be allowed in the extreme, and that a

[3] Pages 39 ff. See also Letter to William Strahan (Hume's publisher), March 1, 1774, in *The Letters of David Hume,* edited by J. Y. T. Greig (Oxford, Clarendon Press, 1932), Vol. II, p. 496.

[4] Pages 41–42.

satisfactory political order requires both to be established in forms and institutions which work together under the law and with the support of the opinion of the nation.

We shall cite here various accounts which Hume gave at different critical junctures in the history of that period, as well as his comments as a philosopher-historian on the events. Hume sympathizes with the advocates of liberty in their struggle against an imperious royal authority, but when those advocates get the upper hand he rebukes their excessive liberty and shows that they assumed absolute authority themselves. There is a chain of such phenomena in the course of eighty-six years—first the king, then Parliament becoming authoritarian; then the army, the sect of Independents and the Levellers, and Cromwell. History shows that the nation came through because there were "bounds" to liberty and authority alike, and because of the structure of the constitution, which defined and limited the role of each part of the government—a structure resting upon the opinion and experience of the people as a whole.

When James I succeeded Elizabeth, in 1603, there was the following situation: The House of Commons represented the interest of property, and therefore privilege, and "the turbulent government of England" during the time between 1603 and 1620 was forever fluctuating between prerogative and privilege.[5] From the start the Commons, finding themselves free from the arbitrary government of Elizabeth, "made application for a conference with the Lords and presented a petition to the King, the purport of which was to procure, in favor of the Puritans, a relaxation of the ecclesiastical laws."[6] For "the votes" of the Commons "show that the House contained a mixture of Puritans, who had gained great authority among them, and who, together with religious prejudices, were continually suggesting ideas more suitable to a popular than a monarchical form of government. The natural appetite for rule made the Commons lend a willing ear to every doctrine which tended to augment their own power and influence."[7]

[5] *History of England,* Vol. IV, Ch. XLIX, p. 469. See also "Of the First Principles of Government," pp. 24 ff.

[6] *History of England,* Vol. IV, Ch. XLV, pp. 397–398.

[7] *Ibid.,* Vol. V, Ch. XLVI, p. 410.

Of the Commons at the beginning of the reign of Charles I Hume reported well:

The House of Commons . . . was almost entirely governed by a set of men of the most uncommon capacity and the largest views; men who were now formed into a regular party, and united as well by fixed aims and projects as by the hardships which some of them had undergone in prosecution of them.[8]

They were "animated with a warm regard to liberty," and used their "undoubted privilege" to grant or refuse supplies as a means of extorting "concessions in favor of civil liberty." Treating with a King who had "so high an idea . . . of kingly prerogative and so contemptible a notion of the rights of those popular assemblies" that, "had he possessed any military force on which he could rely, it is not improbable that he had . . . governed without any regard to Parliamentary privileges,"[9] it was necessary for Parliament to curb his ambitions and resolve upon "some new laws" to that end. Furthermore,

. . . it was requisite to temper by the decency and moderation of their debates the rigor which must necessarily attend their determinations. Nothing can give us a higher idea of the capacity of those men who now guided the Commons and of the great authority which they had acquired than the forming and executing of so judicious and so difficult a plan of operations.[10]

They publicly declared their grievances, however, speaking on behalf of the people, "grievances concerning acts of power against law," such as imprisonment without bail or bond and with no legal redress, forced loans, taxation without consent of Parliament, and martial law. These declarations were formulated in a Petition of Right recalling the Great Charter. There then ensued a great debate between the "partisans of the Commons" and the "partisans of the Court" on personal liberty.[11] In the end the King had to give his assent to the petition and thereupon was voted his funds, which had been held up.

The Commons, however, were still far from satisfied and "con-

[8] *Ibid.*, Vol. V, Ch. L, pp. 4–5.
[9] *Ibid.*, Vol. V, Ch. L, p. 20.
[10] *Ibid.*, Vol. V., Ch. LI, p. 33.
[11] *Ibid.*, Vol. V, Ch. LI, pp. 33–34.

tinued to carry their scrutiny into every part of government. In some particulars, their industry was laudable; in some, it may be liable to censure." [12] The Puritans' parties emerged at this time; they consisted of three distinct groups: "political Puritans," "Puritans in discipline" (who were opposed to the Episcopate), and "doctrinal Puritans." [13] It was then too that Oliver Cromwell began to appear in the debates, a future leader of the Commons; but he bided his time, according to Hume.

Soon thereafter "the Puritans, finding themselves restrained in England, shipped off for America and laid there the foundations of a government which possessed all the liberty, both civil and religious, of which they found themselves bereaved in their native country." [14] Meanwhile at home John Hampden, whose spirit and courage won him popularity throughout the nation, "merited great renown with posterity for the bold stand which he made in defense of the laws and liberties of his country." His subsequent trial was a subject of public concern, and the final decision roused the whole country to "the dangers to which their liberties were exposed." [15]

Scotland, meanwhile, was aroused too when the King attempted to impose a liturgy upon their church; and from this dissension there arose the Covenanters, "who found themselves seconded by the zeal of the whole nation." [16] The leaders here were also men of "vigor and abilities," and the Commons in England were in sympathy with those "refractory opposers of the King and the ministers." [17] The Scots then invaded England and enjoyed a temporary victory, thanks to their "zeal and unanimity" and their "exact discipline." This brought matters to a crisis for the King.

The Commons proceeded to impeach the King's minister, the Earl of Strafford, and Archbishop Laud, on the charge of high treason, for it was supposed that they had the intention "of subverting the laws and constitution of England and introducing

[12] *Ibid.*, Vol. V, Ch. LI, p. 45.
[13] *Ibid.*, Vol. V, Ch. LI, p. 56.
[14] *Ibid.*, Vol. V, Ch. LII, p. 84.
[15] *Ibid.*, Vol. V, Ch. LII, pp. 88 ff.
[16] *Ibid.*, Vol. V, Ch. LIII, pp. 102, 106.
[17] *Ibid.*, Vol. V, Ch. LIII, p. 114.

arbitrary and unlimited authority into the kingdom. . . ." [18] Yet such action really meant that "a new jurisdiction was erected in the nation. . . . What rendered the power of the Commons more formidable was the extreme prudence with which it was conducted." [19] Soon "the whole sovereign power" was "in a manner transferred to the Commons, and the government, without any seeming violence or disorder . . . changed in a moment from a monarchy almost absolute to a pure democracy." [20] At this time, too, "the press, freed from all fear or reserve, swarmed with productions, dangerous by their seditious zeal and calumny. . . ." And Puritan preachers and lecturers had a field day. [21] The Commons encouraged the presenting of grievances and charges against private persons, and so many of these were presented that more than forty committees were set up to pass upon them; "never was so much multiplied," Hume comments, "the use of these committees of the House." [22] And the Commons themselves were again instituting one of the "greatest innovations." One such committee was "a court of inquisition," and was popularly called "the Committee of Scandalous Ministers," whose proceedings were "cruel and arbitrary, and made great havoc both on the church and the universities." [23] Thus the mantle of arbitrary authority had now fallen on the Commons and its forty or more committees. And Hume observed at this juncture that the political disputes about power and liberty, which seemed so much less important to those who wrote about them at the time than the religious issues, were but an example of that persistent problem in each age of the relation of authority and liberty. [24]

In the opinion of the historian, the Commons had already gone too far toward authority, and such a judgment was confirmed by the way they hardened their hearts against the dignified and just defense the Earl of Strafford made before his execution on charge

[18] *Ibid.*, Vol. V, Ch. LIV, p. 132.
[19] *Ibid.*, Vol. V, Ch. LIV, p. 133.
[20] *Ibid.*, Vol. V, Ch. LIV, p. 135.
[21] *Ibid.*, Vol. V, Ch. LIV, p. 137.
[22] *Ibid.*, Vol. V, Ch. LIV, p. 139.
[23] *Ibid.*, Vol. V, Ch. LIV, p. 144.
[24] *Ibid.*, Vol. V, Ch. LIV, pp. 144–145.

of treason. Yet Hume intended to be fair himself in judging this Parliament and recognized that the merits of their performance during the session outweighed their mistakes. "All lovers of liberty" could still (1641) praise the Parliament.[25]

The scene again shifts to the Scots, then bent on "spreading the Presbyterian discipline in England and Ireland." They sought more autonomy for Scotland and demanded that "no member of the Privy Council, in whose hands during the King's absence the whole administration lay, no officer of state, none of the judges should be appointed but by the advice and approbation of [the Scottish] Parliament." The King was forced to agree to this "most fatal blow given to royal authority."[26] Then came Irish Catholic rebellion against the King, accompanied by barbarities against the Protestants. Taking advantage of this predicament of the royal government, the Scots "now considered themselves entirely as a republic, and made no account of the authority of their prince, which they had utterly annihilated."[27]

The English Commons likewise pursued their objective, which was to exalt their own authority and diminish the King's, and "resolved to seek their own security, as well as greatness, by enlarging popular authority in England."[28] The King, being helpless himself, had committed to them the care of Ireland, and this gave them their opportunity.

They had, on other occasions, been gradually encroaching on the executive power of the crown, which forms the principal and most natural branch of authority; but with regard to Ireland, they at once assumed it fully and entirely. . . .[29]

The plight of Ireland was then subordinated to their own interests and ambition. However,

. . . to make the attack on royal authority by regular approaches, it was thought proper to frame a general remonstrance of the state of the nation. The committee brought into the house that remon-

[25] *Ibid.*, Vol. V, Ch. LIV, p. 171.
[26] *Ibid.*, Vol. V, Ch. LV, pp. 174–176.
[27] *Ibid.*, Vol. V, Ch. LV, p. 188.
[28] *Ibid.*, Vol. V, Ch. LV, p. 189.
[29] *Ibid.*, Vol. V, Ch. LV, p. 191.

strance which has become so memorable and which was soon afterward attended with such important consequences. It was not addressed to the King, but was openly declared to be an appeal to the people. . . .[30]

Hume comments at this point that the actual "grievances" cited in the remonstrance "had been already redressed, and even laws enacted for future security against their return," though "the praise of these advantages was ascribed, not to the King, but to the Parliament, who had extorted his consent to such salutary statutes."[31] The remonstrance was but a signal, therefore, for further "unlimited pretensions" on the part of the Commons, so that what was really intended was nothing less, "whatever ancient names might be preserved, than an abolition, almost total, of the monarchical government of England."[32] Their overt plea in the remonstrance, however, was this:

A *right* was indeed acquired to the people, or rather their ancient right was more exactly defined [in the previous petition]; but as the *power* of invading it still remained to the prince, no sooner did an opportunity offer, than he totally disregarded all laws and preceding engagements. . . .[33]

Hence the necessity of eliminating the monarchy.

Among the "best arguments of the royalists against a further attack on the prerogative" was the following:

Let us beware, lest our encroachments, by introducing anarchy, make the people seek shelter under the peaceable and despotic rule of a monarch. Authority, as well as liberty, is requisite to government; and even is requisite to the support of liberty itself, by maintaining the laws which can alone regulate and protect it. What madness, while everything is so happily settled under ancient forms and institutions, now more exactly poised and adjusted, to try the hazardous experience of a new constitution. . . .[34]

This reference by the royalists to liberty is explained later:

[30] *Ibid.*, Vol. V, Ch. LV, p. 192.
[31] *Ibid.*, Vol. V, Ch. LV, pp. 192f.
[32] *Ibid.*, Vol. V, Ch. LV, p. 194.
[33] *Ibid.*, Vol. V, Ch. LV, p. 194.
[34] *Ibid.*, Vol. V, Ch. LV, p. 197.

The bulk of that generous train of nobility and gentry who now attended the King in his distresses breathed the spirit of liberty as well as of loyalty, and in the hopes alone of his submitting to a legal and limited government were they willing in his defense to sacrifice their lives and fortunes. . . .[35]

The civil war came.

The furious zeal for liberty and Presbyterian discipline [on the part of Commons] which had hitherto run uncontrolled throughout the nation now at last excited an equal ardor for monarchy and episcopacy, when the intention of abolishing these ancient modes of government was openly avowed by the Parliament. . . .[36]

Here Hume stops to pay tribute to the character of the whole nation in this war:

Fierce, however, and inflamed as were the dispositions of the English by a war both civil and religious, that great destroyer of humanity, all the events of this period are less distinguished by atrocious deeds, either of treachery or cruelty, than were ever any intestine discords which had so long a continuance, a circumstance which will be found to reflect a great praise on the national character of that people now so unhappily roused to arms. . . .[37]

The intestine struggle between authority and liberty, the main theme of this history, was to illustrate itself in further events during the course of this war and until the settlement of the Revolution in 1688.

Oliver Cromwell and Sir Thomas Fairfax now rose to command and established "a new model of the army," where "citizens and country gentlemen soon became excellent officers." [38] Hume's picture of Cromwell is that of a Machiavellian statesman:

Carried by his natural temper to magnanimity, to grandeur, and to an imperious and domineering polity, he yet knew when necessary to employ the most profound dissimulation, the most oblique and refined artifice, the semblance of the greatest moderation and simplicity. A friend to justice, though his public conduct was one continued violation of it; devoted to religion, though he

[35] *Ibid.*, Vol. V, Ch. LVI, p. 235.
[36] *Ibid.*, Vol. V, Ch. LVI, p. 241.
[37] *Loc. cit.*
[38] *Ibid.*, Vol. V, Ch. LVII, p. 269.

perpetually employed it as the instrument of his ambition; he was engaged in crimes from the prospect of sovereign power, a temptation which is in general irresistible to human nature. . . .[39]

But the affair was not simply one of the personal ambition of one man, for Hume's theme is the inevitable march of events, so that when liberty itself becomes unlimited, it leads to new authority unlimited. Hence the story continues:

The dominion of the Parliament was of short duration. No sooner had they subdued their sovereign than their own servants arose against them, and tumbled them down from their slippery throne. The sacred boundaries of the laws being once violated nothing remained to confine the wild projects of zeal and ambition: and every successive revolution became a precedent for that which followed it.[40]

Thus the Council of Officers in Cromwell's army became "a military Parliament."[41]

Here commenced the encroachments of the military upon the civil authority. The army, in their usurpations on the Parliament, copied exactly the model which the Parliament itself had set them in their recent usurpations on the crown.[42]

The leaders of the army were the sect of Independents:

The whole authority of the nation, they imagined, was now lodged in their hands; and they had a near prospect of molding the government into that imaginary republic which had long been the subject of their wishes . . . and they expected, by the terror of the sword, to impose a more perfect system of liberty on the reluctant nation. . . .

The troops themselves were formed into a kind of republic and the plans of imaginary republics for the settlement of the State were every day the topics of conversation among the armed legislators. Royalty it was agreed to abolish; nobility must be set aside: even all ranks of men be leveled; and a universal equality of property, as well as of power, be introduced among the citizens. The saints, they said, were the salt of the earth. . . .[43]

---

[39] *Ibid.*, Vol. V, Ch. LVII, p. 289.
[40] *Ibid.*, Vol. V, Ch. LIX, p. 330.
[41] *Ibid.*, Vol. V, Ch. LIX, p. 334.
[42] *Ibid.*, Vol. V, Ch. LIX, p. 340.
[43] *Ibid.*, Vol. V, Ch. LIX, pp. 346, 350.

At this juncture Hume draws the moral plainly:

It is seldom that the people gain anything by revolutions in government; because the new government, jealous and insecure, must commonly be supported with more expense and severity than the old . . . the people found themselves loaded with a multiplicity of taxes, formerly unknown; and scarcely an appearance of law and liberty remained in the administration.[44]

Finally comes the open claim to complete power by the military party in the Commons:

Having first established a principle which is noble in itself and seems specious, but is belied by all history and experience, *that the people are the origin of all just power*, they next declared that the Commons of England, assembled in Parliament, being chosen by the people and representing them, are the supreme authority of the nation, and that whatever is enacted and declared to be law by the Commons has the force of law, without the consent of the King or House of Peers. . . .[45]

The Commonwealth was then established, and again the excess of authority appears in the politics of the leading party, which ostensibly was all for freedom. The Levellers "now practiced against their officers the same lesson which they had been taught against the Parliament. They framed a remonstrance and sent five agitators to present it to the general and council of war."[46] And again Hume points out the lesson:

By recent as well as all ancient example it was become evident that illegal violence, with whatever pretenses it may be covered and whatever object it may pursue, must inevitably end at last in the arbitrary and despotic government of a single person.[47]

The military were now, "in appearance as well as in reality, the sole power which prevailed in the nation."[48]

But Cromwell himself now feared their unlimited, excessive liberty and forthwith devised "another scheme of government . . .

[44] *Ibid.*, Vol. V, Ch. LIX, p. 357.
[45] *Ibid.*, Vol. V, Ch. LIX, p. 370.
[46] *Ibid.*, Vol. V, Ch. LX, p. 394.
[47] *Ibid.*, Vol. V, Ch. LX, p. 435.
[48] *Ibid.*, Vol. V, Ch. LXI, p. 444.

to temper the liberty of a commonwealth by the authority of a single person," namely himself as Protector.[49] This adroitly revived the function of the King, the royal authority in another guise. But the "opinion" of the nation manifest in an election would not tolerate it, for "the electing of a discontented Parliament is a proof of a discontented nation."[50] So "Cromwell was at last obliged to refuse that crown" which his party had proferred him. But on the other hand "the Parliament, when the royal dignity was rejected by Cromwell, found themselves obliged to retain the name of a commonwealth and protector."[51]

After the Restoration, "the House of Commons was now regularly divided into two parties, the Court and the Country."[52] The issue as to the succession to the throne was raised by the Country party, the Whigs, who aimed at making each succeeding monarch derive his title from Parliament and who therefore sought the exclusion of the present heir-apparent. In the words of the opposition to this measure are thoughts that Hume had expressed in his *Essays*:

An authority, they said, wholly absolute and uncontrollable is a mere chimera and is nowhere to be found in human institutions. All government is founded on opinion and a sense of duty; and whenever the supreme magistrate, by any law or positive prescription, shocks an opinion regarded as fundamental and established with a firmness equal to that of his own authority, he subverts the principle by which he himself is established and can no longer hope for obedience.[53]

And later, particularly *a propos* of the exclusion bill: "No human schemes can secure the public in all possible imaginable events. . . ."[54]

James II came to the throne and proceeded in the same fatal manner to make much of his prerogative:

[49] *Ibid.*, Vol. V, Ch. LXI, p. 444.
[50] *Ibid.*, Vol. V, Ch. LXI, p. 452.
[51] *Ibid.*, Vol. V, Ch. LXI, pp. 476–477.
[52] *Ibid.*, Vol. VI, Ch. LXVI, p. 147.
[53] *Ibid.*, Vol. VI, Ch. LXVIII, p. 227.
[54] *Loc. cit.*

He was not deterred by the reflection . . . that in a government such as that of England, it was not sufficient that a prerogative be approved by some lawyers and antiquaries: if it was condemned by the general voice of the nation, and yet was still extorted, the victory over the national liberty was no less signal than if obtained by the most flagrant injustice and usurpation. . . . So lofty was the idea which he had entertained of his *legal* authority that it left his subjects little or no right to liberty. . . .[56]

The Whig party in Commons, no less doctrinaire in its own way, voted by a large majority that

King James II, having endeavored to subvert the constitution of the kingdom by breaking the original contract between king and people and having . . . violated the fundamental laws and withdrawn himself from the kingdom has abdicated the government and that the throne is thereby vacant.[57]

Then followed a great debate in Parliament over the "original contract," with which Hume was out of sympathy. But he gave the "managers of the Commons" a brief that they could have used, arguing their case on the surer grounds that everything in government depended on public opinion and that "any scheme of settlement should be adopted in which it was most probable the people would acquiesce and persevere."[58] On this particular occasion, when the Prince of Orange was being considered for the office of king, Hume remarked that the procedure was a singular exception to the general rule in history of government, inasmuch as

. . . new settlements of civil constitutions are commonly conducted with such violence, tumult, and disorder that the public voice can scarcely ever be heard and the opinions of the citizens are at that time less attended to than even in the common course of administration. . . .[59]

The present revolution in government was unique in having such a foundation on public opinion and the popular voice, and Hume proudly wrote:

[56] *Ibid.*, Vol. VI, Ch. LXX, p. 316; Ch. LXXI, p. 353.
[57] *Ibid.*, Vol. VI, Ch. LXXI, p. 356.
[58] *Ibid.*, Vol. VI, Ch. LXXI, p. 360.
[59] *Ibid.*, Vol. VI, Ch. LXXI, p. 361.

. . . it may justly be affirmed, without any danger of exaggeration, that we in this island have ever since enjoyed, if not the best system of government, at least the most entire system of liberty that ever was known amongst mankind.[60]

Thus in 1689 England achieved an ordered liberty and a government at last secure in its rightful authority.

IV. THE SIGNIFICANCE OF HUME'S POLITICAL THOUGHT FOR HIS CONTEMPORARIES IN EUROPE

We shall now consider some of the reasons why Hume first became famous "abroad and at home" through his political writings. On the continent there had been a long-continued interest in the English system of politics. Bodin, the proponent of the modern theory of sovereignty, in his *Six Books of the Republic* (1576) had signalized the unusual limitation on the English monarchy in requiring the prior consent of Parliament in the matter of taxation. Later Milton reported in his *Areopagitica* (1644) how, in the course of his visit to Galileo in Italy, he found men of letters and science full of admiration for the liberty of thought and speech which they believed the English enjoyed and which meant so much for "the dignity of learning." In the course of a hundred years that belief about English liberty was confirmed in the minds of Europeans everywhere. Locke's *Letter Concerning Toleration* (1689) and *Treatise on Civil Government* (1690) established it beyond question. And at Paris in mid-eighteenth century, just when Hume was publishing his political essays, there were men of letters of great prominence or fame who paid their special tribute to England and her freedom—Voltaire, eulogistic and vivid, singing the praises of a land that could produce both a Newton and a Locke; and Montesquieu, imbued with the true spirit of scientific research, who went to visit England and for two years studied its laws and constitution, and then published his monumental *Spirit of the Laws* (1749). Thus all eyes had been constantly turned toward England as an exemplar

[60] *Ibid.*, Vol. VI, Ch. LXXI, p. 363.

of politics and freedom, of thought and learning. But unless those who were thus curious could actually visit the country as Montesquieu had done and investigate at first hand the operations of government under the British Constitution, they had little new material available to them beyond Locke's *Civil Government*, published only two years after the Revolution. The time was ripe for fresh information and reflections on English liberty and the Constitution. This was what Hume offered in both his political and historical writings. His *Essays* were particularly valuable, moreover, for the light they shed on the actual working of the political parties which were so distinctive a phenomenon of the government of Britain.

But Hume satisfied a broader interest than that in the English system of life and politics. The tenor and critical method of his philosophy was in concurrence with that of the *philosophes* of Paris. Speculative metaphysics was not to their taste; they were concerned with knowledge that was of use to man. These men had their own great project under way, an "Encyclopedia of Universal Knowledge" which was intended to collect and to disseminate as widely as possible the established truths of science, history, and philosophy. Optimistically they believed that they were ushering in a new era of happiness for all mankind through such enlightenment. And it was more than factual information that was necessary to this end. Light was needed to dispel, not only ignorance of facts, but also prejudices and false beliefs. Much of their own enlightening work had consisted of attacks on prevalent religious beliefs. Sometimes they offered new beliefs in the form of propositions of deism, supposedly based on reason and experience. Now the special merit of Hume was that he had studied belief as a general phenomenon of human nature and had carried out his inquiry in a cool and systematic manner, without the animus which others had often shown. His *Inquiry Concerning Human Understanding* was first and foremost an examination of the sort of belief which is most common and useful both in daily life and in science, the belief resulting from causal inference.

The inference to remote causes or effects from some immediate perception can only be made because we have had experience of such things conjoined in the past, and abstract reason alone without experience cannot decide anything. It is experience that enables us to draw a conclusion about the existence of something which is not present and directly perceived by us. But strangely enough, too, even when one has had experience of the past, it is still not reason that is operating in the inference but imagination. For on every occasion when man makes use of experience to reach a particular conclusion, he is imaginatively supposing the future to be exactly like the past, as if the course of nature were absolutely the same throughout all time. This is an assumption which human reason cannot prove. It is really a habit of the mind. We have an inveterate propensity to take any order of events we have known in a number of cases to be the rule for situations where we do not have experience, and then to infer a cause or an effect and believe in its existence as firmly as if it were a fact or present observation. This phenomenon of belief intrigued Hume. Belief lacked rational foundation; yet it worked in practice and was an essential part of the equipment of man for dealing with the events of his life.

Besides the belief in particular causes and effects which all men live by and which is also relied upon in science, there are other beliefs which form part of the general outlook of every human being. They are common to mankind. Such, for instance, is the belief in an external world, a world that continues to exist independently of ourselves, though we can actually ascertain only what we perceive precisely when we perceive it. Another remarkable belief is the belief in our "personal identity," that we are a "self," one and the same throughout all the changes in our actual perception and consciousness. The attribution of such unity and identity to ourselves, over and above the diversity of our successive perceptions, is a belief which cannot be explained from the evidence. Neither of these beliefs, not this one in the self nor that in the independent permanent world beyond us, can ever be proved by reason. Yet both beliefs are absolutely inescapable. They too, like the belief in causes or effects, must be referred to some fundamental habit of imagination in human nature.

And Hume investigated another belief, one almost universal, though it had been much more debated than the two which we have noticed—this was the belief in the existence of God. Hume had not expounded all his difficulties with this belief in the early *Treatise;* but in the revision of that work, in his *Inquiry Concerning Human Understanding,* he ventured to add one essay on the belief in a special Providence. An extensive discussion of religious belief had been written in the *Dialogues Concerning Natural Religion,* but this work was not published until after Hume's death. However, Hume had already shown enough in the *Inquiry* so that the other philosophers had some idea of his main point, which was that here, as in the other instances, belief is a judgment beyond the evidence of experience and that it is due to a "presumption of the mind" for which no justifying reason can be given.

Hume's attitude toward all such beliefs that lacked rational foundation was not, however, a negative one. He said nothing against any of these unfounded beliefs. He did not claim that they were false; nor did he even label them "prejudices," as others might have done who pretended to be strictly rational in all that they "believed." Instead, he contented himself simply with the disclosure that these beliefs were not conclusions of the rational mind but products of the human imagination. They are very important for the conduct of life, but remain inexplicable in terms of reason. When one is obliged, too, to refer at the end of the inquiry to something unexplained in the very nature of man, there is also nothing derogatory intended in such a reference, for Hume actually published an essay celebrating the "Dignity of Human Nature." A reasonable and reflective person reading Hume and seeing these disclosures about belief would be made more conscious both of his ignorance and of his presumption in ever judging with great self-assurance, and this would tend to make him less dogmatic in his opinions. The *philosophes* of Paris appreciated this "philosophical scepticism." It combined in a fresh and original way both the critical and the humanistic motifs of the Eighteenth-Century Enlightenment.

But Hume did something else that was surprising to these

philosophers. He questioned a *political* belief which they themselves had been holding without critical examination. This was the doctrine of the reality of the "original contract" in the formation of political society. Hume's essay on this topic was first published in the *Political Discourses* (1752), which, as he said, was an instant success. He continued to discuss the doctrine further in that portion of his *History* which dealt with the period prior to the accession of William of Orange and the settlement of the kingdom in 1689. At the end of this book he complained that the Whig party's notion of an original contract had become such a dogma that it was interfering with a just view of history. For the party had been studiously inculcating that doctrine of contract as the sole basis for the right of government. Their aim was to establish it so firmly as a principle that at every succession to the throne of England there would have to be a solemn act of acknowledgment by the king that he had authority to rule only by the consent of the people. Such consent could only be given, of course, through their "representative," the Parliament. In one sense the idea was a sound one, for, as Hume said in his various essays, all government does in fact rest upon the opinion of the people, or at least upon the credit it has with them. Hume could also see the usefulness of the contract doctrine as a measure of practical politics to check the tendency toward absolute authority on the part of the king. But the same practical consideration led him on the other hand to some doubt about its value, for in the light of history he suspected that the Parliament which has the role of giving or withholding the people's consent can also arrogate to itself an excessive authority. If the theory became really a dogma, if the people actually believed that the contract had been a fact of history, as the Whig party pretended, they would revere it as a basic principle of the constitution and treat any opposition to that party doctrine as something "subversive," which would be very dangerous to the cause of personal liberty. So Hume investigated the doctrine and easily showed that there was no foundation in history for it. It was the exposure of this fact that caused Hume to be labeled a Tory at home, where his *History* evoked such a great clamor. Yet this exposé was no less disturbing abroad.

For, quite independently of English party politics, the doctrine of contract had long been very important to the thinkers and philosophers of that enlightened age. Hume's criticism touched their own political belief.

The idea of a social contract had been part of a whole system of ideas which had developed during the rise of the nation-state in modern Europe as an offset to the new and dominant doctrine of absolute or unlimited monarchical sovereignty. This counter-argument ran as follows: To begin with, individuals and families are possessed of property and their natural liberty. They hold their property by "natural right." They are their own masters in that domain: here is where they enjoy their liberty. The foundation of this property right is the "law of nature," the supreme law of the universe, the law of God. Now, in the course of time, men and families possessing property find it more advantageous, and indeed even necessary, to join together in an association which will be greater and more powerful than their "natural" society, the family, and consequently they form themselves into an "artificial" or political society and establish therein an authority to make the laws and protect the state. The so-called "sovereignty" is thus derived from the agreement or contract of the people. The sovereign is required by this contract to serve the state as is contemplated in the deed of power and authority. He has an obligation here which nobody can indeed enforce upon him, but there stands over him, as over all men, the "law of nature," the law of God. As long as men and kings are God-fearing, the affairs of the state will go well and there will be concord. But what if one party to the contract fails to do his part or even violates it? What if the law of nature and of God ever ceases to awe men, so that they do not faithfully abide by their contract? The parties might then break up and be once again outside the moral and political order, and back in a state of nature resembling the Fall, with its consequences of death. In that case people can only escape their dire predicament by once again making a contract, new and more lasting.—We have sketched here a composite and idealized picture of the political theory in which the social contract figures so significantly.

There was much ambiguity of meaning in the doctrine. For example, it was not always clear in the different versions what precisely the contract was supposed to accomplish. Sometimes it seemed to make or form the very society itself out of a number of separate units or individuals. Again, the contract was an agreement only to the laws of communal life in society. In other cases it was the act of instituting the political authority with power to make and enforce laws. Furthermore the contract idea was also employed with very different interests in view. Thus Althusius used it to favor the sovereignty of the people. Grotius sought to impress upon both the sovereign and people their mutual obligations under the law of nature, although he opposed any resistance to the sovereign on the plea of fighting for liberty. Yet the Puritans of England in their rebellion (1647) cited their Grotius nearly as often as the Scripture, and they arraigned their king before their own military court and struck off his head in defiance of a so-called "divine right." Hobbes, seeing all this and finding the idea of covenant or contract so dominant in the thinking of men during that civil war managed in his *Leviathan* (1651) to turn it all to the advantage of sovereign authority without a trace of power being left to the people. But Spinoza in republican Holland, in his *Theologico-Political Treatise* (1670), countered with the view that no man in his senses and with wit enough to make a contract and to know his own true interests would ever think of surrendering, with the original deed of power, all subsequent right to question or to have a continuing voice in the government or to resist a tyrannical and lawless rule of sovereigns. Spinoza came out openly for a contract establishing a democracy. And then Locke, in 1690, agreed with Spinoza that the community always reserves the right, whenever the delegated political power is abused, to resume that power to itself and to reconstitute the civil government anew.

It was after Locke's *Second Treatise of Government* (1690) that the Whig party became so dogmatic with their political doctrine of original contract. They needed it to justify their revolution and the new government; moreover, Hume suspected that they were using it for their own party advantage. But Locke's theory had gained a vast influence outside of England. It was largely responsible for the belief of the philosophers of Paris in both natural right and the social contract which establishes political right to govern. These men had been too absorbed in their own local campaign for greater intellectual liberty to question a doctrine so useful to their cause. But Hume, who also believed in the "cause of liberty," was able to detach himself from his conviction and go to the root of the historical truth of this doctrine held by all the "liberals" of that time. He subjected their most cherished belief to the very same fearless inquiry which they themselves had been making with respect to the beliefs of religion. Here was a lesson of enlightenment for *them*. It put them very much on their mettle and made them deeply respect Hume.

When Hume went to Paris in 1763, having been preceded there by his reputation gained through his *Essays* and *History,* the name of Rousseau was on everyone's lips. The *Social Contract* had recently appeared in 1762, published in Holland; it was banned in France and burned on the market square in Geneva itself. Rousseau himself had had to flee Paris and take up residence in Neufchâtel. It seemed as if the social contract idea would have a new lease of life through this *cause célèbre.* However, in many respects Rousseau and Hume were really in agreement. For Rousseau had denounced the contract for government as an improper act: the sovereignty of the people is inalienable and cannot be contracted away to any person or a government. Thus there is no special sanctity attached to any established government. It is merely set up as a useful administrative agency. On the other hand, the prior act by which a people acknowledge to each other the reality of their community and the authority over them all of the "general will," which is their own will, that remarkable moral act is the true "social compact," and it is indeed "sacred" and inviolable. Rousseau was here putting new wine into an old vessel.[1] For under the name of the social contract he

---

[1] Cf. C. W. Hendel, *Jean Jacques Rousseau: Moralist* (Oxford University Press, New York and London, 1934), Vol. I, Chs. VI–VII; Vol. II, Chs. XVIII–XIX. See also G. D. H. Cole's Introduction to the *Social Contract* (Everyman's Library).

was introducing wholly different conceptions of man and the community, as well as of sovereignty, law, and obligation. Despite the traditional words in the title of his book, therefore, the older doctrine of social contract was being "liquidated," to use a contemporary colloquialism. Rousseau here led the way for the later insights of Kant and Hegel. Meanwhile Hume's quiet and irresistible examination of the historical aspect of the contract was also to have its effect in gradually bringing about an eventual disuse of the notion. It is worth remarking, however, that Hume himself, in a late edition of his essay on the "Original Contract," inserted a new paragraph opening thus:

> My intention here is not to exclude the consent of the people from being one just foundation of government. Where it has place it is surely the best and most sacred of any. I only contend that it has very seldom had place in any degree, and never almost in its full extent. . . .[2]

Was not Hume tempering here the drastic effect of his criticism? It seems as if he had even been impressed by Rousseau's thought and was willing to use his very term "sacred." In any event, Hume was consistent with himself, for he was doing here, in the case of the belief in the contract, what he had done in the case of all the other beliefs, viz., exposing the inadequacy of their foundation in experience or history while still acknowledging their value for the purposes of life.

When honest thinkers realize an unwitting dogmatism in themselves, they see the need of fresh inquiry to determine what is really true. If the contract is not a fact of history, what then does history actually show to have been the case? Hume's scepticism about the belief in contract thus inspired himself and others to further historical research. In this respect Hume's influence joined with that of Montesquieu, whose *Spirit of the Laws* (1749) was the first great investigation into the nature of historical law and who more than any other modern, perhaps, has taught the lesson that one needs to know the "spirit of the nation" if one is to make good laws and administer them well. Through Montesquieu the

[2] Page 50.

idea of a constitution founded historically in the ways of life of
the people became more important for political science and philosophy than contract. And Hume himself seems to have been
somewhat influenced by Montesquieu, with whom he corres-
ponded and for whose *Esprit des Lois* he tried to secure an English translator; for, as we have seen, he made much of the concept
of the English constitution that took form in the minds of the
people during the years of their struggle with arbitrary authority.

At home Hume's work, both in the *Essays* and in the *History,*
constituted a sober lesson in the values of English society and the
constitution. After him there was to come Edmund Burke, who
continued the new style of historical interpretation and who did
so with such fine imagination and eloquence of the pen that what
had appeared to be only critical thought in Hume's writings later
became a moving and well-founded conviction and an inspiration
to generations. As a pathfinder to the new historical tradition in
politics, Hume richly deserved all the honor paid him during
his lifetime.

V. THE RELEVANCE OF HUME'S POLITICAL
WRITINGS TO AMERICAN THOUGHT

Hume died in August, 1776, a few weeks after the Declaration
of Independence. He had, as he confessed, something of the
interest of a "statesman" at that time and had followed the
development of the rift between the American colonists and
England. In the first volume of his *History,* written years past,
he had said, regarding the first American settlements, that there
was a good prospect of a continued and mutually advantageous
relationship between the colonies and the mother country:

What chiefly renders the reign of James memorable is the
commencement of the English colonies in America, colonies
established on the noblest footing that has been known in any
age or nation. The Spaniards, being the first discoverers of the
New World, immediately took possession of the precious mines
which they found there; and by the allurement of great riches
they were tempted to depopulate their own country as well as
that which they conquered, and added the vice of sloth to those

of avidity and barbarity, which had attended their adventurers in those renowned enterprises. That fine coast was entirely neglected which reaches from St. Augustine to Cape Breton and which lies in all the temperate climates, is watered by noble rivers, and offers a fertile soil, but nothing more, to the industrious planter. Peopled gradually from England by the necessitous and indigent, who at home increased neither wealth nor populousness, the colonies which were planted along that tract have promoted the navigation, encouraged the industry, and even perhaps multiplied the inhabitants of their mother country. The spirit of independency, which was reviving in England, here shone forth in its full luster and received new accession from the aspiring character of those who, being discontented with the established church and monarchy, had sought for freedom amidst those savage deserts. . . .

. . . After supplying themselves with provisions more immediately necessary for the support of life, the new planters began the cultivating of tobacco; and James, notwithstanding his antipathy to that drug, which he affirmed to be pernicious to men's morals as well as their health, gave them permission to enter it in England, and he inhibited by proclamation all importation of it from Spain. By degrees, new colonies were established in that continent and gave new names to the places where they settled, leaving that of Virginia to the province first planted. The Island of Barbadoes was also planted in this reign.

Speculative reasoners during that age raised many objections to the planting of those remote colonies and foretold that, after draining their mother country of inhabitants, they would soon shake off their yoke and erect an independent government in America; but time has shown that the views entertained by those who encouraged such generous undertakings were more just and solid. A mild government and great naval force have preserved and may still preserve during some time the dominion of England over her colonies. And such advantages have commerce and navigation reaped from these establishments that more than a fourth of the English shipping is at present computed to be employed in carrying on the traffic with the American settlements.[3]

Now the tie was about to be severed. It was the fault of the British government.

[3] *History of England*, Vol. IV, Appendix to the Reign of James I, pp. 518–520.

Hume wrote about the matter to his intimate friends, especially to William Strahan, his publisher, to Baron Mure and Adam Smith, and to his brother John Home and his nephew David Hume.[4] To Mure he had said: "I am an American in my principles and wish we could let them alone to govern or misgovern themselves as they think proper."[5] In the same letter he suggested facetiously that "the representative of the county of Renfrew" should "advise the King," and do so namely by putting the question: "Ask him, how he can expect that a form of government will maintain an authority at 3,000 miles distance when it cannot make itself be respected or even treated with common decency at home."[6] He wrote at length to Strahan:

I must, before we part, have a little stroke of politics with you, notwithstanding my resolution to the contrary. We hear that some of the ministers have proposed in Council that both fleet and army be withdrawn from America and these colonists be left entirely to themselves. I wish I had been a member of His Majesty's Cabinet Council that I might have seconded this opinion. I should have said that this measure only anticipates the necessary course of events a few years.[7]

Hume continued with a detail of the extreme measures the government would have to take in order to conquer and then to govern the Americans:

We must . . . annul all the charters, abolish every democratical power in every colony, repeal the habeas corpus act with regard to them, invest every governor with full discretionary or arbitrary powers, confiscate the estates of all the chief planters, and hang three fourths of their clergy. To execute such acts of destructive violence twenty thousand men will not be sufficient; nor thirty thousand to maintain them in so wide and disjointed a territory. . . . Let us therefore lay aside all anger, shake hands, and part

[4] Hume insisted on using the older spelling of family names. His brother used "Home."

[5] Letter to Baron Mure, October 27, 1775, in *The Letters of David Hume*, edited by J. Y. T. Greig (Oxford, Clarendon Press, 1932), Vol. II, p. 303.

[6] *Ibid.*

[7] Letter to William Strahan, October 26, 1775, in Greig, *op. cit.*, Vol. II, p. 300.

friends. Or, if we retain our anger, let it only be against our-selves for our past folly. . . .[8]

Now Hume's sentiments were well known to an American friend with whom he was long acquainted, Benjamin Franklin. That shrewd, gifted diplomat had gone on a mission to England in 1757 when Hume was still at work on his *History*. They had first met in London; later, in 1760, Franklin visited Hume at Edinburgh. In 1762 Franklin sent Hume a paper to be sub-mitted on his behalf to the Philosophical Society of Edinburgh in which he described, as Hume expressed it, "a method of pre-serving houses from thunder." In acknowledging this monograph Hume said:

I am very sorry that you intend soon to leave our hemisphere. America has sent us many good things: gold, silver, sugar, tobacco, indigo, etc. But you are the first philosopher, and indeed the first man of letters from whom we are beholden to her; it is our own fault that we have not kept him. . . .[9]

But Franklin was back again in November 1771, visiting Hume at Edinburgh;[10] and again in February 1772, as this letter wit-nesses:

I was very glad to hear of your safe arrival in London after being exposed to as many perils as St. Paul by land and by water, though to no perils among false brethren, for the good wishes of all your brother philosophers in this place attend you heartily and sincerely, together with much regret that your business would not allow you to pass more time among them.[11]

Then, after speaking of the continuing "prejudice" in England against his work, Hume said:

[8] *Ibid.*, Vol. II, pp. 301.

[9] Letter to Benjamin Franklin, Edinburgh, May 10, 1762, in *The Letters of David Hume*, edited by R. Klibansky and E. C. Mossner (Oxford, Clarendon Press, 1952), pp. 67–68. This is a supplementary volume to Greig's edition of Hume's letters.

[10] Letter to William Strahan, November 12, 1771, in Greig, *op. cit.*, Vol. II, p. 251.

[11] Letter to Benjamin Franklin, Edinburgh, February 7, 1772, in Kliban-sky and Mossner, *op. cit.*, p. 194.

I fancy that I must have recourse to America for justice. You told me, I think, that your countrymen in that part of the world intended to do me the honor of giving an edition of my writings, and you promised that you should recommend to them to follow this last edition which is in the press. I now use the freedom of reminding you of it.[12]

This was apparently the last of their correspondence. A letter from Hume to Adam Smith in 1774 tells of the shock he felt at hearing rumors that Franklin had been accused before the Privy Council of having surreptitiously obtained official papers to which he was not entitled and forwarding them to America, thereby fomenting trouble between the royal governor and the Massachusetts Assembly. "What a pity!" Hume exclaimed.[13] To Strahan he wrote a few days later: "Dr. Franklin wishes to emancipate them [the colonies] too soon from their mother country." [14]

The recommendation of Franklin would certainly make Hume's work known in America. There are various indications, too, that when the Americans were struggling with that difficulty of which Hume had spoken in the "Idea of a Perfect Commonwealth," of *establishing* a republic, Franklin introduced some ideas seemingly learned through his association with Hume in Edinburgh. For example, during the Federal Convention of 1787, when they were discussing how to make a more perfect union than the existing Confederation of United States, the then elderly Franklin urged two articles: (1) that the legislature should be a single house like that of Scotland; (2) that high officers of the national government, legislative, judicial, and executive alike, should not receive any salary, which was one of the articles in Hume's revision of *Oceana*.[15]

But Franklin was by no means the only possible channel

[12] *Ibid.* The editors identify the edition mentioned here as *Essays and Treatises* (1772), 2 vols.

[13] Letter to A. Smith, February 13, 1774, in Greig, *op. cit.*, Vol. II, p. 286. The editor gives details in footnote 3 of the accusation and the consequences.

[14] Letter to William Strahan, March 1, 1774, in Greig, *op. cit.*, Vol. II, p. 288.

[15] See Debates in the Federal Convention of 1787, in *Documents Illustrative of the Formation of the Union of the American States* (Wash-

through which Hume's ideas might have reached Americans. The *literati* and *philosophes* of France had been the first to see the merit of his political essays and to give him a reputation. The ties between America and France were not only of a military nature. A civilization that would send a Lafayette to aid America in her struggle for independence would also be likely to recommend to Americans men such as Hume from whom they themselves were learning their political science and philosophy.

It is true that there was much in Hume's writings which might not ingratiate him with some Americans. For one thing he had mercilessly criticized Puritan "cant, hypocrisy, and bigotry." But in the century and a half since the first Puritan settlements, Americans themselves had acquired some experience of religious sects and their shortcomings. Moreover, there were many freethinkers among them, like Franklin and Jefferson. And whereas the original Puritans, in the Council of Officers at Whitehall in 1648, debated as to whether to lay down guarantees regarding religion in their "settlement of the kingdom" and hedged against doing so,[16] Hume honored the sect of Independents for their adoption of the principle of toleration and for their unflinching loyalty to it. In America this group was known as the Congregationalists. And eventually, as we know, the American founders laid down in the Constitution the guarantees of religious liberty and toleration. Thus in spite of his oft-expressed irony and irritation at the vices of fanaticism and hypocrisy, Hume was not out of harmony with American principles concerning the relation of religion and politics.

On the subject of liberty, however—a cause truly "noble and

---

ington, D. C., United States Government Printing Office, 1927). For Franklin's position on these matters, see pp. 92, 125, 127, 137, 731, and 751.

[16] See A. S. Woodhouse, *Puritanism and Liberty* (Chicago, University of Chicago Press, 1951). The questions before the Council on December 14, 1648, were: "Whether the magistrate have, or ought to have, any compulsive and restrictive power in matters of religion," and "Whether to have [in the Agreement of the People] any reserve to except religious things, or only to give power in natural and civil things and to say nothing of religion" [p. 125].

generous," as Hume had written to one of his critics at home and as he had said many times publicly in the *Essays* and the *History*[17]—there was complete accord.

The prejudice against Hume in England had largely been due, as he believed, to his criticism of the Whig theory and practice of government, as well as to his own seeming espousal of Tory politics. But Americans from 1776 onward were not at all disposed to fight out England's party battles on their own soil. They had no intention of blindly re-enacting in their own land the animosities of the old country; they had their own particular quarrel with the English government, indeed with Parliament itself.

The opening words of the Declaration and Resolves of the First Continental Congress (October 14, 1774) complained especially of the British Parliament. Again the Declaration of the Causes and Necessity of Taking up Arms (July 6, 1775) accused the legislature of Great Britain of "an inordinate passion for power."[18] Both "King and Parliament" were associated in the tyrannies enumerated in the Declaration of Independence, July 4, 1776. "We have warned them ["our British brethren"] from time to time of attempts by their legislature to extend an unwarrantable jurisdiction over us."[19] The very representative of the people in Great Britain, the Parliament, was guilty of the grave fault of excessive and arbitrary authority. In this respect Hume's *History of England* was like a mirror in which Americans could read themselves and their situation. They could see their own case in it, as when Hume says:

At the same time that the boroughs of England were deprived of their privileges, a like attempt was made on the colonies. King James recalled the charters by which their liberties were secured, and he sent over governors invested with absolute power. The arbitrary principles of that monarch appear in every part of his administration.[20]

[17] See Letter to Catherine Macaulay, Paris, March 29, 1764, in Klibansky and Mossner, *op. cit.*, p. 81.
[18] *Documents Illustrative of the Union of the American States, op. cit.*, pp. 1, 10.
[19] *Ibid.*, pp. 24–25.
[20] *History of England*, Vol. VI, Ch. LXXI, p. 371.

And now it had happened again under George III, this time with King and Parliament associated in iniquity and doing precisely what Hume had warned them against in his early essay on the science of politics, "That Politics May Be Reduced to a Science," when he said that even free governments can become "the most ruinous and oppressive to their provinces."[21]

The story of authority and liberty in the *History* contained lessons to be heeded by the Americans as they went about designing their Constitution. Here one could see the importance of a well-founded Constitution, with balanced powers for the sake of regulated liberty and authority. The nemesis of power without limit is here relentlessly exposed by Hume: First the King claimed divine right and supremacy, but acted so arbitrarily and imperiously that the nation rose in rebellion under the leadership of Parliament. Then the Commons, ostensibly in the cause of liberty, gained authority, with much merit to commend them; but having full power, they too became "cruel and arbitrary" and oppressive. Waging civil war, the army subject to Parliament developed within it a Council of Officers, who constituted themselves a "military Parliament" and carried on in the same way as their predecessors had done. Then the Levellers, very radical in their aim to secure equal liberty for all, overturned the Army authority and also exercised arbitrary power. Oliver Cromwell could only check their unbounded license with another authority of his own as Protector, and so the history had come round in a full circle to the rule of one man, as it was in the beginning.

This is not the place to go into the actual historical connections between the work of Hume in his *Essays* and *History* and the debates of the American statesmen who were engaged upon their great task of establishing a republic that would endure. There were grave fears and predictions at the time that the new commonwealth would not last. The men who drew up the resolutions, those who spoke at the Federal Convention, as well as the citizens and country gentlemen who had made a Revolution and were now seeking to govern themselves had little time to docu-

[21] Page 15.

ment their words and identify the sources of their opinion or inspiration. They were constantly referring to the "experience" of the British Constitution, and quite often in the very phrases of Hume, as when Madison spoke of "the republican principle." [22] There are some more specific clues, as when John Adams refers to Hume's *History* and the "Idea of a Perfect Commonwealth," and the very temper of his expression asserting independence betrays how much authority Hume really had with him: Americans in his age "are too enlightened to be bubbled out of their liberties, even by such mighty names as Locke, Milton, Turgot, or Hume. . . ." [23]

What will impress any present-day American, however, in reading the records of the founders of the Republic is their besetting concern in the Convention with "the fury of democracy." [24] "The evils we experience," said Gerry, "flow from the excess of democracy." [25] Randolph also observed that "the general object was to provide a cure for the evils under which the United States labored, that in tracing these evils to their origin every man had found it in the turbulence and follies of democracy." [26] But Mason retorted later: "Notwithstanding the oppressions and injustice experienced among us from democracy, the genius of the people is in favor of it, and the genius of the people must be consulted." [27] That is exactly the way Hume spoke of the people in his *History*, deploring their extreme behavior and yet recognizing that the spirit of liberty was characteristic of the genius of the nation.

Delegates to the Convention were far from thinking that the representatives of the people could do no wrong. They remem-

---

[22] *Ibid.*, p. 116.

[23] Quoted in Alfred Iacuzzi, *John Adams: Scholar* (New York, S. F. Vanni, 1952), pp. 85f.

[24] Randolph quoted in notes of Major William Pierce, in *Documents Illustrative of the Formation of the Union of the American States* (Washington, D. C., United States Government Printing Office, 1927), p. 88. See Note 1, Introduction, p. 159.

[25] Quoted in *ibid.*, p. 127. See Note 2, Introduction, p. 159.

[26] Quoted in *ibid.*, p. 159

[27] Quoted in *ibid.*, p. 150. See Note 3, Introduction, p. 159.

bered the English Parliament and the Commons, and how those parties who cried for liberty were the very ones to deny it by exercising absolute and arbitrary authority. "The lesson we are to draw from the whole," said Madison on another occasion, "is that where a majority are united by a common sentiment and have an opportunity the rights of the minority become insecure."[28] They spent long hours debating the principles of a constitution for the United States which would perfect their union and give it strength, and at the same time secure the rights and liberties of all. They knew that they wanted "the republican form" of government. But in drawing up the particulars, they faced the ever-present problem of politics of which Hume had given so vivid an account in his *History:* the problem of the relation of liberty and authority. One after another of the delegates confessed to being in a dilemma similar to that of Gouveneur Morris:

I avow myself the advocate of a strong government; still I admit that the influence of the rich must be guarded; and a pure democracy is equally oppressive. . . . This remark is founded on the experience of history.[29]

Alexander Hamilton also drew upon the experience of history and was very explicit about his source of knowledge. In speaking against a proposal to make legal provisions against possible venality and corruption on the part of those who hold office, Hamilton said:

Hume's opinion of the British Constitution confirms the remark that there is always a body of firm patriots who often shake a corrupt administration.[30]

And later, when Hamilton was working with Madison and John Jay on the *Federalist* papers, in an endeavor to assure the adoption of the newly designed Constitution, he concluded the very last paper with "judicious reflections" from Hume's essay, "The Rise of the Arts and Sciences":

[28] Quoted in *ibid.,* p. 163.
[29] Quoted in *ibid.,* p. 839. See Note 4, Introduction, pp. 159f.
[30] Quoted in *ibid.,* p. 799.

To balance a large state or society (says he) whether monarchical or republican, on general laws, is a work of so great difficulty, that no human genius, however comprehensive, is able by the mere dint of reason and reflection, to effect it. The judgments of many must unite in the work; experience must guide their labour; time must bring it to perfection, and the feeling of inconveniences must correct the mistakes which they *inevitably* fall into in their first trials and experiments.[31]

The Americans of that time were making their "first experiment" with a republic. They sought balance of power in the government and "peace and order," always in the interest of free men and the general welfare. They established by their labors, not only a workable government, but above all the tradition of a "government of laws, not of men." In all this they had proceeded in the spirit of Hume.

"I am American in my principles,"[30] Hume was not given to making mistakes. He was a man of discernment, in politics as well as in philosophy.

CHARLES W. HENDEL

Yale University
January, 1953

[31] Quoted in *The Federalist*, No. LXXXV, Modern Library edition, p. 574.
[30] Letter to Baron Mure, October 27, 1775, in *The Letters of David Hume*, edited by J. Y. T. Greig (Oxford, Clarendon Press, 1932), Vol. II, p. 303.

SELECTED BIBLIOGRAPHY

HUME'S WORKS AND LETTERS

A Treatise of Human Nature (1739).
Essays, Moral and Political (vol. I: 1741; vol. II: 1742).
An Enquiry Concerning Human Understanding (1748).
  (First published as *Philosophical Essays Concerning Human Understanding.*)
  Second edition with additions and corrections, 1750.
An Enquiry Concerning the Principles of Morals (1751).
Political Discourses (1752).
History of England (1754–62).
Four Dissertations (1757):
  (1) Natural History of Religion
  (2) Of the Passions
  (3) Of Tragedy
  (4) Of the Standard of Taste
Dialogues Concerning Natural Religion (1779).
The Letters of David Hume, edited by J. Y. T. Greig. Oxford, 1932.
The Letters of David Hume, edited by R. Klibansky and E. C. Mossner. Oxford, 1952.

COLLECTED WORKS

The Philosophical Works of David Hume. 4 vols. Adam Black and William Tait, Edinburgh, 1826.
The Philosophical Works of David Hume. 4 vols. Little, Brown and Company, Boston, 1854.
The Philosophical Works of David Hume, edited by T. H. Green and T. H. Grose. 4 vols. Longmans, Green and Company, London, 1898.
Hume's Moral and Political Philosophy, edited by Henry D. Aiken. Hafner Publishing Company, New York, 1948.

WORKS ON HUME

Black, John Bennett, *The Art of History; A Study of Four Great Historians of the Eighteenth Century.* Vol. III: David Hume. London, 1926.

Burton, J. H., *Life and Correspondence of David Hume.* 2 volumes. Edinburgh, 1846.

Hedenius, Ingemar, *Studies in Hume's Ethics,* Upsala and Stockholm, 1935.

Hendel, C. W., *Jean Jacques Rousseau: Moralist.* New York and London, 1934.

————*Selections from Hume,* Scribner's "Modern Student's Library." New York, 1927.

————*Studies in the Philosophy of David Hume.* Princeton, 1925.

Kemp Smith, Norman, *The Philosophy of Hume.* London, 1941.

Kuypers, M. S., *Studies in the Eighteenth Century Background of Hume's Empiricism.* Minneapolis, 1930.

Kydd, Rachael M., *Reason and Conduct in Hume's Treatise.* London, 1946.

Laing, B. M., *David Hume.* London, 1932.

Lechartier, Georges, *David Hume; Moraliste et Sociologue.* Paris, 1900.

Mossner, Ernest Campbell, "Was Hume a Tory Historian?" *Journal of the History of Ideas,* II, 225–36. Lancaster, 1941.

Oake, Roger B., "Montesquieu and Hume," *Modern Language Quarterly,* II, 25–41. Seattle, 1941.

Sabine, George H., *A History of Political Theory.* New York, 1937; revised edition, 1950.

————"Hume's Contribution to the Historical Method," *Philosophical Review,* XV, 17–38. New York, 1905.

Shearer, E. A., *Hume's Place in Ethics.* Bryn Mawr, 1915.

Stephen, L., *History of English Thought in the Eighteenth Century.* London, 1876.

NOTE ON THE TEXT

The present edition of *David Hume's Political Essays* is a selection from *Essays Moral, Political, and Literary*. All essays follow the last edition prepared during Hume's lifetime and are, with a few exceptions, reprinted entire. Omissions, in the few instances where they occur, are clearly marked. They are for the most part digressions or seem irrelevant to the presentation of Hume's political theory. A number of essays have been appended by significant quotations from the *History of England*. These selections have been quoted from the edition of Harper and Brothers (n.d.).

The *Essays Moral, Political, and Literary* were extremely successful (cf. Introduction, pp. ivi, xli) and went through many reprints, in the course of which Hume constantly made changes —rephrasing passages, adding material and entire essays, and dropping others. For the first edition of Hume's collected philosophical writings, published in 1826 by Adam Black and William Tait, Edinburgh, the editor carefully compared the various editions of the *Essays* and noted in footnotes "the successive variations of sentiment and tastes," which in general, in the words of the editor, show a "gradual and most observable increase of caution in his [Hume's] expressions of these sentiments." In the present edition, these editorial notes have been retained wherever Hume's modifications have seemed significant. It has become customary also to designate the various editions which are not merely reprints of preceding editions by letter, from *A* to *O* (fourteen in all). A complete list of these editions, as given in the edition of 1826, is here reprinted (page lxviii).

The editorial staff of the publishers has supplied translations of foreign-language passages and helpful supplementary references, in addition to appendix notes on important historical and political figures and events referred to in the text. All such contributions appearing in footnotes have been bracketed, to distinguish them from Hume's own notes. Spelling and punctuation have been revised throughout to conform to present-day American usage.

O. P.

EDITIONS A TO O

Essays, Moral and Political. Edinburgh, Kincaid, 1741. *(A)*

Essays, Moral and Political, Vol. II. Edinburgh, Kincaid, 1742. *(B)*

Essays, Moral and Political. Second edition, corrected. Edinburgh, Kincaid, 1742. *(C)*

Essays, Moral and Political. By D. Hume, Esq. Third edition, corrected, with additions. London, Millar, 1748. *(D)*

Three Essays, Moral and Political, never before published, which completes the former edition. By D. Hume, Esq. London, Millar, 1748. *(E)*

Political Discourses. By D. Hume, Esq. Edinburgh, Kincaid, 1752. *To this edition there is sometimes added "a list of Scotticisms." (F)*

Political Discourses. By D. Hume, Esq. Second edition. Edinburgh, Kincaid, 1752. *Merely a reprint of the preceding. (G)*

Essays and Treatises on several Subjects. By D. Hume, Esq. Vol. IV containing Political Discourses. Third edition, with additions and corrections. London, Millar, 1754. *(H)*

Four Dissertations: 1st, Natural History of Religion; 2nd, Of the Passions; 3rd, Of Tragedy; 4th, Of the Standard of Taste. By D. Hume, Esq. London, Millar, 1757. *(I)*

Philosophical Essays concerning Human Understanding. By the Author of the Essays, Moral and Political. London, Millar, 1748. *(K)*

Philosophical Essays concerning Human Understanding. By D. Hume, Esq. Second edition, with additions and corrections. London, Millar, 1750. *(L)*

An Enquiry concerning the Principles of Morals. By D. Hume, Esq. London, Millar, 1751. *(M)*

Essays and Treatises on several Subjects. By D. Hume, Esq. London, Millar, 1768. 2 vols. *(N)*

Essays and Treatises on several Subjects. By D. Hume, Esq. London, Cadell, 1777. 2 vols. *(O)*

DAVID HUME'S POLITICAL ESSAYS

I

OF THE LIBERTY OF THE PRESS

NOTHING IS MORE APT to surprise a foreigner than the extreme liberty which we enjoy in this country of communicating whatever we please to the public and of openly censuring every measure entered into by the king or his ministers. If the administration resolve upon war, it is affirmed that, either willfully or ignorantly, they mistake the interests of the nation; and that peace, in the present situation of affairs, is infinitely preferable. If the passion of the ministers lie toward peace, our political writers breathe nothing but war and devastation, and represent the specific conduct of the government as mean and pusillanimous. As this liberty is not indulged in any other government, either republican or monarchical—in Holland and Venice more than in France or Spain—it may very naturally give occasion to the question: *How it happens that Great Britain alone enjoys this peculiar privilege?* [a]

The reason why the laws indulge us in such a liberty seems to be derived from our mixed form of government, which is neither wholly monarchical nor wholly republican. It will be found, if I mistake not, a true observation in politics that the two extremes in government, liberty and slavery, commonly approach nearest to each other; and that, as you depart from the extremes and mix a little of monarchy with liberty, the government becomes always the more free, and on the other hand, when you mix a little of liberty with monarchy, the yoke becomes always the more grievous and intolerable. In a government, such as that of France, which is absolute and where law, custom, and religion concur, all of them, to make the people fully satisfied with their

[a] "And whether the unlimited exercise of this liberty be advantageous or prejudicial to the public."—Editions A, C, D, N.

3

condition, the monarch cannot entertain any *jealousy* against his subjects and therefore is apt to indulge them in great *liberties*, both of speech and action. In a government altogether republican, such as that of Holland, where there is no magistrate so eminent as to give *jealousy* to the state, there is no danger in entrusting the magistrates with large discretionary powers; and though many advantages result from such powers, in preserving peace and order, yet they lay a considerable restraint on men's actions and make every private citizen pay a great respect to the government. Thus it seems evident that the two extremes of absolute monarchy and of a republic approach near to each other in some material circumstances. In the *first* the magistrate has no jealousy of the people, in the *second* the people have none of the magistrate; which want of jealousy begets a mutual confidence and trust in both cases and produces a species of liberty in monarchies and of arbitrary power in republics.

To justify the other part of the foregoing observation—that, in every government, the means are most wide of each other, and that the mixtures of monarchy and liberty render the yoke either more grievous—I must take notice of a remark in Tacitus, with regard to the Romans under the emperors, that they neither could bear total slavery nor total liberty: "*Nec totam servitutem, nec totam libertatem pati possunt.*" This remark a celebrated poet [1] has translated and applied to the English in his lively description of Queen Elizabeth's policy and government:

> Et fit aimer son joug à l'Anglois indompté,
> Qui ne peut ni servir, ni vivre en liberté.
> —*Henriade*, liv. i.

According to these remarks, we are to consider the Roman government under the emperors as a mixture of despotism and liberty where the despotism prevailed, and the English government as a mixture of the same kind where the liberty predominates. The consequences are conformable to the foregoing observation and such as may be expected from those mixed forms of government which beget a mutual watchfulness and jealousy. The Roman emperors were, many of them, the most frightful tyrants that ever disgraced human nature; and it is evident that their cruelty was chiefly excited by their *jealousy,* and by their observing that all the great men of Rome bore with impatience the dominion of a family which, but a little before, was nowise superior to their own. On the other hand, as the republican part [2] of the government prevails in England, though with a great mixture of monarchy, it is obliged, for its own preservation, to maintain a watchful *jealousy* over the magistrates, to remove all discretionary powers, and to secure everyone's life and fortune by general and inflexible laws. No action must be deemed a crime but what the law has plainly determined to be such; no crime must be imputed to a man but from a legal proof before his judges, and even these judges must be his fellow subjects, who are obliged by their own interest to have a watchful eye over the encroachments and violence of the ministers. From these causes it proceeds that there is as much liberty, and even perhaps licentiousness, in Great Britain as there were formerly slavery and tyranny in Rome.

These principles account for the great liberty of the press in these kingdoms beyond what is indulged in any other government. It is apprehended that arbitrary power would steal in upon us were we not careful to prevent its progress and were there not an easy method of conveying the alarm from one end of the kingdom to the other. The spirit of the people must frequently be roused in order to curb the ambition of the court, and the dread of rousing this spirit must be employed to prevent that ambition. Nothing so effectual to this purpose as the liberty of the press, by which all the learning, wit, and genius of the nation may be employed on the side of freedom and everyone be animated to its defense. As long, therefore, as the republican part of our government can maintain itself against the monarchical, it will naturally be careful to keep the press open, as of importance to its own preservation.[b]

[b] [The following passage, from "Since, therefore . . ." to ". . . attempts shall succeed," here incorporated as text, appears as a footnote in Editions A, C, D, and N.]

Since, therefore, the liberty of the press is so essential to the support of our mixed government, this sufficiently decides the second question: *Whether this liberty be advantageous or prejudicial,* there being nothing of greater importance in every state than the preservation of the ancient government, especially if it be a free one. But I would fain go a step further and assert that such a liberty is attended with so few inconveniences that it may be claimed as the common right of mankind and ought to be indulged them almost in every government except the ecclesiastical, to which, indeed, it would be fatal. We need not dread from this liberty any such ill consequences as followed from the harangues of the popular demagogues of Athens and tribunes of Rome. A man reads a book or pamphlet alone and coolly. There is none present from whom he can catch the passion by contagion. He is not hurried away by the force and energy of action. And should he be wrought up to never so seditious a humor, there is no violent resolution presented to him by which he can immediately vent his passion. The liberty of the press, therefore, however abused, can scarce ever excite popular tumults or rebellion. And as to those murmurs or secret discontents it may occasion, it is better they should get vent in words, that they may come to the knowledge of the magistrate before it be too late, in order to his providing a remedy against them. Mankind, it is true, have always a greater propension to believe what is said to the disadvantage of their governors than the contrary; but this inclination is inseparable from them whether they have liberty or not. A whisper may fly as quick and be as pernicious as a pamphlet. Nay, it will be more pernicious where men are not accustomed to think freely or distinguish betwixt truth and falsehood.

It has also been found, as the experience of mankind increases, that the *people* are no such dangerous monsters as they have been represented, and that it is in every respect better to guide them like rational creatures than to lead or drive them like brute beasts. Before the United Provinces set the example, toleration was deemed incompatible with good government; and it was thought impossible that a number of religious sects could live together in harmony and peace, and have all of them an equal affection to their common country and to each other. *England* has set a like example of civil liberty, and though this liberty seems to occasion some small ferment at present, it has not as yet produced any pernicious effects; and it is to be hoped that men, being every day more accustomed to the free discussion of public affairs, will improve in their judgment of them and be with greater difficulty seduced by every idle rumor and popular clamor.

It is a very comfortable reflection to the lovers of liberty that this peculiar privilege of *Britain* is of a kind that cannot easily be wrested from us and must last as long as our government remains in any degree free and independent. It is seldom that liberty of any kind is lost all at once. Slavery has so frightful an aspect to men accustomed to freedom that it must steal in upon them by degrees and must disguise itself in a thousand shapes in order to be received. But if the liberty of the press ever be lost, it must be lost at once. The general laws against sedition and libeling are at present as strong as they possibly can be made. Nothing can impose a further restraint but either the clapping an imprimatur upon the press or the giving very large discretionary powers to the court to punish whatever displeases them. But these concessions would be such a barefaced violation of liberty that they will probably be the last efforts of a despotic government. We may conclude that the liberty of *Britain* is gone forever when these attempts shall succeed.

It must however be allowed that the unbounded liberty of the press, though it be difficult—perhaps impossible—to propose a suitable remedy for it, is one of the evils attending those mixed forms of government.

FROM THE *HISTORY OF ENGLAND*

Hume, though devoted to liberty, reminds his readers of the need of historical perspective:

The severity of the Star Chamber [3] . . . was perhaps in itself blamable, but will naturally to us appear enormous who enjoy in the utmost latitude that liberty of the press which is esteemed so necessary in every monarchy confined by strict legal limitations. But as these limitations were not regularly fixed during the age of Charles, nor at any time before, so was this liberty totally unknown and was generally deemed, as well as religious toleration, incompatible with all good government. No age or nation among the moderns had ever set an example of such an indulgence; and it seems unreasonable to judge of the measures embraced during one period by the maxims which prevail in another. [Vol. V, Ch. LII, pp. 83–84.]

The press, freed from all fear or reserve, swarmed with productions, dangerous by their seditious zeal and calumny more than by any art or eloquence of composition. Noise and fury, cant and hypocrisy formed the sole rhetoric which, during this tumult of various prejudices and passions, could be heard or attended to. [Vol. V, Ch. LIV, p. 137.]

Hume declares toward the end of his history of the revolution:

Till the revolution, the liberty of the press was very imperfectly enjoyed in England and during a very short period. The Star Chamber, while that court subsisted, put effectual restraints upon printing. On the suppression of that tribunal in 1641, the long Parliament, after their rupture with the King, assumed the same power with regard to the licensing of books, and this authority was continued during all the period of the republic and protectorship. Two years after the restoration, an act was passed reviving the republican ordinances. This act expired in 1679, but was revived in the first of King James. The liberty of the press did not even commence with the revolution. It was not till 1694 that the restraints were taken off, to the great displeasure of the King and his ministers, who, seeing nowhere in any government during present or past ages any example of such unlimited freedom, doubted much of its salutary effects and probably thought that no books or writings would ever so much improve the general understanding of men as to render it safe to intrust them with an indulgence so easily abused. [Vol. VI, Ch. LXXI, p. 372.]

Hume himself was free to publish, in this volume of the History of England *(1757), the following opinion:*

The Whig party, for a course of near seventy years, has almost without interruption enjoyed the whole authority of government, and no honors or offices could be obtained but by their countenance and protection. But this event, which in some particulars has been advantageous to the state, has proved destructive to the truth of history. [Vol. VI, Ch. LXXI, p. 365.]

Liberty of conscience was as basic to Hume as personal and political liberty. In the following passages from the History, *he traces the development of religious toleration:*

In a word, that liberty of conscience which we so highly and so justly value at present was totally suppressed, and no exercise of any religion but the established was permitted throughout the kingdom. [Vol. IV, Appendix to the Reign of James I, p. 497.]

We have had occasion to remark in so many instances the bigotry which prevailed in that age that we can look for no toleration among the different sects. Two Arians, under the title of heretics, were punished by fire during this period; and no one reign since the Reformation had been free from the like barbarities. Stowe says that these Arians were offered their pardon at the stake if they would merit it by a recantation. A madman who called himself the Holy Ghost was, without any indulgence for his frenzy, condemned to the same punishment. Twenty pounds a month could, by law, be levied on everyone who frequented not the established worship. This rigorous law, however, had one indulgent clause, that the fines exacted should not exceed two thirds of the yearly income of the person. It had been usual for Elizabeth to allow those penalties to run on for several years and to levy them all at once, to the utter ruin of such Catholics as had incurred her displeasure. James was more humane in this as in every other respect. The Puritans formed a sect which secretly lurked in the church but pretended not to any separate worship or discipline. An attempt of that kind would have been universally regarded as the most unpardonable enormity. And had the King been disposed to grant the Puritans a full toleration for a separate exercise of their religion, it is certain, from the spirit of the times, that this sect itself would have despised and hated him for it, and would have reproached him with lukewarmness and indifference in the cause of religion. They maintained that they themselves were the only pure church, that their principles and practices ought to be established by law, and that no others ought to be tolerated. It may be questioned, therefore, whether the administration at this time could with propriety deserve the appellation of persecutors with regard to the Puritans. Such of the clergy indeed as refused to comply with the legal ceremonies were deprived of their livings, and sometimes, in Elizabeth's reign, were otherwise punished; and ought any man to accept of an office or benefice in an establishment while he declines compliance with the fixed and known rules of that establishment? But Puritans were never punished for frequenting separate congregations because there were none such in the kingdom, and no Protestant ever assumed or pretended to the right of erecting them. The greatest well-wishers of the Puritanical sect would have condemned a practice which in that age was universally, by statesmen and ecclesiastics, philosophers and zealots, regarded as subversive of civil society. Even so great a reasoner as Lord Bacon thought that uniformity in religion was absolutely necessary to the support of government and that no toleration could with safety be given to sectaries. Nothing but the imputation of idolatry, which was thrown on the Catholic religion, could justify, in the eyes of the Puritans themselves, the schism made by the Huguenots and other Protestants who lived in Popish countries.

In all former ages, not wholly excepting even those of Greece and Rome, religious sects and heresies and schisms had been esteemed dangerous, if not pernicious, to civil government, and were regarded as the source of faction and private combination and opposition to the laws. The magistrate, therefore, applied himself directly to the cure of this evil, as of every other; and very naturally attempted, by penal statutes, to suppress those separate communities and punish the obstinate innovators. But it was found by fatal experience and after spilling an ocean of blood in those theological quarrels that the evil was of a peculiar nature, and was both inflamed by violent remedies and diffused itself more rapidly throughout the whole society. Hence, though late, arose the paradoxical principle and salutary practice of toleration.

The liberty of the press was incompatible with such maxims and such principles of government as then prevailed, and was therefore quite unknown in that age. [Vol. IV, Appendix to the Reign of James I, pp. 500–502.]

Of all Christian sects, this [the Independents] was the first which, during its prosperity as well as its adversity, always adopted the principle of toleration; and it is remarkable that so reasonable a doctrine owed its origin, not to reasoning, but to the height of extravagance and fanaticism. [Vol. V, Ch. LVII, p. 282.]

An unlimited *toleration*, after sects have diffused themselves and are strongly rooted, is the only expedient which can allay their fervor and make the civil union acquire a superiority above religious distinctions. [Vol. VI, Ch. LXVI, p. 162.]

II

THAT POLITICS MAY BE REDUCED
TO A SCIENCE

IT IS A QUESTION with several whether there be any essential difference between one form of government and another, and whether every form may not become good or bad, according as it is well or ill administered?[a] Were it once admitted that all governments are alike and that the only difference consists in the character and conduct of the governors, most political disputes would be at an end, and all *zeal* for one constitution above another must be esteemed mere bigotry and folly. But, though a friend to moderation, I cannot forbear condemning this sentiment and should be sorry to think that human affairs admit of no greater stability than what they receive from the casual humors and characters of particular men.

It is true, those who maintain that the goodness of all government consists in the goodness of the administration may cite many particular instances in history where the very same government, in different hands, has varied suddenly into the two opposite extremes of good and bad. Compare the French government under Henry III and under Henry IV.[1] Oppression, levity, artifice on the part of the rulers, faction, sedition, treachery, rebellion, disloyalty on the part of the subjects—these compose the character of the former miserable era. But when the patriot and heroic prince who succeeded was once firmly seated on the throne, the government, the people, everything seemed to be totally changed; and all from the difference of the temper and conduct of these two sovereigns.[b] Instances of this kind may be multiplied, almost

a "For forms of government let fools contest,
   Whate'er is best administered is best"—[Pope,] *Essay on Man,* Book 3.
   b An equal difference of a contrary kind may be found in comparing the reigns of Elizabeth and James, at least with regard to foreign affairs.

12

without number, from ancient as well as modern history, foreign as well as domestic.

But here it may be proper to make a distinction. All absolute governments must very much depend on the administration, and this is one of the great inconveniences attending that form of government. But a republican and free government would be an obvious absurdity if the particular checks and controls provided by the constitution had really no influence and made it not the interest, even of bad men, to act for the public good. Such is the intention of these forms of government, and such is their real effect where they are wisely constituted; as, on the other hand, they are the source of all disorder and of the blackest crimes where either skill or honesty has been wanting in their original frame and institution.

So great is the force of laws and of particular forms of government, and so little dependence have they on the humors and tempers of men, that consequences almost as general and certain may sometimes be deduced from them as any which the mathematical sciences afford us.

The constitution of the Roman republic gave the whole legislative power to the people, without allowing a negative voice either to the nobility or consuls. This unbounded power they possessed in a collective, not in a representative body. The consequences were: when the people, by success and conquest, had become very numerous and had spread themselves to a great distance from the capital, the city tribes, though the most contemptible, carried almost every vote; they were, therefore, most cajoled by everyone that affected popularity; they were supported in idleness by the general distribution of corn and by particular bribes which they received from almost every candidate. By this means they became every day more licentious, and the Campus Martius was a perpetual scene of tumult and sedition; armed slaves were introduced among these rascally citizens, so that the whole government fell into anarchy, and the greatest happiness which the Romans could look for was the despotic power of the Caesars. Such are the effects of democracy without a representative.

A nobility may possess the whole or any part of the legislative power of a state in two different ways. Either every nobleman shares the power as a part of the whole body or the whole body enjoys the power as composed of parts which have each a distinct power and authority. The Venetian aristocracy is an instance of the first kind of government, the Polish of the second. In the Venetian government the whole body of nobility possesses the whole power, and no nobleman has any authority which he receives not from the whole. In the Polish government every nobleman, by means of his fiefs, has a distinct hereditary authority over his vassals, and the whole body has no authority but what it receives from the concurrence of its parts. The different operations and tendencies of these two species of government might be made apparent even a priori. A Venetian nobility is preferable to a Polish, let the humors and education of men be ever so much varied. A nobility who possess their power in common will preserve peace and order both among themselves and their subjects, and no member can have authority enough to control the laws for a moment. The nobles will preserve their authority over the people, but without any grievous tyranny or any breach of private property, because such a tyrannical government promotes not the interests of the whole body, however it may that of some individuals. There will be a distinction of rank between the nobility and people, but this will be the only distinction in the state. The whole nobility will form one body and the whole people another, without any of those private feuds and animosities which spread ruin and desolation everywhere. It is easy to see the disadvantages of a Polish nobility in every one of these particulars.

It is possible so to constitute a free government as that a single person, call him a doge, prince, or king, shall possess a large share of power and shall form a proper balance or counterpoise to the other parts of the legislature. This chief magistrate may be either *elective* or *hereditary*; and though the former institution may to a superficial view appear the most advantageous, yet a more accurate inspection will discover in it greater inconveniences than in the latter, and such as are founded on causes and principles eternal and immutable. The filling of the throne in such a government is a point of too great and too general interest not to divide the whole people into factions. Whence a civil war, the greatest of ills, may be apprehended almost with certainty upon every vacancy. The prince elected must be either a *foreigner* or a *native*. The former will be ignorant of the people whom he is to govern, suspicious of his new subjects and suspected by them, giving his confidence entirely to strangers who will have no other care but of enriching themselves in the quickest manner, while their master's favor and authority are able to support them. A native will carry into the throne all his private animosities and friendships and will never be viewed in his elevation without exciting the sentiment of envy in those who formerly considered him as their equal. Not to mention that a crown is too high a reward ever to be given to merit alone, and will always induce the candidates to employ force or money or intrigue to procure the votes of the electors, so that such an election will give no better chance for superior merit in the prince than if the state had trusted to birth alone for determining the sovereign.

It may, therefore, be pronounced as a universal axiom in politics *that a hereditary prince, a nobility without vassals, and a people voting by their representatives form the best monarchy, aristocracy, and democracy.* But in order to prove more fully that politics admit of general truths which are invariable by the humor or education either of subject or sovereign, it may not be amiss to observe some other principles of this science which may seem to deserve that character.

It may easily be observed that though free governments have been commonly the most happy for those who partake of their freedom, yet are they the most ruinous and oppressive to their provinces.[2] And this observation may, I believe, be fixed as a maxim of the kind we are here speaking of. When a monarch extends his dominions by conquest, he soon learns to consider his old and his new subjects as on the same footing, because, in reality, all his subjects are to him the same, except the few friends and favorites with whom he is personally acquainted. He does not, therefore, make any distinction between them in his *general* laws, and at the same time is careful to prevent all *particular* acts of oppression on the one as well as the other. But a free state necessarily makes a great distinction, and must always do so till men learn to love their neighbors as well as themselves. The conquerors in such a government are all legislators and will be sure to contrive matters by restrictions on trade and by taxes so as to draw some private as well as public advantage from their conquests. Provincial governors have also a better chance in a republic to escape with their plunder by means of bribery or intrigue; and their fellow citizens who find their own state to be enriched by the spoils of the subject provinces will be the more inclined to tolerate such abuses. Not to mention that it is a necessary precaution in a free state to change the governors frequently, which obliges these temporary tyrants to be more expeditious and rapacious, that they may accumulate sufficient wealth before they give place to their successors. What cruel tyrants were the Romans over the world during the time of their commonwealth! It is true they had laws to prevent oppression in their provincial magistrates, but Cicero informs us that the Romans could not better consult the interests of the provinces than by repealing these very laws. For in that case, says he, our magistrates, having entire impunity, would plunder no more than would satisfy their own rapaciousness, whereas at present they must also satisfy that of their judges and of all the great men in Rome of whose protection they stand in need. Who can read of the cruelties and oppressions of Verres without horror and astonishment? And who is not touched with indignation to hear that, after Cicero had exhausted on that abandoned criminal all the thunders of his eloquence and had prevailed so far as to get him condemned to the utmost extent of the laws, yet that cruel tyrant lived peaceably to old age, in opulence and ease, and, thirty years afterward, was put into the proscription by Mark Antony on account of his exorbitant wealth, where he fell with Cicero himself and all the most virtuous men of Rome? After the dissolution of the commonwealth, the Roman yoke became easier upon the provinces, as Tacitus informs us; [c] and it may be observed that many of the

c *Ann.* lib. i. cap. 2.

worst emperors, Domitian,[d] for instance, were careful to prevent all oppression on the provinces. In Tiberius'[e] time Gaul was esteemed richer than Italy itself; nor do I find during the whole time of the Roman monarchy that the empire became less rich or populous in any of its provinces, though indeed its valor and military discipline were always upon the decline. The oppression and tyranny of the Carthaginians over their subject states in Africa went so far, as we learn from Polybius,[f] that, not content with exacting the half of all the produce of the land, which of itself was a very high rent, they also loaded them with many other taxes. If we pass from ancient to modern times, we shall still find the observation to hold. The provinces of absolute monarchies are always better treated than those of free states. Compare the *Païs conquis* of France with Ireland, and you will be convinced of this truth, though this latter kingdom, being in a good measure peopled from England, possesses so many rights and privileges as should naturally make it challenge better treatment than that of a conquered province. Corsica is also an obvious instance to the same purpose.

There is an observation of Machiavel with regard to the conquests of Alexander the Great which I think may be regarded as one of those eternal political truths which no time nor accidents can vary. It may seem strange, says that politician, that such sudden conquests as those of Alexander should be possessed so peaceably by his successors and that the Persians, during all the confusions and civil wars among the Greeks, never made the smallest effort toward the recovery of their former independent government. To satisfy us concerning the cause of this remark-

[d] Suet. in *Vita Domit.*

[e] "Egregium resumendae libertati tempus, si ipsi florentes, quam inops Italia, quam imbellis urbana plebs, nihil validum in exercitibus, nisi quod externum cogitarent." [This was a unique opportunity to regain their freedom, if they would consider that, while they were prospering, Italy was poor and the city population unwarlike; with the exception of the foreign troops, there was no element of strength in the armies.] —Tacit. *Ann.* lib. iii.

[f] Lib. i. cap. 72.

able event, we may consider that a monarch may govern his subjects in two different ways. He may either follow the maxims of the Eastern princes and stretch his authority so far as to leave no distinction of rank among his subjects but what proceeds immediately from himself: no advantages of birth, no hereditary honors and possessions, and, in a word, no credit among the people except from his commission alone. Or a monarch may exert his power after a milder manner, like other European princes, and leave other sources of honor beside his smile and favor: birth, titles, possessions, valor, integrity, knowledge, or great and fortunate achievements. In the former species of government, after a conquest, it is impossible ever to shake off the yoke, since no one possesses among the people so much personal credit and authority as to begin such an enterprise, whereas, in the latter, the least misfortune or discord among the victors will encourage the vanquished to take arms, who have leaders ready to prompt and conduct them in every undertaking.

Such is the reasoning of Machiavel, which seems solid and conclusive, though I wish he had not mixed falsehood with truth in asserting that monarchies governed according to Eastern policy, though more easily kept when once subdued, yet are the most difficult to subdue, since they cannot contain any powerful subject whose discontent and faction may facilitate the enterprises of an enemy. For besides that such a tyrannical government enervates the courage of men and renders them indifferent toward the fortunes of their sovereign—besides this, I say, we find by experience that even the temporary and delegated authority of the generals and magistrates, being always in such governments as absolute within its sphere as that of the prince himself, is able with barbarians accustomed to a blind submission to produce the most dangerous and fatal revolutions. So that in every respect a gentle government is preferable and gives the greatest security to the sovereign as well as to the subject.

Legislators, therefore, ought not to trust the future government of a state entirely to chance, but ought to provide a system of laws to regulate the administration of public affairs to the latest posterity. Effects will always correspond to causes, and wise regulations in any commonwealth are the most valuable legacy that can be left to future ages. In the smallest court or office the stated forms and methods by which business must be conducted are found to be a considerable check on the natural depravity of mankind. Why should not the case be the same in public affairs? Can we ascribe the stability and wisdom of the Venetian government, through so many ages, to anything but the form of government? And is it not easy to point out those defects in the original constitution which produced the tumultuous governments of Athens and Rome, and ended at last in the ruin of these two famous republics? And so little dependence has this affair on the humors and education of particular men that one part of the same republic may be wisely conducted and another weakly by the very same men, merely on account of the differences of the forms and institutions by which these parts are regulated. Historians inform us that this was actually the case with Genoa. For while the state was always full of sedition and tumult and disorder, the bank of St. George, which had become a considerable part of the people, was conducted for several ages with the utmost integrity and wisdom.g

The ages of greatest public spirit are not always most eminent for private virtue. Good laws may beget order and moderation in the government where the manners and customs have instilled little humanity or justice into the tempers of men. The most illus-

g "Esempio veramente raro, et da' filosofi in tante loro immaginate e vedute Repubbliche mai non trovato, vedere dentro ad un medesimo cerchio, fra medesimi cittadini, la libertà e la tirannide, la vita civile e la corrotta, la giustizia e la licenza; perche quello ordine solo mantiene quella città piena di costumi antichi e venerabili. E s'egli avvenisse, che col tempo in ogni modo avverrà, che San Giorgio tutta quella città occupasse, sarebbe quella una Repubblica più che la Veneziana memorabile." [A really rare example, one which the philosophers never found in all their imagined or visualized republics, to see in the same circle, among the same citizens, liberty and tyranny, civil life and corruption, justice and license; because that order alone maintains that city full of ancient and venerable customs. And if it would come about, which is going to happen anyway, that Saint George occupies that whole city, it then would be a republic more memorable than Venice.]—Delle Istorie Fiorentine, lib. viii. 437. Florent. 1782.

trious period of the Roman history, considered in a political view, is that between the beginning of the first and end of the last Punic War,[3] the due balance between the nobility and people being then fixed by the contests of the tribunes, and not being yet lost by the extent of conquests. Yet at this very time the horrid practice of poisoning was so common that during part of the season a praetor punished capitally for this crime above three thousand[h] persons in a part of Italy, and found informations of this nature still multiplying upon him. There is a similar or rather a worse instance[i] in the more early times of the commonwealth, so depraved in private life were that people whom in their histories we so much admire. I doubt not but they were really more virtuous during the time of the two triumvirates,[4] when they were tearing their common country to pieces and spreading slaughter and desolation over the face of the earth, merely for the choice of tyrants.[j]

Here, then, is a sufficient inducement to maintain with the utmost zeal in every free state those forms and institutions by which liberty is secured, the public good consulted, and the avarice or ambition of particular men restrained and punished. Nothing does more honor to human nature than to see it susceptible of so noble a passion, as nothing can be greater indication of meanness of heart in any man than to see him destitute of it. A man who loves only himself, without regard to friendship and desert, merits the severest blame; and a man who is only susceptible of friendship, without public spirit or a regard to the community, is deficient in the most material part of virtue.

But this is a subject which needs not be longer insisted on at present. There are enough of zealots on both sides who kindle up the passions of their partisans and, under pretense of public good, pursue the interests and ends of their particular faction. For my part I shall always be more fond of promoting moderation than zeal, though perhaps the surest way of producing modera-

[h] T. Livii, lb. xl. cap. 43.
[i] T. Livii, lib. viii. cap. 18.
[j] "L'Aigle contre l'Aigle, Romains contre Romains,
  Combatans seulement pour le choix de tyrans."—CORNEILLE

tion in every party is to increase our zeal for the public. Let us therefore try, if it be possible from the foregoing doctrine, to draw a lesson of moderation with regard to the parties into which our country is at present divided, at the same time that we allow not this moderation to abate the industry and passion with which every individual is bound to pursue the good of his country.

Those who either attack or defend a minister [5] in such a government as ours, where the utmost liberty is allowed, always carry matters to an extreme and exaggerate his merit or demerit with regard to the public. His enemies are sure to charge him with the greatest enormities, both in domestic and foreign management; and there is no meanness or crime of which, in their account, he is not capable. Unnecessary wars, scandalous treaties, profusion of public treasure, oppressive taxes, every kind of maladministration is ascribed to him. To aggravate the charge, his pernicious conduct, it is said, will extend its baneful influence even to posterity, by undermining the best constitution in the world and disordering that wise system of laws, institutions, and customs by which our ancestors during so many centuries have been so happily governed. He is not only a wicked minister in himself, but has removed every security provided against wicked ministers for the future.

On the other hand, the partisans of the minister make his panegyric run as high as the accusation against him and celebrate his wise, steady, and moderate conduct in every part of his administration. The honor and interest of the nation supported abroad, public credit maintained at home, persecution restrained, faction subdued—the merit of all these blessings is ascribed solely to the minister. At the same time he crowns all his other merits by a religious care of the best constitution in the world, which he has preserved in all its parts and has transmitted entire to be the happiness and security of the latest posterity.

When this accusation and panegyric are received by the partisans of each party, no wonder they beget an extraordinary ferment on both sides and fill the nation with violent animosities. But I would fain persuade these party zealots that there is a flat contradiction both in the accusation and panegyric, and that it were impossible for either of them to run so high were it not for this contradiction. If our constitution be really *that noble fabric, the pride of Britain, the envy of our neighbors, raised by the labor of so many centuries, repaired at the expense of so many millions, and cemented by such a profusion of blood*[k]—I say, if our constitution does in any degree deserve these eulogies, it would never have suffered a wicked and weak minister to govern triumphantly for a course of twenty years when opposed by the greatest geniuses in the nation, who exercised the utmost liberty of tongue and pen in Parliament and in their frequent appeals to the people. But if the minister be wicked and weak to the degree so strenuously insisted on, the constitution must be faulty in its original principles, and he cannot consistently be charged with undermining the best form of government in the world. A constitution is only so far good as it provides a remedy against maladministration; and if the British, when in its greatest vigor and repaired by two such remarkable events as the *Revolution* and *Accession*,[6] by which our ancient royal family was sacrificed to it—if our constitution, I say, with so great advantages does not, in fact, provide any such remedy, we are rather beholden to any minister who undermines it and affords us an opportunity of erecting a better in its place.

I would employ the same topics to moderate the zeal of those who defend the minister. *Is our constitution so excellent?* Then a change of ministry can be no such dreadful event, since it is essential to such a constitution in every ministry, both to preserve itself from violation and to prevent all enormities in the administration. *Is our constitution very bad?* Then so extraordinary a jealousy and apprehension on account of changes is ill placed, and a man should no more be anxious in this case than a husband who had married a woman from the stews should be watchful to prevent her infidelity. Public affairs in such a government must necessarily go to confusion by whatever hands they are conducted, and the zeal of *patriots* is in that case much less requisite than the patience and submission of *philosophers*. The virtue and

[k] "Dissertations on Parties," [by Lord Bolingbroke,] Letter X.

good intention of Cato and Brutus [7] are highly laudable; but to what purpose did their zeal serve? Only to hasten the fatal period of the Roman government, and render its convulsions and dying agonies more violent and painful.

It would not be understood to mean that public affairs deserve no care and attention at all. Would men be moderate and consistent, their claims might be admitted, at least might be examined. The *Country party* might still assert that our constitution, though excellent, will admit of maladministration to a certain degree; and therefore, if the minister be bad, it is proper to oppose him with a *suitable* degree of zeal. And on the other hand the *Court party* [8] may be allowed, upon the supposition that the minister were good, to defend, and with *some* zeal too, his administration. I would only persuade men not to contend as if they were fighting *pro aris et focis,* and change a good constitution into a bad one by the violence of their factions.

I have not here considered anything that is personal in the present controversy. In the best civil constitution, where every man is restrained by the most rigid laws, it is easy to discover either the good or bad intentions of a minister and to judge whether his personal character deserve love or hatred. But such questions are of little importance to the public and lay those who employ their pens upon them under a just suspicion either of malevolence or of flattery.

III

OF THE FIRST PRINCIPLES
OF GOVERNMENT

NOTHING APPEARS MORE SURPRISING to those who consider human affairs with a philosophical eye than the easiness with which the many are governed by the few and the implicit submission with which men resign their own sentiments and passions to those of their rulers. When we inquire by what means this wonder is effected, we shall find that, as force is always on the side of the governed, the governors have nothing to support them but opinion. It is, therefore, on opinion only that government is founded, and this maxim extends to the most despotic and most military governments as well as to the most free and most popular. The sultan of Egypt or the emperor of Rome might drive his harmless subjects like brute beasts against their sentiments and inclination. But he must, at least, have led his *mamelukes* or *praetorian bands*, like men, by their opinion.

Opinion is of two kinds, to wit, opinion of *interest* and opinion of *right*. By opinion of interest I chiefly understand the sense of general advantage which is reaped from government, together with the persuasion that the particular government which is established is equally advantageous with any other that could easily be settled. When this opinion prevails among the generality of a state or among those who have the force in their hands, it gives great security to any government.

Right is of two kinds: right to *power* and right to *property*. What prevalence opinion of the first kind has over mankind may easily be understood by observing the attachment which all nations have to their ancient government and even to those names which have had the sanction of antiquity. Antiquity always begets the opinion of right; and whatever disadvantageous sentiments we may entertain of mankind, they are always found to be prodigal both of blood and treasure in the maintenance of public justice.[a] There is, indeed, no particular in which, at first sight, there may appear a greater contradiction in the frame of the human mind than the present. When men act in a faction, they are apt, without shame or remorse, to neglect all the ties of honor and mortality in order to serve their party; and yet, when a faction is formed upon a point of right or principle, there is no occasion where men discover a greater obstinacy and a more determined sense of justice and equity. The same social disposition of mankind is the cause of these contradictory appearances.

It is sufficiently understood that the opinions or right to property is of moment in all matters of government. A noted author has made property the foundation of all government,[1] and most of our political writers seem inclined to follow him in that particular. This is carrying the matter too far, but still it must be owned that the opinion of right to property has a great influence in this subject.

Upon these three opinions, therefore, of public *interest*, of *right to power*, and of *right to property*, are all governments founded and all authority of the few over the many. There are, indeed, other principles which add force to these and determine, limit, or alter their operation, such as *self-interest*, *fear*, and *affection*. But still we may assert that these other principles can have no influence alone, but suppose the antecedent influence of those opinions above mentioned. They are, therefore, to be esteemed the secondary, not the original, principles of government.

For, *first*, as to *self-interest*, by which I mean the expectation of particular rewards, distinct from the general protection which we receive from government, it is evident that the magistrate's authority must be antecedently established, at least be hoped for, in order to produce this expectation. The prospect of reward may augment his authority with regard to some particular persons, but can never give birth to it with regard to the public. Men natur-

[a] This passion we may denominate "enthusiasm," or we may give it what appellation we please; but a politician who should overlook its influence on human affairs would prove himself to have but a very limited understanding.

ally look for the greatest favors from their friends and acquaintance, and, therefore, the hopes of any considerable number of
the state would never center in any particular set of men if these
men had no other title to magistracy and had no separate influence
over the opinions of mankind. The same observation may be extended to the other two principles of *fear* and *affection*. No man
would have any reason to *fear* the fury of a tyrant if he had no
authority over any but from fear, since, as a single man, his
bodily force can reach but a small way, and all the farther power
he possesses must be founded either on our own opinion or on
the presumed opinion of others. And though *affection* to wisdom
and virtue in a *sovereign* extends very far and has great influence,
yet he must antecedently be supposed invested with a public
character; otherwise the public esteem will serve him in no stead;
nor will his virtue have any influence beyond a narrow sphere.

A government may endure for several ages, though the balance
of power and the balance of property do not coincide. This
chiefly happens where any rank or order of the state has acquired
a large share in the property, but, from the original constitution
of the government, has no share in the power. Under what pretense would any individual of that order assume authority in
public affairs? As men are commonly much attached to their ancient government, it is not to be expected that the public would
ever favor such usurpations. But where the original constitution
allows any share of power, though small, to an order of men who
possess a large share of property, it is easy for them gradually to
stretch their authority and bring the balance of power to coincide
with that of property. This has been the case with the House of
Commons in England.

Most writers that have treated of the British government have
supposed that, as the Lower House represents all the Commons
of Great Britain, its weight in the scale is proportioned to the
property and power of all whom it represents. But this principle
must not be received as absolutely true. For though the people
are apt to attach themselves more to the House of Commons than
to any other member of the constitution, that House being chosen
by them as their representatives and as the public guardians of

their liberty, yet are there instances where the House, even when in opposition to the crown, has not been followed by the people, as we may particularly observe of the *Tory* House of Commons in the reign of King William.[2] Were the members obliged to receive instructions from their constituents, like the Dutch deputies, this would entirely alter the case; and if such immense power and riches as those of all the Commons of Great Britain were brought into the scale, it is not easy to conceive that the crown could either influence that multitude of people or withstand that balance of property. It is true the crown has great influence over the collective body in the elections of members; but were this influence, which at present is only exerted once in seven years, to be employed in bringing over the people to every vote, it would soon be wasted, and no skill, popularity, or revenue could support it. I must, therefore, be of opinion that an alteration in this particular would introduce a total alteration in our government and would soon reduce it to a pure republic and, perhaps, to a republic of no inconvenient form. For though the people, collected in a body like the Roman tribes, be quite unfit for government, yet, when dispersed in small bodies, they are more susceptible both of reason and order; the force of popular currents and tides is in a great measure broken, and the public interest may be pursued with some method and constancy. But it is needless to reason any farther concerning a form of government which is never likely to have place in Great Britain and which seems not to be the aim of any party among us. Let us cherish and improve our ancient government as much as possible, without encouraging a passion for such dangerous novelties.

IV

OF THE ORIGIN OF JUSTICE
AND PROPERTY [a]

WE NOW PROCEED TO EXAMINE two questions, viz., *concerning
the manner in which the rules of justice are established by the
artifice of men*. . . .

Of all the animals with which this globe is peopled there is
none toward whom nature seems, at first sight, to have exercised
more cruelty than toward man, in the numberless wants and necessities with which she has loaded him and in the slender means
which she affords to the relieving these necessities. In other
creatures these two particulars generally compensate each other.
If we consider the lion as a voracious and carnivorous animal, we
shall easily discover him to be very necessitous; but if we turn
our eye to his make and temper, his agility, his courage, his arms,
and his force, we shall find that his advantages hold proportion
with his wants. The sheep and ox are deprived of all these advantages, but their appetites are moderate and their food is of easy
purchase. In man alone this unnatural conjunction of infirmity
and of necessity may be observed in its greatest perfection. Not
only the food which is required for his sustenance flies his search
and approach, or at least requires his labor to be produced, but
he must be possessed of clothes and lodging to defend him against
the injuries of the weather; though, to consider him only in himself, he is provided neither with arms nor force nor other natural
abilities which are in any degree answerable to so many
necessities.

It is by society alone he is able to supply his defects and raise
himself up to an equality with his fellow creatures, and even
acquire a superiority above them. By society all his infirmities are

[a] [*Treatise of Human Nature*, Bk. III, Pt. II, Sec. II.]

28

compensated; and though in that situation his wants multiply every moment upon him, yet his abilities are still more augmented and leave him in every respect more satisfied and happy than it is possible for him in his savage and solitary condition ever to become. When every individual person labors apart and only for himself, his force is too small to execute any considerable work; his labor being employed in supplying all his different necessities, he never attains a perfection in any particular art; and as his force and success are not at all times equal, the least failure in either of these particulars must be attended with inevitable ruin and misery. Society provides a remedy for these *three* inconveniences. By the conjunction of forces our power is augmented; by the partition of employments our ability increases; and by mutual succor we are less exposed to fortune and accidents. It is by this additional *force, ability,* and *security* that society becomes advantageous.

But in order to form society, it is requisite not only that it be advantageous but also that men be sensible of these advantages; and it is impossible in their wild uncultivated state that by study and reflection alone they should ever be able to attain this knowledge. Most fortunately, therefore, there is conjoined to those necessities whose remedies are remote and obscure another necessity, which, having a present and more obvious remedy, may justly be regarded as the first and original principle of human society. This necessity is no other than that natural appetite betwixt the sexes which unites them together and preserves their union till a new tie takes place in their concern for their common offspring. This new concern becomes also a principle of union betwixt the parents and offspring, and forms a more numerous society where the parents govern by the advantage of their superior strength and wisdom, and at the same time are restrained in the exercise of their authority by that natural affection which they bear their children. In a little time, custom and habit, operating on the tender minds of the children, makes them sensible of the advantages which they may reap from society, as well as fashions them by degrees for it by rubbing off those rough corners and untoward affections which prevent their coalition.

For it must be confessed that however the circumstances of human nature may render a union necessary, and however those passions of lust and natural affection may seem to render it unavoidable, yet there are other particulars in our *natural temper* and in our *outward circumstances* which are very incommodious, and are even contrary to the requisite conjunction. Among the former we may justly esteem our *selfishness* to be the most considerable. I am sensible that, generally speaking, the representations of this quality have been carried much too far, and that the descriptions which certain philosophers delight so much to form of mankind in this particular are as wide of nature as any accounts of monsters which we meet with in fables and romances. So far from thinking that men have no affection for anything beyond themselves, I am of opinion that, though it be rare to meet with one who loves any single person better than himself, yet it is as rare to meet with one in whom all the kind affections, taken together, do not overbalance all the selfish. Consult common experience; do you not see that, though the whole expense of the family be generally under the direction of the master of it, yet there are few that do not bestow the largest part of their fortunes on the pleasures of their wives and the education of their children, reserving the smallest portion for their own proper use and entertainment? This is what we may observe concerning such as have those endearing ties, and may presume that the case would be the same with others were they placed in a like situation.

But though this generosity must be acknowledged to the honor of human nature, we may at the same time remark that so noble an affection, instead of fitting men for large societies, is almost as contrary to them as the most narrow selfishness. For while each person loves himself better than any other single person, and in his love to others bears the greatest affection to his relations and acquaintance, this must necessarily produce an opposition of passions and a consequent opposition of actions which cannot but be dangerous to the new-established union.

It is, however, worth while to remark that this contrariety of passions would be attended with but small danger did it not concur with a peculiarity in our *outward circumstances* which affords it an opportunity of exerting itself. There are three different species of goods which we are possessed of: the internal satisfaction of our minds, the external advantages of our body, and the enjoyment of such possessions as we have acquired by our industry and good fortune. We are perfectly secure in the enjoyment of the first. The second may be ravished from us, but can be of no advantage to him who deprives us of them. The last only are both exposed to the violence of others and may be transferred without suffering any loss or alteration, while at the same time there is not a sufficient quantity of them to supply everyone's desires and necessities. As the improvement, therefore, of these goods is the chief advantage of society, so the *instability* of their possession, along with their *scarcity,* is the chief impediment.

In vain should we expect to find in *uncultivated nature* a remedy to this inconvenience, or hope for any inartificial principle of the human mind which might control those partial affections and make us overcome the temptations arising from our circumstances. The idea of justice can never serve to this purpose or be taken for a natural principle capable of inspiring men with an equitable conduct toward each other. That virtue, as it is now understood, would never have been dreamed of among rude and savage men. For the notion of injury or injustice implies an immorality or vice committed against some other person. And as every immorality is derived from some defect or unsoundness of the passions, and as this defect must be judged of in a great measure from the ordinary course of nature in the constitution of the mind, it will be easy to know whether we be guilty of any immorality with regard to others by considering the natural and usual force of those several affections which are directed toward them. Now it appears that in the original frame of our mind our strongest attention is confined to ourselves; our next is extended to our relations and acquaintance; and it is only the weakest which reaches to strangers and indifferent persons. This partiality, then, and unequal affection must not only have an influence on our behavior and conduct in society, but even on our ideas of vice and virtue, so as to make us regard any remarkable transgression of such a degree of partiality, either by too great an enlargement or contraction of the affections, as vicious and immoral. This we may observe in our common judgments concerning actions, where we blame a person who either centers all his affections in his family or is so regardless of them as, in any opposition of interest, to give the preference to a stranger or mere chance acquaintance. From all which it follows that our natural uncultivated ideas of morality, instead of providing a remedy for the partiality of our affections, do rather conform themselves to that partiality and give it an additional force and influence.

The remedy, then, is not derived from nature but from *artifice;* or, more properly speaking, nature provides a remedy in the judgment and understanding for what is irregular and incommodious in the affections. For when men, from their early education in society, have become sensible of the infinite advantages that result from it and have besides acquired a new affection to company and conversation, and when they have observed that the principal disturbance in society arises from those goods which we call external and from their looseness and easy transition from one person to another, they must seek for a remedy by putting these goods as far as possible on the same footing with the fixed and constant advantages of the mind and body. This can be done after no other manner than by a convention entered into by all the members of the society to bestow stability on the possession of those external goods and leave everyone in the peaceable enjoyment of what he may acquire by his fortune and industry. By this means everyone knows what he may safely possess, and the passions are restrained in their partial and contradictory motions. Nor is such a restraint contrary to these passions, for if so it could never be entered into nor maintained; but it is only contrary to their heedless and impetuous movement. Instead of departing from our own interest or from that of our nearest friends by abstaining from the possessions of others, we cannot better consult both these interests than by such a convention, because it is by that means we maintain society, which is so necessary to their well-being and subsistence as well as to our own.

This convention is not of the nature of a *promise;* for even promises themselves, as we shall see afterward, arise from human conventions. It is only a general sense of common interest, which sense all the members of the society express to one another and which induces them to regulate their conduct by certain rules. I observe that it will be for my interest to leave another in the possession of his goods *provided* he will act in the same manner with regard to me. He is sensible of a like interest in the regulation of his conduct. When this common sense of interest is mutually expressed and is known to both, it produces a suitable resolution and behavior. And this may properly enough be called a convention or agreement betwixt us, though without the interposition of a promise, since the actions of each of us have a reference to those of the other and are performed upon the supposition that something is to be performed on the other part. Two men who pull the oars of a boat do it by an agreement or convention, though they have never given promises to each other. Nor is the rule concerning the stability of possessions the less derived from human conventions that it arises gradually and acquires force by a slow progression and by our repeated experience of the inconveniences of transgressing it. On the contrary, this experience assures us still more that the sense of interest has become common to all our fellows and gives us a confidence of the future regularity of their conduct; and it is only on the expectation of this that our moderation and abstinence are founded. In like manner are languages gradually established by human conventions, without any promise. In like manner do gold and silver become the common measures of exchange and are esteemed sufficient payment for what is of a hundred times their value.

After this convention concerning abstinence from the possessions of others is entered into, and everyone has acquired a stability in his possessions, there immediately arise the ideas of *justice* and *injustice,* as also those of *property, right,* and *obligation.* The latter are altogether unintelligible without first understanding the former. Our property is nothing but those goods whose constant possession is established by the laws of society— that is, by the laws of justice. Those, therefore, who make use of the words *"property,"* or *"right,"* or *"obligation"* before they have explained the origin of justice, or even make use of them in that explication, are guilty of a very gross fallacy and can never reason upon any solid foundation. A man's property is some object related to him. This relation is not natural but moral, and founded on justice. It is very preposterous, therefore, to imagine that we can have any idea of property without fully comprehending the nature of justice and showing its origin in the artifice and contrivance of men. The origin of justice explains that of property. The same artifice gives rise to both. As our first and most natural sentiment of morals is founded on the nature of our passions and gives the preference to ourselves and friends above strangers, it is impossible there can be naturally any such thing as a fixed right or property, while the opposite passions of men impel them in contrary directions and are not restrained by any convention or agreement.

No one can doubt that the convention for the distinction of property and for the stability of possession is of all circumstances the most necessary to the establishment of human society, and that after the agreement for the fixing and observing of this rule there remains little or nothing to be done toward settling a perfect harmony and concord. All the other passions, beside this of interest, are either easily restrained or are not of such pernicious consequences when indulged. *Vanity* is rather to be esteemed a social passion and a bond of union among men. *Pity* and *love* are to be considered in the same light. And as to *envy* and *revenge,* though pernicious, they operate only by intervals and are directed against particular persons whom we consider our superiors or enemies. This avidity alone of *acquiring* goods and possessions for ourselves and our nearest friends is insatiable, perpetual, universal, and directly destructive of society. There scarce is anyone who is not actuated by it; and there is no one who has not reason to fear from it when it acts without any restraint and gives way to its first and most natural movements. So that, upon the whole, we are to esteem the difficulties in the establishment of society to be greater or less according to those we encounter in regulating and restraining this passion.

It is certain that no affection of the human mind has both a sufficient force and a proper direction to counterbalance the love of gain and render men fit members of society by making them abstain from the possessions of others. Benevolence to strangers is too weak for this purpose; and as to the other passions, they rather inflame this avidity, when we observe that the larger our possessions are the more ability we have of gratifying all our appetites. There is no passion, therefore, capable of controlling the interested affection but the very affection itself, by an alteration of its direction. Now this alteration must necessarily take place upon the least reflection, since it is evident that the passion is much better satisfied by its restraint than by its liberty and that, in preserving society, we make much greater advances in the acquiring possessions than in the solitary and forlorn condition which must follow upon violence and a universal license. The question, therefore, concerning the wickedness or goodness of human nature enters not in the least into that other question concerning the origin of society; nor is there anything to be considered but the degrees of men's sagacity or folly. For whether the passion of self-interest be esteemed vicious or virtuous, it is all a case, since itself alone restrains it; so that if it be virtuous men become social by their virtue, if vicious their vice has the same effect.

Now, as it is by establishing the rule for the stability of possession that this passion restrains itself, if that rule be very abstruse and of difficult invention, society must be esteemed in a manner accidental and the effect of many ages. But if it be found that nothing can be more simple and obvious than that rule that every parent, in order to preserve peace among his children, must establish it, and that these first rudiments of justice must every day be improved as the society enlarges—if all this appear evident, as it certainly must, we may conclude that it is utterly impossible for men to remain any considerable time in that savage condition which precedes society, but that his very first state and situation may justly be esteemed social. This, however, hinders not but that philosophers may, if they please, extend their reasoning to the supposed *state of nature*, provided they allow it to be a mere philosophical fiction which never had and never could have reality. Human nature being composed of two principal parts, which are requisite in all its actions—the affections and understanding—it is certain that the blind motions of the former, without the direction of the latter, incapacitate men for society; and it may be allowed us to consider separately the effects that result from the separate operations of these two component parts of the mind. The same liberty may be permitted to moral, which is allowed to natural philosophers; and it is very usual with the latter to consider any motion as compounded and consisting of two parts separate from each other, though at the same time they acknowledge it to be in itself uncompounded and inseparable.

This *state of nature*, therefore, is to be regarded as a mere fiction, not unlike that of the *golden age* which poets have invented, only with this difference, that the former is described as full of war, violence, and injustice, whereas the latter is painted out to us as the most charming and most peaceable condition that can possibly be imagined. The seasons in that first age of nature were so temperate, if we may believe the poets, that there was no necessity for men to provide themselves with clothes and houses as a security against the violence of heat and cold. The rivers flowed with wine and milk, the oaks yielded honey, and nature spontaneously produced her greatest delicacies. Nor were these the chief advantages of that happy age. The storms and tempests were not alone removed from nature, but those more furious tempests were unknown to human breasts which now cause such uproar and engender such confusion. Avarice, ambition, cruelty, selfishness were never heard of; cordial affection, compassion, sympathy were the only movements with which the human mind was yet acquainted. Even the distinction of *mine* and *thine* was banished from that happy race of mortals, and carried with them the very notions of property and obligation, justice and injustice.

This, no doubt, is to be regarded as an idle fiction, but yet deserves our attention because nothing can more evidently show the origin of those virtues which are the subjects of our present inquiry. I have already observed that justice takes its rise from human conventions, and that these are intended as a remedy to some inconveniences which proceed from the concurrence of certain *qualities* of the human mind with the *situation* of external objects. The qualities of the mind are *selfishness* and *limited generosity;* and the situation of external objects is their *easy change,* joined to their *scarcity* in comparison of the wants and desires of men. But however philosophers may have been bewildered in those speculations, poets have been guided more infallibly by a certain taste or common instinct which, in most kinds of reasoning, goes further than any of that art and philosophy with which we have been yet acquainted. They easily perceived, if every man had a tender regard for another or if nature supplied abundantly all our wants and desires, that the jealousy of interest, which justice supposes, could no longer have place; nor would there be any occasion for those distinctions and limits of property and possession which at present are in use among mankind. Increase to a sufficient degree the benevolence of men or the bounty of nature, and you render justice useless by supplying its place with much nobler virtues and more valuable blessings. The selfishness of men is animated by the few possessions we have in proportion to our wants, and it is to restrain this selfishness that men have been obliged to separate themselves from the community and to distinguish betwixt their own goods and those of others.

Nor need we have recourse to the fictions of poets to learn this, but, beside the reason of the thing, may discover the same truth by common experience and observation. It is easy to remark that a cordial affection renders all things common among friends, and that married people in particular mutually lose their property and are unacquainted with the *mine* and *thine,* which are so necessary and yet cause such disturbance in human society. The same effect arises from any alteration in the circumstances of mankind, as when there is such a plenty of anything as satisfies all the desires of men; in which case the distinction of property is entirely lost and everything remains in common. This we may observe with regard to air and water, though the most valuable of all external objects, and may easily conclude that if men were supplied with everything in the same abundance, or if *everyone* had the same affection and tender regard for *everyone* as for himself, justice and injustice would be equally unknown among mankind.

Here then is a proposition which, I think, may be regarded as certain, *that it is only from the selfishness and confined generosity of man, along with the scanty provision nature has made for his wants, that justice derives its origin.* . . .

V

OF THE ORIGIN OF GOVERNMENT

MAN, BORN IN A FAMILY, is compelled to maintain society from necessity, from natural inclination, and from habit. The same creature, in his farther progress, is engaged to establish political society in order to administer justice, without which there can be no peace among them, nor safety, nor mutual intercourse. We are, therefore, to look upon all the vast apparatus of our government as having ultimately no other object or purpose but the distribution of justice, or, in other words, the support of the twelve judges. Kings and parliaments, fleets and armies, officers of the court and revenue, ambassadors, ministers, and privy councilors are all subordinate in their end to this part of administration. Even the clergy, as their duty leads them to inculcate morality, may justly be thought, so far as regards this world, to have no other useful object of their institution.

All men are sensible of the necessity of justice to maintain peace and order, and all men are sensible of the necessity of peace and order for the maintenance of society. Yet notwithstanding this strong and obvious necessity—such is the frailty or perverseness of our nature!—it is impossible to keep men faithfully and unerringly in the paths of justice. Some extraordinary circumstances may happen in which a man finds his interests to be more promoted by fraud or rapine than hurt by the breach which his injustice makes in the social union. But much more frequently he is seduced from his great and important, but distant, interests by the allurement of present, though often very frivolous, temptations. This great weakness is incurable in human nature.

Men must, therefore, endeavor to palliate what they cannot cure. They must institute some persons under the appellation of magistrates whose peculiar office it is to point out the decrees of equity, to punish transgressors, to correct fraud and violence, and to oblige men, however reluctant, to consult their own real and permanent interests. In a word, obedience is a new duty which must be invented to support that of justice, and the ties of equity must be corroborated by those of allegiance.

But still, viewing matters in an abstract light, it may be thought that nothing is gained by this alliance, and that the factitious duty of obedience, from its very nature, lays as feeble a hold of the human mind as the primitive and natural duty of justice. Peculiar interests and present temptations may overcome the one as well as the other. They are equally exposed to the same inconvenience, and the man who is inclined to be a bad neighbor must be led by the same motives, well or ill understood, to be a bad citizen or subject. Not to mention that the magistrate himself may often be negligent, or partial, or unjust in his administration.

Experience, however, proves that there is a great difference between the cases. Order in society, we find, is much better maintained by means of government, and our duty to the magistrate is more strictly guarded by the principles of human nature than our duty to our fellow citizens. The love of dominion is so strong in the breast of man that many not only submit to but court all the dangers and fatigues and cares of government; and men, once raised to that station, though often led astray by private passions, find in ordinary cases a visible interest in the impartial administration of justice. The persons who first attain this distinction by the consent, tacit or express, of the people must be endowed with superior personal qualities of valor, force, integrity, or prudence, which command respect and confidence; and, after government is established, a regard to birth, rank, and station has a mighty influence over men and enforces the decrees of the magistrate. The prince or leader exclaims against every disorder which disturbs his society. He summons all his partisans and all men of probity to aid him in correcting and redressing it, and he is readily followed by all indifferent persons in the execution of his office. He soon acquires the power of rewarding these services; and, in the progress of society, he establishes subordinate ministers, and often a military force, who find an immediate and a visible interest in supporting his authority. Habit soon consolidates what other principles of human nature had imperfectly founded, and men, once accustomed to obedience, never think of departing from that path in which they and their ancestors have constantly trod and to which they are confined by so many urgent and visible motives.

But though this progress of human affairs may appear certain and inevitable, and though the support which allegiance brings to justice be founded on obvious principles of human nature, it cannot be expected that men should beforehand be able to discover them or foresee their operation. Government commences more casually and more imperfectly. It is probable that the first ascendant of one man over multitudes began during a state of war, where the superiority of courage and of genius discovers itself most visibly, where unanimity and concert are most requisite, and where the pernicious effects of disorder are most sensibly felt. The long continuance of that state, an incident common among savage tribes, inured the people to submission; and if the chieftain possessed as much equity as prudence and valor, he became, even during peace, the arbiter of all differences and could gradually, by a mixture of force and consent, establish his authority. The benefit sensibly felt from his influence made it be cherished by the people, at least by the peaceable and well-disposed among them; and if his son enjoyed the same good qualities, government advanced the sooner to maturity and perfection, but was still in a feeble state till the farther progress of improvement procured the magistrate a revenue and enabled him to bestow rewards on the several instruments of his administration, and to inflict punishments on the refractory and disobedient.

Before that period, each exertion of his influence must have been particular and founded on the peculiar circumstances of the case. After it, submission was no longer a matter of choice in the bulk of the community, but was rigorously exacted by the authority of the supreme magistrate.

In all governments there is a perpetual intestine struggle, open or secret, between Authority and Liberty, and neither of them can ever absolutely prevail in the contest. A great sacrifice of liberty must necessarily be made in every government; yet even the authority which confines liberty can never, and perhaps ought never, in any constitution to become quite entire and uncontrollable. The sultan is master of the life and fortune of any individual, but will not be permitted to impose new taxes on his subjects; a French monarch can impose taxes at pleasure, but would find it dangerous to attempt the lives and fortunes of individuals. Religion also, in most countries, is commonly found to be a very intractable principle; and other principles or prejudices frequently resist all the authority of the civil magistrate, whose power, being founded on opinion, can never subvert other opinions equally rooted with that of his title to dominion. The government which, in common appellation, receives the appellation of "free" is that which admits of a partition of power among several members whose united authority is no less, or is commonly greater, than that of any monarch, but who, in the usual course of administration, must act by general and equal laws that are previously known to all the members and to all their subjects. In this sense it must be owned that liberty is the perfection of civil society, but still authority must be acknowledged essential to its very existence. And in those contests which so often take place between the one and the other, the latter may, on that account, challenge the preference. Unless perhaps one may say—and it may be said with some reason—that a circumstance which is essential to the existence of civil society must always support itself and needs be guarded with less jealousy than one that contributes only to its perfection, which the indolence of men is so apt to neglect or their ignorance to overlook.

VI

OF THE ORIGINAL CONTRACT

As NO PARTY, in the present age, can well support itself without a philosophical or speculative system of principles annexed to its political or practical one, we accordingly find that each of the factions into which this nation is divided has reared up a fabric of the former kind in order to protect and cover that scheme of actions which it pursues. The people being commonly very rude builders, especially in this speculative way, and more especially still when actuated by party zeal, it is natural to imagine that their workmanship must be a little unshapely, and discover evident marks of that violence and hurry in which it was raised. The one party,[1] by tracing up government to the Deity, endeavor to render it so sacred and inviolate that it must be little less than sacrilege, however tyrannical it may become, to touch or invade it in the smallest article. The other party,[2] by founding government altogether on the consent of the people, suppose that there is a kind of *original contract* by which the subjects have tacitly reserved the power of resisting their sovereign whenever they find themselves aggrieved by that authority with which they have, for certain purposes, voluntarily entrusted him. These are the speculative principles of the two parties, and these, too, are the practical consequences deduced from them.

I shall venture to affirm *that both these systems of speculative principles are just, though not in the sense intended by the parties;* and *that both the schemes of practical consequences are prudent, though not in the extremes to which each party, in opposition to the other, has commonly endeavored to carry them.*

That the Deity is the ultimate author of all government will never be denied by any who admit a general providence and allow that all events in the universe are conducted by a uniform plan and directed to wise purposes. As it is impossible for the human race to subsist, at least in any comfortable or secure state, without the protection of government, this institution must certainly have been intended by that beneficent Being who means the good of all his creatures. And as it has universally, in fact, taken place in all countries and all ages, we may conclude, with still greater certainty, that it was intended by that omniscient Being who can never be deceived by any event or operation. But since he gave rise to it, not by any particular or miraculous interposition, but by his concealed and universal efficacy, a sovereign cannot, properly speaking, be called his vicegerent in any other sense than every power or force, being derived from him, may be said to act by his commission. Whatever actually happens is comprehended in the general plan or intention of Providence; nor has the greatest and most lawful prince any more reason, upon that account, to plead a peculiar sacredness or inviolable authority than an inferior magistrate, or even a usurper, or even a robber and a pirate. The same Divine Superintendent who, for wise purposes, invested a Titus or a Trajan with authority did also, for purposes no doubt equally wise though unknown, bestow power on a Borgia or an Angria. The same causes which gave rise to the sovereign power in every state established likewise every petty jurisdiction in it and every limited authority. A constable, therefore, no less than a king, acts by a divine commission and possesses an indefeasible right.

When we consider how nearly equal all men are in their bodily force, and even in their mental powers and faculties, till cultivated by education, we must necessarily allow that nothing but their own consent could at first associate them together and subject them to any authority. The people, if we trace government to its first origin in the woods and deserts, are the source of all power and jurisdiction, and voluntarily, for the sake of peace and order, abandoned their native liberty and received laws from their equal and companion. The conditions upon which they were willing to submit were either expressed or were so clear and obvious that it might well be esteemed superfluous to express them. If this, then, be meant by the *original contract*, it cannot be denied that all government is, at first, founded on a contract and that the most ancient rude combinations of mankind were formed chiefly by that principle. In vain are we asked in what records this charter of our liberties is registered. It was not written on parchment, nor yet on leaves or barks of trees. It preceded the use of writing and all the other civilized arts of life. But we trace it plainly in the nature of man and in the equality, or something approaching equality, which we find in all the individuals of that species. The force which now prevails, and which is founded on fleets and armies, is plainly political and derived from authority, the effect of established government. A man's natural force consists only in the vigor of his limbs and the firmness of his courage, which could never subject multitudes to the command of one. Nothing but their own consent and their sense of the advantages resulting from peace and order could have had that influence.

Yet even this consent was long very imperfect and could not be the basis of a regular administration. The chieftain, who had probably acquired his influence during the continuance of war, ruled more by persuasion than command; and till he could employ force to reduce the refractory and disobedient, the society could scarcely be said to have attained a state of civil government. No compact or agreement, it is evident, was expressly formed for general submission, an idea far beyond the comprehension of savages. Each exertion of authority in the chieftain must have been particular and called forth by the present exigencies of the case. The sensible utility resulting from his interposition made these exertions become daily more frequent; and their frequency gradually produced a habitual and, if you please to call it so, a voluntary and therefore precarious acquiescence in the people.

But philosophers who have embraced a party—if that be not a contradiction in terms—are not content with these concessions. They assert not only that government in its earliest infancy arose from consent, or rather the voluntary acquiescence of the people, but also that, even at present, when it has attained its full maturity, it rests on no other foundation. They affirm that all men are still born equal and owe allegiance to no prince or government unless bound by the obligation and sanction of a *promise*. And as no man, without some equivalent, would forego the advantages of his native liberty and subject himself to the will of another, this promise is always understood to be conditional and imposes on him no obligation, unless he meet with justice and protection from his sovereign. These advantages the sovereign promises him in return; and if he fail in the execution, he has broken on his part the articles of engagement, and has thereby freed his subject from all obligations to allegiance. Such, according to these philosophers, is the foundation of authority in every government, and such the right of resistance possessed by every subject.[3]

But would these reasoners look abroad into the world, they would meet with nothing that in the least corresponds to their ideas or can warrant so refined and philosophical a system. On the contrary, we find everywhere princes who claim their subjects as their property and assert their independent right of sovereignty from conquest or succession. We find also everywhere subjects who acknowledge this right in their prince and suppose themselves born under obligations of obedience to a certain sovereign, as much as under the ties of reverence and duty to certain parents. These connections are always conceived to be equally independent of our consent, in Persia and China, in France and Spain, and even in Holland and England, wherever the doctrines above mentioned have not been carefully inculcated. Obedience or subjection becomes so familiar that most men never make any inquiry about its origin or cause, more than about the principle of gravity, resistance, or the most universal laws of nature. Or if curiosity ever move them, as soon as they learn that they themselves and their ancestors have, for several ages, or from time immemorial, been subject to such a form of government or such a family, they immediately acquiesce and acknowledge their obligation to allegiance. Were you to preach, in most parts of the world, that political connections are founded altogether on voluntary consent or a mutual promise, the magistrate would soon imprison you as seditious for loosening the ties of obedience, if your friends did not before shut you up as delirious for advancing such absurdities. It is strange that an act of the mind which every individual is supposed to have formed, and after he came to the use of reason too—otherwise it could have no authority—that this act, I say, should be so much unknown to all of them that over the face of the whole earth there scarcely remain any traces or memory of it.

But the contract on which government is founded is said to be the *original contract,* and consequently may be supposed too old to fall under the knowledge of the present generation. If the agreement by which savage men first associated and conjoined their force be here meant, this is acknowledged to be real; but being so ancient and being obliterated by a thousand changes of government and princes, it cannot now be supposed to retain any authority. If we would say anything to the purpose, we must assert that every particular government which is lawful and which imposes any duty of allegiance on the subject was at first founded on consent and a voluntary compact. But besides that this supposes the consent of the fathers to bind the children, even to the most remote generations—which republican writers[4] will never allow—besides this, I say, it is not justified by history or experience in any age or country of the world.

Almost all the governments which exist at present, or of which there remains any record in story, have been founded originally either on usurpation or conquest or both, without any pretense of a fair consent or voluntary subjection of the people. When an artful and bold man is placed at the head of an army or faction, it is often easy for him, by employing sometimes violence, sometimes false pretenses, to establish his dominion over a people a hundred times more numerous than his partisans. He allows no such open communication that his enemies can know with certainty their number or force. He gives them no leisure to assemble together in a body to oppose him. Even all those who are the instruments of his usurpation may wish his fall, but their ignorance of each other's intention keeps them in awe and is the sole cause of his security. By such arts as these many governments have been established, and this is all the *original contract* which they have to boast of.

The face of the earth is continually changing by the increase of small kingdoms into great empires, by the dissolution of great empires into smaller kingdoms, by the planting of colonies, by the migration of tribes. Is there anything discoverable in all these events but force and violence? Where is the mutual agreement or voluntary association so much talked of?

Even the smoothest way by which a nation may receive a foreign master, by marriage or a will, is not extremely honorable for the people, but supposes them to be disposed of like a dowry or a legacy, according to the pleasure or interest of their rulers.

But where no force interposes and election takes place, what is this election so highly vaunted? It is either the combination of a few great men who decide for the whole and will allow of no opposition or it is the fury of a multitude that follow a seditious ringleader who is not known, perhaps, to a dozen among them and who owes his advancement merely to his own impudence or to the momentary caprice of his fellows.

Are these disorderly elections, which are rare too, of such mighty authority as to be the only lawful foundation of all government and allegiance?

In reality there is not a more terrible event than a total dissolution of government, which gives liberty to the multitude and makes the determination or choice of a new establishment depend upon a number which nearly approaches to that of the body of the people. For it never comes entirely to the whole body of them. Every wise man, then, wishes to see at the head of a powerful and obedient army a general who may speedily seize the prize and give to the people a master which they are so unfit to choose for themselves—so little correspondent is fact and reality to those philosophical notions.

Let not the establishment at the Revolution [5] deceive us or make us so much in love with a philosophical origin to government as to imagine all others monstrous and irregular. Even that event was far from corresponding to these refined ideas. It was only the succession, and that only in the regal part of the government, which was then changed. And it was only the majority of seven hundred who determined that change for near ten millions. [6] I doubt not, indeed, but the bulk of those ten millions acquiesced willingly in the determination. But was the matter left in the least to their choice? Was it not justly supposed to be from that moment decided and every man punished who refused to submit to the new sovereign? How otherwise could the matter have ever been brought to any issue or conclusion?

The republic of Athens was, I believe, the most extensive democracy that we read of in history. Yet if we make the requisite allowances for the women, the slaves, and the strangers, we shall find that that establishment was not at first made, nor any law ever voted, by a tenth part of those who were bound to pay obedience to it, not to mention the islands and foreign dominions which the Athenians claimed as theirs by right of conquest. And as it is well known that popular assemblies in that city were always full of license and disorder, notwithstanding the institutions and laws by which they were checked, how much more disorderly must they prove where they form not the established constitution, but meet tumultuously on the dissolution of the ancient government in order to give rise to a new one? How chimerical must it be to talk of a choice in such circumstances?

The Achaeans enjoyed the freest and most perfect democracy of all antiquity; yet they employed force to oblige some cities to enter into their league, as we learn from Polybius.[a]

Harry IV and Harry VII[7] of England had really no title to the throne but a parliamentary election; yet they never would acknowledge it, lest they should thereby weaken their authority. Strange if the only real foundation of all authority be consent and promise.

It is in vain to say that all governments are or should be at first founded on popular consent as much as the necessity of human affairs will admit. This favors entirely my pretension. I maintain that human affairs will never admit of this consent, seldom of the appearance of it; but that conquest or usurpation— that is, in plain terms, force—by dissolving the ancient governments, is the origin of almost all the new ones which were ever established in the world. And that in the few cases where consent may seem to have taken place, it was commonly so irregular, so confined, or so much intermixed either with fraud or violence that it cannot have any great authority.

[a] Lib. ii. cap. 38.

My intention here is not to exclude the consent of the people from being one just foundation of government. Where it has place, it is surely the best and most sacred of any. I only contend that it has very seldom had place in any degree, and never almost in its full extent, and that, therefore, some other foundation of government must also be admitted.

Were all men possessed of so inflexible a regard to justice that of themselves they would totally abstain from the properties of others, they had forever remained in a state of absolute liberty, without subjection to any magistrate or political society. But this is a state of perfection of which human nature is justly deemed incapable. Again, were all men possessed of so perfect an understanding as always to know their own interests, no form of government had ever been submitted to but what was established on consent and was fully canvassed by every member of the society. But this state of perfection is likewise much superior to human nature. Reason, history, and experience show us that all political societies have had an origin much less accurate and regular; and were one to choose a period of time when the people's consent was the least regarded in public transactions, it would be precisely on the establishment of a new government. In a settled constitution their inclinations are often consulted, but during the fury of revolutions, conquests, and public convulsions, military force or political craft usually decides the controversy.

When a new government is established, by whatever means, the people are commonly dissatisfied with it and pay obedience more from fear and necessity than from any idea of allegiance or of moral obligation. The prince is watchful and jealous, and must carefully guard against every beginning or appearance of insurrection. Time, by degrees, removes all these difficulties and accustoms the nation to regard as their lawful or native princes that family which at first they considered as usurpers or foreign conquerors. In order to found this opinion, they have no recourse to any notion of voluntary consent or promise which, they know, never was in this case either expected or demanded. The original establishment was formed by violence and submitted to from necessity. The subsequent administration is also supported by power and acquiesced in by the people, not as a matter of choice but of obligation. They imagine not that their consent gives their prince a title. But they willingly consent because they think that, from long possession, he has acquired a title independent of their choice or inclination.

Should it be said that, by living under the dominion of a prince which one might leave, every individual has given a *tacit* consent to his authority and promised him obedience, it may be answered that such an implied consent can only have place where a man imagines that the matter depends on his choice. But where he thinks—as all mankind do who are born under established governments—that by his birth he owes allegiance to a certain prince or certain form of government, it would be absurd to infer a consent or choice which he expressly in this case renounces and disclaims.

Can we seriously say that a poor peasant or artisan has a free choice to leave his country when he knows no foreign language or manners and lives from day to day by the small wages which he acquires? We may as well assert that a man, by remaining in a vessel, freely consents to the dominion of the master, though he was carried on board while asleep and must leap into the ocean and perish the moment he leaves her.

What if the prince forbid his subjects to quit his dominions, as in Tiberius' time it was regarded as a crime in a Roman knight that he had attempted to fly to the Parthians in order to escape the tyranny of that emperor?[b] Or as the ancient Muscovites prohibited all traveling under pain of death? And did a prince observe that many of his subjects were seized with the frenzy of migrating to foreign countries, he would doubtless, with great reason and justice, restrain them in order to prevent the depopulation of his own kingdom. Would he forfeit the allegiance of all his subjects by so wise and reasonable a law? Yet the freedom of their choice is surely, in that case, ravished from them.

[b] Tacit. *Ann.* lib. vi. cap. 14.

A company of men who should leave their native country in order to people some uninhabited region might dream of recovering their native freedom, but they would soon find that their prince still laid claim to them and called them his subjects even in their new settlement. And in this he would but act conformably to the common ideas of mankind.

The truest *tacit* consent of this kind that is ever observed is when a foreigner settles in any country and is beforehand acquainted with the prince and government and laws to which he must submit; yet is his allegiance, though more voluntary, much less expected or depended on than that of a natural-born subject. On the contrary, his native prince still asserts a claim to him. And if he punish not the renegade when he seizes him in war with his new prince's commission, this clemency is not founded on the municipal law, which in all countries condemns the prisoner, but on the consent of princes, who have agreed to this indulgence in order to prevent reprisals.

Did one generation of men go off the stage at once and another succeed, as is the case with silkworms and butterflies, the new race, if they had sense enough to choose their government, which surely is never the case with men, might voluntarily and by general consent establish their own form of civil polity without any regard to the laws or precedents which prevailed among their ancestors. But as human society is in perpetual flux, one man every hour going out of the world, another coming into it, it is necessary in order to preserve stability in government that the new brood should conform themselves to the established constitution and nearly follow the path which their fathers, treading in the footsteps of theirs, had marked out to them. Some innovations must necessarily have place in every human institution; and it is happy where the enlightened genius of the age give these a direction to the side of reason, liberty, and justice. But violent innovations no individual is entitled to make. They are even dangerous to be attempted by the legislature. More ill than good is ever to be expected from them. And if history affords examples to the contrary, they are not to be drawn into precedent and are only to be regarded as proofs that the science of politics affords few rules which will not admit of some exception and which may not sometimes be controlled by fortune and accident. The violent innovations in the reign of Henry VIII[8] proceeded from an imperious monarch seconded by the appearance of legislative authority; those in the reign of Charles I[9] were derived from faction and fanaticism; and both of them have proved happy in the issue. But even the former were long the source of many disorders, and still more dangers; and if the measures of allegiance were to be taken from the latter, a total anarchy must have place in human society and a final period at once be put to every government.

Suppose that a usurper, after having banished his lawful prince and royal family, should establish his dominion for ten or a dozen years in any country and should preserve so exact a discipline in his troops and so regular a disposition in his garrisons that no insurrection had ever been raised or even murmur heard against his administration. Can it be asserted that the people, who in their hearts abhor his treason, have tacitly consented to his authority and promised him allegiance merely because, from necessity, they live under his dominion? Suppose again their native prince restored by means of an army which he levies in foreign countries. They receive him with joy and exultation, and show plainly with what reluctance they had submitted to any other yoke. I may now ask upon what foundation the prince's title stands? Not on popular consent surely; for though the people willingly acquiesce in his authority, they never imagine that their consent made him sovereign. They consent because they apprehend him to be already, by birth, their lawful sovereign. And as to tacit consent, which may now be inferred from their living under his dominion, this is no more than what they formerly gave to the tyrant and usurper.

When we assert that all lawful government arises from the consent of the people, we certainly do them a great deal more honor than they deserve or even expect and desire from us. After the Roman dominions became too unwieldy for the republic to govern them, the people over the whole known world were extremely grateful to Augustus for that authority which, by violence, he had established over them; and they showed an equal disposition to submit to the successor whom he left them by his last will and testament. It was afterward their misfortune that there never was, in one family, any long regular succession, but that their line of princes was continually broken either by private assassinations or public rebellions. The *praetorian* bands, on the failure of every family, set up one emperor, the legions in the East a second, those in Germany, perhaps, a third; and the sword alone could decide the controversy. The condition of the people in that mighty monarchy was to be lamented, not because the choice of the emperor was never left to them, for that was impracticable, but because they never fell under any succession of masters who might regularly follow each other. As to the violence and wars and bloodshed occasioned by every new settlement, these were not blamable because they were inevitable.

The house of Lancaster ruled in this island about sixty years; yet the partisans of the White Rose [10] seemed daily to multiply in England. The present establishment has taken place during a still longer period. Have all views of right in another family been utterly extinguished, even though scarce any man now alive had arrived at the years of discretion when it was expelled, or could have consented to its dominion or have promised it allegiance?—a sufficient indication, surely, of the general sentiment of mankind on this head. For we blame not the partisans of the abdicated family merely on account of the long time during which they have preserved their imaginary loyalty. We blame them for adhering to a family which we affirm has been justly expelled and which, from the moment the new settlement took place, had forfeited all title to authority.

But would we have a more regular, at least a more philosophical, refutation of this principle of an original contract or popular consent, perhaps the following observations may suffice.

All *moral* duties may be divided into two kinds. The *first* are those to which men are impelled by a natural instinct or immediate propensity which operates on them, independent of all ideas of obligation and of all views either to public or private utility. Of this nature are love of children, gratitude to benefactors, pity to the unfortunate. When we reflect on the advantage which results to society from such humane instincts, we pay them the just tribute of moral approbation and esteem. But the person actuated by them feels their power and influence antecedent to any such reflection.

The *second* kind of moral duties are such as are not supported by any original instinct of nature, but are performed entirely from a sense of obligation, when we consider the necessities of human society and the impossibility of supporting it if these duties were neglected. It is thus *justice*, or a regard to the property of others, *fidelity*, or the observance of promises, become obligatory and acquire an authority over mankind. For as it is evident that every man loves himself better than any other person, he is naturally impelled to extend his acquisitions as much as possible; and nothing can restrain him in this propensity but reflection and experience, by which he learns the pernicious effects of that license and the total dissolution of society which must ensue from it. His original inclination, therefore, or instinct, is here checked and restrained by a subsequent judgment or observation.

The case is precisely the same with the political or civil duty of *allegiance* as with the natural duties of justice and fidelity. Our primary instincts lead us either to indulge ourselves in unlimited freedom or to seek dominion over others; and it is reflection only which engages us to sacrifice such strong passions to the interests of peace and public order. A small degree of experience and observation suffices to teach us that society cannot possibly be maintained without the authority of magistrates, and that this authority must soon fall into contempt where exact obedience is not paid to it. The observation of these general and obvious interests is the source of all allegiance and of that moral obligation which we attribute to it.

What necessity, therefore, is there to found the duty of *allegiance*, or obedience to magistrates, on that of *fidelity*, or a regard to promises, and to suppose that it is the consent of each individual which subjects him to government, when it appears that both allegiance and fidelity stand precisely on the same foundation and are both submitted to by mankind on account of the apparent interests and necessities of human society? We are bound to obey our sovereign, it is said, because we have given a tacit promise to that purpose. But why are we bound to observe our promise? It must here be asserted that the commerce and intercourse of mankind, which are of such mighty advantage, can have no security where men pay no regard to their engagements. In like manner may it be said that men could not live at all in society, at least in a civilized society, without laws and magistrates and judges to prevent the encroachments of the strong upon the weak, of the violent upon the just and equitable. The obligation to allegiance being of like force and authority with the obligation to fidelity, we gain nothing by resolving the one into the other. The general interests or necessities of society are sufficient to establish both.

If the reason be asked of that obedience which we are bound to pay to government, I readily answer, "Because society could not otherwise subsist"; and this answer is clear and intelligible to all mankind. Your answer is, "Because we should keep our word." But besides that nobody, till trained in a philosophical system, can either comprehend or relish this answer; besides this, I say, you find yourself embarrassed when it is asked, *Why we are bound to keep our word?* Nor can you give any answer but what would immediately, without any circuit, have accounted for our obligation to allegiance.

But *to whom is allegiance due, and who is our lawful sovereign?* This question is often the most difficult of any and liable to infinite discussions. When people are so happy that they can answer, "Our present sovereign, who inherits, in a direct line, from ancestors that have governed us for many ages," this answer admits of no reply, even though historians in tracing up to the remotest antiquity the origin of that royal family may find, as commonly happens, that its first authority was derived from usurpation and violence. It is confessed that private justice, or the abstinence from the properties of others, is a most cardinal virtue. Yet reason tells us that there is no property in durable objects, such as land or houses, when carefully examined in passing from hand to hand, but must in some period have been founded on fraud and injustice. The necessities of human society, neither in private nor public life, will allow of such an accurate inquiry; and there is no virtue or moral duty but what may with facility be refined away, if we indulge a false philosophy in sifting and scrutinizing it, by every captious rule of logic, in every light or position in which it may be placed.

The questions with regard to private property have filled infinite volumes of law and philosophy if in both we add the commentators to the original text; and in the end we may safely pronounce that many of the rules there established are uncertain, ambiguous, and arbitrary. The like opinion may be formed with regard to the succession and rights of princes and forms of government. Several cases no doubt occur, especially in the infancy of any constitution, which admit of no determination from the laws of justice and equity; and our historian Rapin pretends that the controversy between Edward the Third and Philip de Valois [11] was of this nature and could be decided only by an appeal to heaven, that is, by war and violence.

Who shall tell me whether Germanicus or Drusus ought to have succeeded to Tiberius, had he died while they were both alive without naming any of them for his successor? Ought the right of adoption to be received as equivalent to that of blood in a nation where it had the same effect in private families and had already, in two instances, taken place in the public? Ought Germanicus to be esteemed the elder son because he was born before Drusus, or the younger because he was adopted after the birth of his brother? Ought the right of the elder to be regarded in a nation where he had no advantage in the succession of private families? Ought the Roman Empire at that time to be deemed hereditary because of two examples; or ought it, even so early, to be regarded as belonging to the stronger or to the present possessor, as being founded on so recent a usurpation?

Commodus mounted the throne after a pretty long succession of excellent emperors who had acquired their title, not by birth or public election, but by the fictitious rite of adoption. The bloody debauche being murdered by a conspiracy suddenly

formed between his wench and her gallant, who happened at
that time to be praetorian praefect, these immediately deliberated
about choosing a master to human kind, to speak in the style
of those ages, and they cast their eyes on Pertinax. Before the
tyrant's death was known, the praefect went secretly to that
senator who, on the appearance of the soldiers, imagined that
his execution had been ordered by Commodus. He was immediately saluted emperor by the officer and his attendants, cheer-
fully proclaimed by the populace, unwillingly submitted to by
the guards, formally recognized by the senate, and passively received by the provinces and armies of the empire.

The discontent of the praetorian bands broke out in a sudden
sedition, which occasioned the murder of that excellent prince;
and the world being now without a master and without government, the guards thought proper to set the empire formally to
sale. Julian, the purchaser, was proclaimed by the soldiers,
recognized by the senate, and submitted to by the people; and
must also have been submitted to by the provinces had not the
envy of the legions begotten opposition and resistance. Pescennius
Niger in Syria elected himself emperor, gained the tumultuary
consent of his army, and was attended with the secret good will
of the senate and people of Rome. Albinus in Britain found an
equal right to set up his claim, but Severus, who governed
Pannonia, prevailed in the end above both of them. That able
politician and warrior, finding his own birth and dignity too
much inferior to the imperial crown, professed at first an intention only of revenging the death of Pertinax. He marched as
general into Italy, defeated Julian, and without our being able to
fix any precise commencement even of the soldiers' consent he
was from necessity acknowledged emperor by the senate and
people, and fully established in his violent authority by subduing
Niger and Albinus.[c]

"*Inter haec Gordianus Caesar,*" says Capitolinus, speaking of
another period, "*sublatus a militibus. Imperator est appellatus,
quia non erat alius in praesenti.*" [12] It is to be remarked that Gordian was a boy of fourteen years of age.

[c] Herodian, lib. ii.

Frequent instances of a like nature occur in the history of the emperors, in that of Alexander's successors, and of many other countries. Nor can anything be more unhappy than a despotic government of this kind where the succession is disjointed and irregular and must be determined on every vacancy by force or election. In a free government the matter is often unavoidable, and is also much less dangerous. The interests of liberty may there frequently lead the people, in their own defense, to alter the succession of the crown. And the constitution, being compounded of parts, may still maintain a sufficient stability by resting on the aristocratical or democratical members, though the monarchical be altered from time to time in order to accommodate it to the former.

In an absolute government, when there is no legal prince who has a title to the throne, it may safely be determined to belong to the first occupant. Instances of this kind are but too frequent, especially in the eastern monarchies. When any race of princes expires, the will or destination of the last sovereign will be regarded as a title. Thus the edict of Louis XIV, who called the bastard princes to the succession in case of the failure of all the legitimate princes, would in such an event have some authority.[d] Thus the will of Charles the Second disposed of the whole Spanish monarchy. The cession of the ancient proprietor, especially when joined to conquest, is likewise deemed a good title.

---

[d] It is remarkable that, in the remonstrance of the Duke of Bourbon and the legitimate princes against this destination of Louis XIV, the doctrine of the *original contract* is insisted on, even in that absolute government. The French nation, say they, choosing Hugh Capet and his posterity to rule over them and their posterity, where the former line fails, there is a tacit right reserved to choose a new royal family; and this right is invaded by calling the bastard princes to the throne without the consent of the nation. But the Comte de Boulainvilliers, who wrote in defense of the bastard princes, ridicules this notion of an original contract, especially when applied to Hugh Capet, who mounted the throne, says he, by the same arts which have ever been employed by all conquerors and usurpers. He got his title, indeed, recognized by the states after he had put himself in possession. But is this a choice or contract? The Comte de Boulainvilliers, we may observe, was a noted republican;

The general obligation which binds us to government is the interest and necessities of society; and this obligation is very strong. The determination of it to this or that particular prince or form of government is frequently more uncertain and dubious. Present possession has considerable authority in these cases, and greater than in private property because of the disorders which attend all revolutions and changes of government.

We shall only observe, before we conclude, that though an appeal to general opinion may justly, in the speculative sciences of metaphysics, natural philosophy, or astronomy, be deemed unfair and inconclusive, yet in all questions with regard to morals, as well as criticism, there is really no other standard by which any controversy can ever be decided. And nothing is a clearer proof that a theory of this kind is erroneous than to find that it leads to paradoxes repugnant to the common sentiments of mankind and to the practice and opinion of all nations and all ages. The doctrine which founds all lawful government on an *original contract,* or consent of the people, is plainly of this kind; nor has the most noted of its partisans, in prosecution of it, scrupled to affirm *that absolute monarchy is inconsistent with civil society and so can be no form of civil government at all,*[e] and *that the supreme power in a state cannot take from any man by taxes and impositions any part of his property without his own consent or that of his representatives.*[f] What authority any moral reasoning can have which leads into opinions so wide of the general practice of mankind in every place but this single kingdom, it is easy to determine.

The only passage I meet with in antiquity where the obligation of obedience to government is ascribed to a promise is in Plato's *Crito,* where Socrates refuses to escape from prison be-

but being a man of learning and very conversant in history, he knew that the people were almost never consulted in these revolutions and new establishments, and that time alone bestowed right and authority on what was commonly at first founded on force and violence. See *Etat de la France,* Vol. III.

e See Locke, *On Government,* Chap. VII, § 90.

f Locke, *On Government,* Chap. XI, §§ 138, 139, 140.

cause he had tacitly promised to obey the laws. Thus he builds a *Tory* consequence of passive obedience on a *Whig*[13] foundation of the original contract.

New discoveries are not to be expected in these matters. If scarce any man, till very lately, ever imagined that government was founded on compact, it is certain that it cannot in general have any such foundation.

The crime of rebellion among the ancients was commonly expressed by the terms νεωτερίζειν (*novas res moliri*).

FROM THE *HISTORY OF ENGLAND*

In his History of England *Hume repeatedly discussed the notion of original contract and consent:*

These latter [the prelatical clergy], while they claimed to themselves a divine right, admitted of a like origin to civil authority; the former [the Independents] challenging to their own order a celestial pedigree, derived the legislative power from a source no more dignified than the voluntary association of the people. [Vol. V, Ch. LVIII, p. 320.]

The English convention was assembled; and it immediately appeared that the House of Commons, both from the prevailing humor of the people and from the influence of present authority, were mostly chosen from among the Whig party. After thanks were unanimously given by both houses to the Prince of Orange for the deliverance which he had brought them, a less decisive vote than that of the Scottish convention was in a few days passed by a great majority of the Commons and sent up to the Peers for their concurrence. It was contained in these words: "That King James II, having endeavored to subvert the constitution of the kingdom by breaking the original contract between king and people. . . ." [Vol. VI, Ch. LXXI, p. 355.]

The House of Peers proceeded next to examine piecemeal the votes sent up to them by the Commons. They debated, "Whether there were an original contract between king and people?" and the affirmative was carried by fifty-three against forty-six, a proof that the Tories were already losing ground. The next question was, "Whether King James had broken that original contract?" and after a slight opposition, the affirmative prevailed. The Lords proceeded to take into consideration the word "abdicated"; and it was carried that "deserted" was more proper. The concluding question was, "Whether King James having broken the original contract and deserted the government, the throne was thereby vacant?" This question was debated with more heat and contention than any of the former; and upon a division, the Tories prevailed by eleven voices, and it was carried to omit the last article with regard to the vacancy of the throne. The vote was sent back to the Commons with these amendments. [Vol. VI, Ch. LXXI, p. 358.]

It happens unluckily for those who maintain an original contract between the magistrate and people that great revolutions of government and new settlements of civil constitutions are commonly conducted with such violence, tumult, and disorder that the public voice can scarcely ever be heard; and the opinions of the citizens are at that time less attended to than even in the common course of administration. The present [1689] transactions in England, it must be confessed, are a singular exception to this observation. [Vol. VI, Ch. LXXI, p. 361.]

The opposite views in the debate were well represented. There was the argument of the "partisans of the court" in the reign of Charles I:

The true rule of government, said they, during any period is that to which the people from time immemorial have been accustomed and to which they naturally pay a prompt obedience. . . . A law, to have any authority, must be derived from a legislature which has right. And whence do all legislatures derive their right but from long custom and established practice? [Vol. V, Ch. LI, p. 38.]

The Commons . . . having established [1649] a principle which is noble in itself and seems specious, but is belied by all history and experience, "that the people are the origin of all just power," they next declared that the Commons of England, assembled in Parliament, being chosen by the people and representing them, are the supreme authority of the nation, and that whatever is enacted and declared to be the law by the Commons has the force of law, without the consent of the King or House of Peers. The ordinance for the trial of Charles Stuart, King of England (so they called him), was again read and unanimously assented to. [Vol. V, Ch. LIX, p. 370.]

All government is founded on opinion and sense of duty. . . . No human schemes can secure the public in all possible imaginable events. [Vol. VI, Ch. LXVIII, p. 227.]

The managers for the Commons might have opposed this reasoning by many specious and even solid arguments. They might have said that the great security for allegiance being merely opinion, any scheme of settlement should be adopted in which it was most probable the people would acquiesce and persevere; that though, upon the natural death of a king whose administration had been agreeable to the laws, many and great inconveniences would be endured rather than exclude his lineal successor, yet the case was not the same when the people had been obliged by their revolt to dethrone a prince whose illegal measures had, in every circumstance, violated the constitution; that in these extraordinary revolutions the government reverted, in some degree, to its first principles, and the community acquired a right of providing for the public interest by expedients which, on other occasions, might be deemed violent and irregular. . . . [Vol. VI, Ch. LXXI, p. 360.]

Compare Hume's remarks with the concluding words of Locke's Second Treatise of Government:

. . . when by the miscarriages of those in authority it [the legislative power] is forfeited; upon the forfeiture of the rulers . . . it reverts to the society, and the people have the right to act as supreme and continue the legislature in themselves or place it in a new form, or new hands, as they think good. [§243.]

VII

OF PASSIVE OBEDIENCE

In the former Essay,[a] we endeavored to refute the *specula-tive* systems of politics advanced in this nation, as well the religious system of the one party as the philosophical of the other. We now come to examine the *practical* consequences deduced by each party with regard to the measures of submission due to sovereigns.

As the obligation to justice is founded entirely on the interests of society, which require mutual abstinence from property in order to preserve peace among mankind, it is evident that, when the execution of justice would be attended with very pernicious consequences, that virtue must be suspended and give place to public utility in such extraordinary and such pressing emergencies. The maxim *fiat Justitia, ruat Coelum,* "let justice be performed though the universe be destroyed," is apparently false, and by sacrificing the end to the means shows a preposterous idea of the subordination of duties. What governor of a town makes any scruple of burning the suburbs when they facilitate the approaches of the enemy? Or what general abstains from plundering a neutral country when the necessities of war require it and he cannot otherwise subsist his army? The case is the same with the duty of allegiance; and common sense teaches us that, as government binds us to obedience only on account of its tendency to public utility, that duty must always, in extraordinary cases when public ruin would evidently attend obedience, yield to the primary and original obligation. *Salus populi suprema Lex*—the safety of the people is the supreme law. This maxim is agreeable to the sentiments of mankind in all ages; nor is anyone, when he reads of the insurrections against Nero or Philip

a ["Of the Original Contract," pp. 43 ff].

the Second, so infatuated with party systems as not to wish success to the enterprise and praise the undertakers. Even our high monarchical party, in spite of their sublime theory, are forced in such cases to judge and feel and approve in conformity to the rest of mankind.

Resistance, therefore, being admitted in extraordinary emergencies, the question can only be among good reasoners with regard to the degree of necessity which can justify resistance and render it lawful or commendable. And here I must confess that I shall always incline to their side who draw the bond of allegiance very close and consider an infringement of it as the last refuge in desperate cases, when the public is in the highest danger from violence and tyranny. For besides the mischiefs of a civil war, which commonly attends insurrection, it is certain that, where a disposition to rebellion appears among any people, it is one chief cause of tyranny in the rulers and forces them into many violent measures which they never would have embraced had everyone been inclined to submission and obedience. Thus the *tyrannicide*, or assassination, approved of by ancient maxims, instead of keeping tyrants and usurpers in awe, made them ten times more fierce and unrelenting and is now justly, upon that account, abolished by the laws of nations and universally condemned as a base and treacherous method of bringing to justice these disturbers of society.

Besides we must consider that as obedience is our duty in the common course of things, it ought chiefly to be inculcated; nor can anything be more preposterous than an anxious care and solicitude in stating all the cases in which resistance may be allowed. In like manner, though a philosopher reasonably acknowledges, in the course of an argument, that the rules of justice may be dispensed with in cases of urgent necessity, what should we think of a preacher or casuist who should make it his chief study to find out such cases and enforce them with all the vehemence of argument and eloquence? Would he not be better employed in inculcating the general doctrine than in displaying the particular exceptions, which we are, perhaps, but too much inclined of ourselves to embrace and to extend?

There are, however, two reasons which may be pleaded in defense of that party among us who have, with so much industry, propagated the maxims of resistance—maxims which, it must be confessed, are in general so pernicious and so destructive of civil society. The *first* is that their antagonists, carrying the doctrine of obedience to such an extravagant height as not only never to mention the exceptions in extraordinary cases (which might, perhaps, be excusable) but even positively to exclude them, it became necessary to insist on these exceptions and defend the rights of injured truth and liberty. The *second* and perhaps better reason is founded on the nature of the British constitution and form of government.

It is almost peculiar to our constitution to establish a first magistrate with such high pre-eminence and dignity that, though limited by the laws, he is in a manner, so far as regards his own person, above the laws and can neither be questioned nor punished for any injury or wrong which may be committed by him. His ministers alone, or those who act by his commission, are obnoxious to justice; and while the prince is thus allured by the prospect of personal safety to give the laws their free course, an equal security is in effect obtained by the punishment of lesser offenders; and at the same time a civil war is avoided, which would be the infallible consequence were an attack at every turn made directly upon the sovereign. But though the constitution pays this salutary compliment to the prince, it can never be reasonably understood by that maxim to have determined its own destruction or to have established a tame submission where he protects his ministers, perseveres in injustice, and usurps the whole power of the commonwealth. This case, indeed, is never expressly put by the laws, because it is impossible for them, in their ordinary course, to provide a remedy for it or establish any magistrate with superior authority to chastise the exorbitances of the prince. But as a right without a remedy would be an absurdity, the remedy in this case is the extraordinary one of resistance, when affairs come to that extremity that the constitution can be defended by it alone. Resistance, therefore, must of course become more frequent in the British government than in others which are simpler and consist of fewer parts and movements. Where the king is an absolute sovereign, he has little temptation to commit such enormous tyranny as may justly provoke rebellion. But where he is limited, his imprudent ambition, without any great vices, may run him into that perilous situation. This is frequently supposed to have been the case with Charles the First; and if we may now speak truth, after animosities are ceased, this was also the case with James the Second.[1] These were harmless if not, in their private character, good men; but mistaking the nature of our constitution and engrossing the whole legislative power, it became necessary to oppose them with some vehemence and even to deprive the latter formally of that authority which he had used with such imprudence and indiscretion.

VIII

OF THE INDEPENDENCE OF PARLIAMENT

POLITICAL WRITERS HAVE ESTABLISHED IT as a maxim that, in contriving any system of government and fixing the several checks and controls of the constitution, every man ought to be supposed a *knave* and to have no other end, in all his actions, than private interest. By this interest we must govern him and, by means of it, make him, notwithstanding his insatiable avarice and ambition, cooperate to public good. Without this, say they, we shall in vain boast of the advantages of any constitution and shall find in the end that we have no security for our liberties or possessions except the good will of our rulers; that is, we shall have no security at all.

It is, therefore, a just *political* maxim *that every man must be supposed a knave*, though at the same time it appears somewhat strange that a maxim should be true in *politics* which is false in *fact*. But to satisfy us on this head we may consider that men are generally more honest in their private than in their public capacity, and will go greater lengths to serve a party than when their own private interest is alone concerned. Honor is a great check upon mankind; but where a considerable body of men act together, this check is in a great measure removed, since a man is sure to be approved of by his own party for what promotes the common interest, and he soon learns to despise the clamors of adversaries. To which we may add that every court or senate is determined by the greater number of voices, so that, if self-interest influences only the majority (as it will always do), the whole senate follows the allurements of this separate interest and acts as if it contained not one member who had any regard to public interest and liberty.

When there offers, therefore, to our censure and examination any plan of government, real or imaginary, where the power is distributed among several courts and several orders of men, we should always consider the separate interest of each court and each order; and if we find that, by the skillful division of power, this interest must necessarily in its operation concur with the public, we may pronounce that government to be wise and happy. If, on the contrary, separate interest be not checked and be not directed to the public, we ought to look for nothing but faction, disorder, and tyranny from such a government. In this opinion I am justified by experience, as well as by the authority of all philosophers and politicians, both ancient and modern.

How much, therefore, would it have surprised such a genius as Cicero or Tacitus to have been told that, in a future age, there should arise a very regular system of *mixed* government, where the authority was so distributed that one rank, whenever it pleased, might swallow up all the rest and engross the whole power of the constitution! Such a government, they would say, will not be a mixed government. For so great is the natural ambition of men that they are never satisfied with power; and if one order of men, by pursuing its own interest, can usurp upon every other order, it will certainly do so and render itself, as far as possible, absolute and uncontrollable.

But in this opinion experience shows they would have been mistaken. For this is actually the case with the British constitution. The share of power allotted by our constitution to the House of Commons is so great that it absolutely commands all the other parts of the government. The king's legislative power is plainly no proper check to it. For though the king has a negative in framing laws, yet this in fact is esteemed of so little moment that whatever is voted by the two houses is always sure to pass into a law, and the royal assent is little better than a form. The principal weight of the crown lies in the executive power. But besides that the executive power in every government is altogether subordinate to the legislative, besides this I say, the exercise of this power requires an immense expense, and the Commons have assumed to themselves the sole right of granting money. How easy, therefore, would it be for that house to wrest from the crown all these powers, one after another, by making every grant conditional and choosing their time so well that their refusal of supply should only distress the government, without giving foreign powers any advantage over us! Did the House of Commons depend in the same manner upon the king and had none of the members any property but from his gift, would not he command all their resolutions and be from that moment absolute? As to the House of Lords, they are a very powerful support to the crown so long as they are, in their turn, supported by it; but both experience and reason show that they have no force or authority sufficient to maintain themselves alone without such support.

How, therefore, shall we solve this paradox? And by what means is this member of our constitution confined within the proper limits, since, from our very constitution, it must necessarily have as much power as it demands and can only be confined by itself? How is this consistent with our experience of human nature? I answer that the interest of the body is here restrained by that of the individuals, and that the House of Commons stretches not its power, because such a usurpation would be contrary to the interest of the majority of its members. The crown has so many offices at its disposal that, when assisted by the honest and disinterested part of the House, it will always command the resolutions of the whole, so far, at least, as to preserve the ancient constitution from danger. We may therefore give to this influence what name we please; we may call it by the invidious appellations of *corruption* and *dependence;* but some degree and some kind of it are inseparable from the very nature of the constitution and necessary to the preservation of our mixed government.

Instead, then, of asserting [a] absolutely that the dependence of Parliament, in every degree, is an infringement of British liberty, the Country party should have made some concessions to their adversaries and have only examined what was the proper degree of this dependence beyond which it became dangerous to liberty. But such a moderation is not to be expected in party men of any kind. After a concession of this nature, all declamation must be

[a] See "Dissertation on Parties," [by Lord Bolingbroke,] throughout.

abandoned; and a calm inquiry into the proper degree of court influence and parliamentary dependence would have been expected by the readers. And though the advantage in such a controversy might possibly remain to the Country party, yet the victory would not be so complete as they wish for; nor would a true patriot have given an entire loose to his zeal, for fear of running matters into a contrary extreme by diminishing too far the influence of the crown. It was therefore thought best to deny that this extreme could ever be dangerous to the constitution or that the crown could ever have too little influence over members of Parliament.

All questions concerning the proper medium between extremes are difficult to be decided, both because it is not easy to find *words* proper to fix this medium and because the good and ill, in such cases, run so gradually into each other as even to render our *sentiments* doubtful and uncertain. But there is a peculiar difficulty in the present case, which would embarrass the most knowing and most impartial examiner. The power of the crown is always lodged in a single person, either king or minister; and as this person may have either a greater or less degree of ambition, capacity, courage, popularity, or fortune, the power, which is too great in one hand, may become too little in another. In pure republics, where the authority is distributed among several assemblies or senates, the checks and controls are more regular in their operation, because the members of such numerous assemblies may be presumed to be always nearly equal in capacity and virtue, and it is only their number, riches, or authority which enter into consideration. But a limited monarchy admits not of any such stability; nor is it possible to assign to the crown such a determinate degree of power as will, in every hand, form a proper counterbalance to the other parts of the constitution. This is an unavoidable disadvantage among the many advantages attending that species of government.

IX

WHETHER THE BRITISH GOVERNMENT INCLINES MORE TO ABSOLUTE MONARCHY OR TO A REPUBLIC

IT AFFORDS A VIOLENT PREJUDICE against almost every science that no prudent man, however sure of his principles, dares prophesy concerning any event or foretell the remote consequences of things. A physician will not venture to pronounce concerning the condition of his patient a fortnight or a month after, and still less dares a politician foretell the situation of public affairs a few years hence. Harrington[1] thought himself so sure of his general principles, *that the balance of power depends on that of property,* that he ventured to pronounce it impossible ever to re-establish monarchy in England, but his book was scarcely published when the king was restored, and we see that monarchy has ever since subsisted upon the same footing as before. Notwithstanding this unlucky example, I will venture to examine an important question, to wit: *Whether the British government inclines more to absolute monarchy or to a republic, and in which of these two species of government it will most probably terminate?* As there seems not to be any great danger of a sudden revolution either way, I shall at least escape the shame attending my temerity if I should be found to have been mistaken.

Those who assert that the balance of our government inclines toward absolute monarchy may support their opinion by the following reasons: That property has a great influence on power cannot possibly be denied; but yet the general maxim *that the balance of the one depends on the balance of the other* must be received with several limitations. It is evident that much less property in a single hand will be able to counterbalance a greater property in several, not only because it is difficult to make many persons combine in the same views and measures, but because property when united causes much greater dependence than the same property when dispersed. A hundred persons of £1,000 a year apiece can consume all their income and nobody shall ever be the better for them except their servants and tradesmen, who justly regard their profits as the product of their own labor. But a man possessed of £100,000 a year, if he has either any generosity or any cunning, may create a great dependence by obligations and still a greater by expectations. Hence we may observe that, in all free governments, any subject exorbitantly rich has always created jealousy, even though his riches bore no proportion to those of the state. Crassus' fortune, if I remember well, amounted only to about two millions and a half of our money, yet we find that, though his genius was nothing extraordinary, he was able by means of his riches alone to counterbalance during his lifetime the power of Pompey as well as that of Caesar, who afterward became master of the world. The wealth of the Medici made them masters of Florence, though it is probable it was not considerable compared to the united property of that opulent republic.

These considerations are apt to make one entertain a magnificent idea of the British spirit and love of liberty, since we could maintain our free government during so many centuries against our sovereigns, who, besides the power and dignity and majesty of the crown, have always been possessed of much more property than any subject has ever enjoyed in any commonwealth. But it may be said that this spirit, however great, will never be able to support itself against that immense property which is now lodged in the king and which is still increasing. Upon a moderate computation there are near three millions a year at the disposal of the crown. The civil list amounts to near a million; the collection of all taxes to another; and the employments in the army and navy, together with ecclesiastical preferments, to above a third million—an enormous sum, and what may fairly be computed to be more than a thirtieth part of the whole income and labor of the kingdom. When we add to this great property the increasing luxury of the nation, our proneness to corruption, together with the great power and prerogatives of the crown and the command of military force, there is no one but must despair of being able, without extraordinary efforts, to support our free government much longer under these disadvantages.

On the other hand, those who maintain that the bias of the British government leans toward a republic may support their opinions by specious arguments. It may be said that, though this immense property in the crown be joined to the dignity of first magistrate and to many other legal powers and prerogatives which should naturally give it greater influence, yet it really becomes less dangerous to liberty upon that very account. Were England a republic and were any private man possessed of a revenue a third or even a tenth part as large as that of the crown, he would very justly excite jealousy, because he would infallibly have great authority in the government. And such an irregular authority, not avowed by the laws, is always more dangerous than a much greater authority derived from them. A man possessed of usurped power can set no bounds to his pretensions: his partisans have liberty to hope for everything in his favor; his enemies provoke his ambition with his fears by the violence of their opposition; and the government being thrown into a ferment, every corrupted humor in the state naturally gathers to him. On the contrary, a legal authority, though great, has always some bounds which terminate both the hopes and pretensions of the person possessed of it: the laws must have provided a remedy against its excesses; such an eminent magistrate has much to fear and little to hope from his usurpations; and as his legal authority is quietly submitted to, he has small temptation and small opportunity of extending it further. Besides, it happens with regard to ambitious aims and projects what may be observed with regard to sects of philosophy and religion. A new sect excites such a ferment and is both opposed and defended with such vehemence that it always spreads faster and multiplies its partisans with greater rapidity than any old established opinion recommended by the sanction of the laws and of antiquity. Such is the nature of novelty that, where anything pleases, it becomes doubly agreeable if new; but if it displeases, it is doubly displeasing upon that very account.

And, in most cases, the violence of enemies is favorable to ambitious projects as well as the zeal of partisans.

It may further be said that, though men be much governed by interest, yet even interest itself and all human affairs are entirely governed by *opinion*. Now there has been a sudden and sensible change in the opinions of men within these last fifty years by the progress of learning and of liberty. Most people in this Island have divested themselves of all superstitious reverence to names and authority; the clergy have much lost their credit, their pretensions and doctrines have been ridiculed, and even religion can scarcely support itself in the world. The mere name of "king" commands little respect; and to talk of a king as God's vicegerent on earth, or to give him any of those magnificent titles which formerly dazzled mankind, would but excite laughter in everyone. Though the crown, by means of its large revenue, may maintain its authority in times of tranquillity upon private interest and influence, yet, as the least shock or convulsion must break all these interests to pieces, the royal power, being no longer supported by the settled principles and opinions of men, will immediately dissolve. Had men been in the same disposition at the Revolution as they are at present, monarchy would have run a great risk of being entirely lost in this Island.

Durst I venture to deliver my own sentiments amidst these opposite arguments, I would assert that, unless there happens some extraordinary convulsion, the power of the crown, by means of its large revenue, is rather upon the increase, though at the same time I own that its progress seems very slow and almost insensible. The tide has run long and with some rapidity to the side of popular government and is just beginning to turn toward monarchy.

It is well known that every government must come to a period and that death is unavoidable to the political as well as to the animal body. But, as one kind of death may be preferable to another, it may be inquired whether it be more desirable for the British constitution to terminate in a popular government or in an absolute monarchy? Here I would frankly declare that, though liberty be preferable to slavery in almost every case, yet I should

rather wish to see an absolute monarch than a republic in this
Island. For let us consider what kind of republic we have reason
to expect. The question is not concerning any fine imaginary
republic of which a man forms a plan in his closet. There is no
doubt but a popular government may be imagined more perfect
than an absolute monarchy or even than our present constitution.
But what reason have we to expect that any such government will
ever be established in Great Britain upon the dissolution of our
monarchy? If any single person acquire power enough to take
our constitution to pieces and put it up anew, he is really an
absolute monarch; and we have already had an instance of this
kind sufficient to convince us that such a person will never resign
his power or establish any free government. Matters, therefore,
must be trusted to their natural progress and operation; and the
House of Commons, according to its present constitution, must
be the only legislature in such a popular government. The inconveniences attending such a situation of affairs present themselves
by thousands. If the House of Commons in such a case ever dissolve itself, which is not to be expected, we may look for a civil
war every election. If it continue itself, we shall suffer all the
tyranny of a faction subdivided into new factions. And as such a
violent government cannot long subsist, we shall at last, after
many convulsions and civil wars, find repose in absolute monarchy, which it would have been happier for us to have established
peaceably from the beginning. Absolute monarchy, therefore, is
the easiest death, the true *Euthanasia* of the British constitution.

Thus if we have reason to be more jealous of monarchy because
the danger is more imminent from that quarter, we have also
reason to be more jealous of popular government because that
danger is more terrible. This may teach us a lesson of moderation
in all our political controversies.

X

OF PARTIES IN GENERAL

OF ALL MEN THAT DISTINGUISH THEMSELVES by memorable achievements, the first place of honor seems due to legislators and founders of states who transmit a system of laws and institutions to secure the peace, happiness, and liberty of future generations. The influence of useful inventions in the arts and sciences may, perhaps, extend further than that of wise laws, whose effects are limited both in time and place; but the benefit arising from the former is not so sensible as that which results from the latter. Speculative sciences do indeed improve the mind, but this advantage reaches only to a few persons who have leisure to apply themselves to them. And as to practical arts, which increase the commodities and enjoyments of life, it is well known that men's happiness consists not so much in an abundance of these as in the peace and security with which they possess them, and those blessings can only be derived from good government. Not to mention that general virtue and good morals in a state, which are so requisite to happiness, can never arise from the most refined precepts of philosophy or even the severest injunctions of religion, but must proceed entirely from the virtuous education of youth, the effect of wise laws and institutions. I must therefore presume to differ from Lord Bacon in this particular and must regard antiquity as somewhat unjust in its distribution of honors when it made gods of all the inventors of useful arts, such as Ceres, Bacchus, Aesculapius, and dignified legislators such as Romulus and Theseus only with the appellation of demigods and heroes.

As much as legislators and founders of states ought to be honored and respected among men, as much ought the founders of sects and factions to be detested and hated, because the influence of faction is directly contrary to that of laws. Factions subvert government, render laws impotent, and beget the fiercest animosi-

77

ties among men of the same nation, who ought to give mutual assistance and protection to each other. And what should render the founders of parties more odious is the difficulty of extirpating these weeds when once they have taken root in any state. They naturally propagate themselves for many centuries, and seldom end but by the total dissolution of that government in which they are sown. They are, besides, plants which grow most plentiful in the richest soil; and though absolute governments be not wholly free from them, it must be confessed that they rise more easily and propagate themselves faster in free governments, where they always infect the legislature itself, which alone could be able, by the steady application of rewards and punishments, to eradicate them.

Factions may be divided into *personal* and *real,* that is, into factions founded on personal friendship or animosity among such as compose the contending parties and into those founded on some real difference of sentiment or interest. The reason of this distinction is obvious, though I must acknowledge that parties are seldom found pure and unmixed, either of the one kind or the other. It is not often seen that a government divides into factions where there is no difference in the views of the constituent members, either real or apparent, trivial or material; and in those factions which are founded on the most real and most material difference there is always observed a great deal of personal animosity or affection. But notwithstanding this mixture, a party may be denominated either personal or real according to that principle which is predominant and is found to have the greatest influence.

Personal factions arise most easily in small republics. Every domestic quarrel there becomes an affair of state. Love, vanity, emulation, any passion, as well as ambition and resentment, begets public division. The *Neri* and *Bianchi* of Florence, the *Fregosi* and *Adorni* of Genoa, the *Colonnesi* and *Orsini* of modern Rome were parties of this kind.

Men have such a propensity to divide into personal factions that the smallest appearance of real difference will produce them. What can be imagined more trivial than the difference between one color of livery and another in horse races? Yet this difference begat two most inveterate factions in the Greek Empire, the *Prasini* and *Veneti*, who never suspended their animosities till they ruined that unhappy government.

We find in the Roman history a remarkable dissension between two tribes, the *Pollia* and *Papiria*, which continued for the space of near three hundred years and discovered itself in their suffrages at every election of magistrates.[a] This faction was the more remarkable as it could continue for so long a tract of time, even though it did not spread itself nor draw any of the other tribes into a share of the quarrel. If mankind had not a strong propensity to such divisions, the indifference of the rest of the community must have suppressed this foolish animosity that had not any aliment of new benefits and injuries, of general sympathy and antipathy, which never fail to take place when the whole state is rent into equal factions.

[a] As this fact has not been much observed by antiquaries or politicians, I shall deliver it in the words of the Roman historian:

"Populus Tusculanus cum conjugibus ac liberis Romam venit: Ea multitudo veste mutata, et specie reorum, tribus circuit, genibus se omnium advolvens. Plus itaque misericordia ad poenae veniam impetrandam, quam causa ad crimen purgandum valuit. Tribus omnes, praeter Polliam, antiquarunt legem. Polliae sententia fuit, puberes verberatos necari; liberos conjugesque sub corona lege belli venire: Memoriamque ejus irae Tusculanis in poenae tam atrocis auctores, mansisse ad patrum aetatem constat, nec quemquam ferme ex Pollia tribu candidatum Papiriam ferre solitum." [The people of Tusculum came to Rome with their women and children. They put on garments to make them look like defendants, and, in a crowd, went from one tribe to the next and clasped the knees of all citizens in supplication. As a result, pity had more effect in obtaining for them remission of their punishment than did argument in absolving them from the charges against them. All the tribes, except the Pollian, voted to reject the law. The Pollian voted to have the adults scourged and killed, and to sell the children and wives as slaves under the laws of war. As a matter of fact, the Tusculans, down to the time of our fathers, have not forgotten their wrath against the advocates of so cruel a punishment, and hardly ever has a candidate of the Pollian tribe received their vote.]— T. Livii, lib. 8.

The *Castelani* and *Nicolloti* are two mobbish factions in Venice who frequently box together and then lay aside their quarrels presently.

Nothing is more usual than to see parties which have begun upon a real difference continue even after that difference is lost. When men are once enlisted on opposite sides, they contract an affection to the persons with whom they are united and an animosity against their antagonists, and these passions they often transmit to their posterity. The real difference between Guelf and Ghibelline was long lost in Italy before these factions were extinguished. The Guelfs adhered to the Pope, the Ghibellines to the Emperor; yet the family of Sforza, who were in alliance with the Emperor though they were Guelfs, being expelled [from] Milan by the King of France,[b] assisted by Jacomo Trivulzio and the Ghibellines, the Pope concurred with the latter and they formed leagues with the Pope against the Emperor.[1]

The civil wars which arose some few years ago in Morocco between the *Blacks* and *Whites,* merely on account of their complexion, are founded on a pleasant difference. We laugh at them; but I believe, were things rightly examined, we afford much more occasion of ridicule to the Moors. For what are all the wars of religion which have prevailed in this polite and knowing part of the world? They are certainly more absurd than the Moorish civil wars. The difference of complexion is a sensible and a real difference; but the controversy about an article of faith, which is utterly absurd and unintelligible, is not a difference in sentiment but in a few phrases and expressions which one party accepts of without understanding them and the other refuses in the same manner.[c]

Real factions may be divided into those from *interest,* from *principle,* and from *affection.* Of all factions the first are the most reasonable and the most excusable. Where two orders of

---

[b] [Louis XII.]

[c] Besides I do not find that the Whites in Morocco ever imposed on the Blacks any necessity of altering their complexion or frightened them with inquisitions and penal laws in case of obstinacy. Nor have the Blacks been more unreasonable in this particular. But is a man's opinion—where he is able to form a real opinion—more at his disposal than his complexion? And can one be induced by force or fear to do more than paint and disguise in the one case as well as in the other?--Editions A, C, D, N.

men, such as the nobles and people, have a distinct authority in a government not very accurately balanced and modeled, they naturally follow a distinct interest; nor can we reasonably expect a different conduct, considering that degree of selfishness implanted in human nature. It requires great skill in a legislator to prevent such parties; and many philosophers are of opinion that this secret, like the *grand elixir* or *perpetual motion*, may amuse men in theory but can never possibly be reduced to practice. In despotic governments, indeed, factions often do not appear, but they are not the less real; or rather, they are more real and more pernicious upon that very account. The distinct orders of men— nobles and people, soldiers and merchants—have all a distinct interest; but the more powerful oppresses the weaker with impunity and without resistance, which begets a seeming tranquillity in such governments.

There has been an attempt in England to divide the *landed* and *trading* part of the nation, but without success. The interests of these two bodies are not really distinct, and never will be so till our public debts increase to such a degree as to become altogether oppressive and intolerable.

Parties from *principle*, especially abstract speculative principle, are known only to modern times and are, perhaps, the most extraordinary and unaccountable phenomenon that has yet appeared in human affairs. Where different principles beget a contrariety of conduct, which is the case with all different political principles, the matter may be more easily explained. A man who esteems the true right of government to lie in one man or one family cannot easily agree with his fellow citizen who thinks that another man or family is possessed of this right. Each naturally wishes that right may take place according to his own notions of it. But where the difference of principle is attended with no contrariety of action, but everyone may follow his own way without interfering with his neighbor, as happens in all religious controversies, what madness, what fury can beget such an unhappy and such fatal divisions?

Two men traveling on the highway—the one east, the other west—can easily pass each other if the way be broad enough;

but two men reasoning upon opposite principles of religion cannot so easily pass without shocking, though one should think that the way were also in that case sufficiently broad and that each might proceed without interruption in his own course. But such is the nature of the human mind that it always lays hold on every mind that approaches it, and as it is wonderfully fortified by a unanimity of sentiments, so it is shocked and disturbed by any contrariety. Hence the eagerness which most people discover in a dispute, and hence their impatience of opposition even in the most speculative and indifferent opinions.

This principle, however frivolous it may appear, seems to have been the origin of all religious wars and divisions. But as this principle is universal in human nature, its effects would not have been confined to one age and to one sect of religion did it not there concur with other more accidental causes, which raise it to such a height as to produce the greatest misery and devastation. Most religions of the ancient world arose in the unknown ages of government when men were as yet barbarous and uninstructed, and the prince, as well as peasant, was disposed to receive with implicit faith every pious tale or fiction which was offered him. The magistrate embraced the religion of the people and, entering cordially into the care of sacred matters, naturally acquired an authority in them and united the ecclesiastical with the civil power. But the *Christian* religion arising while principles directly opposite to it were firmly established in the polite part of the world, who despised the nation that first broached this novelty, no wonder that in such circumstances it was but little countenanced by the civil magistrate and that the priesthood was allowed to engross all the authority in the new sect. So bad a use did they make of this power, even in those early times, that the primitive persecutions may, perhaps *in part,*[d] be ascribed to the violence instilled by them into their followers.

---

[d] I say *in part,* for it is a vulgar error to imagine that the ancients were as great friends to toleration as the English or Dutch are at present. The laws against external superstition among the Romans were as ancient as the time of the Twelve Tables; and the Jews, as well as Christians, were sometimes punished by them, though in general these laws were not rigor-

And the same principles of priestly government continuing after Christianity became the established religion, they have engendered a spirit of persecution which has ever since been the poison of human society and the source of the most inveterate factions in every government. Such divisions, therefore, on the part of the people may justly be esteemed factions of *principle*; but on the part of the priests, who are the prime movers, they are really factions of *interest*.

There is another cause (beside the authority of the priests and the separation of the ecclesiastical and civil powers) which has contributed to render Christendom the scene of religious wars and divisions. Religions that arise in ages totally ignorant and barbarous consist mostly of traditional tales and fictions, which may be different in every sect without being contrary to each other; and even when they are contrary, everyone adheres to the tradition of his own sect without much reasoning or disputation. But as philosophy was widely spread over the world at the time when Christianity arose, the teachers of the new sect were obliged to form a system of speculative opinions; to divide, with some accuracy, their articles of faith; and to explain, comment, confute, and defend with all the subtlety of argument and science. Hence naturally arose keenness in dispute when the Christian religion came to be split into new divisions and heresies; and this keen-

---

ously executed. Immediately after the conquest of Gaul, they forbade all but the natives to be initiated into the religion of the Druids; and this was a kind of persecution. In about a century after this conquest, the Emperor Claudius quite abolished that superstition by penal laws, which would have been a very grievous persecution if the imitation of the Roman manners had not, beforehand, weaned the Gauls from their ancient prejudices. Suetonius in *Vita Claudii*. Pliny ascribes the abolition of the Druidical superstitions to Tiberius, probably because that emperor had taken some steps toward restraining them (lib. xxx. cap. i). This is an instance of the usual caution and moderation of the Romans in such cases, and very different from their violent and sanguinary method of treating the Christians. Hence we may entertain a suspicion that those furious persecutions of *Christianity* were in some measure owing to the imprudent zeal and bigotry of the first propagators of that sect, and ecclesiastical history affords us many reasons to confirm this suspicion.

ness assisted the priests in their policy of begetting a mutual hatred and antipathy among their deluded followers. Sects of philosophy in the ancient world were more zealous than parties of religion, but in modern times parties of religion are more furious and enraged than the most cruel factions that ever arose from interest and ambition.

I have mentioned parties from *affection* as a kind of *real* parties beside those from *interest* and *principle*. By parties from affection I understand those which are founded on the different attachments of men toward particular families and persons whom they desire to rule over them. These factions are often very violent, though I must own it may seem unaccountable that men should attach themselves so strongly to persons with whom they are nowise acquainted, whom perhaps they never saw, and from whom they never received nor can ever hope for any favor. Yet this we often find to be the case, and even with men who, on other occasions, discover no great generosity of spirit nor are found to be easily transported by friendship beyond their own interest. We are apt to think the relation between us and our sovereign very close and intimate. The splendor of majesty and power bestows an importance on the fortunes even of a single person. And when a man's good nature does not give him this imaginary interest, his ill nature will, from spite and opposition to persons whose sentiments are different from his own.

XI

OF THE PARTIES OF GREAT BRITAIN

WERE THE BRITISH GOVERNMENT proposed as a subject of speculation, one would immediately perceive in it a source of division and party which it would be almost impossible for it, under any administration, to avoid. The just balance between the republican [1] and monarchical part of our constitution is really in itself so extremely delicate and uncertain that, when joined to men's passions and prejudices, it is impossible but different opinions must arise concerning it, even among persons of the best understanding. Those of mild tempers who love peace and order, and detest sedition and civil wars, will always entertain more favorable sentiments of monarchy than men of bold and generous spirits who are passionate lovers of liberty and think no evil comparable to subjection and slavery. And though all reasonable men agree in general to preserve our mixed government, yet, when they come to particulars, some will incline to trust greater powers to the crown, to bestow on it more influence, and to guard against its encroachments with less caution than others who are terrified at the most distant approaches of tyranny and despotic power. Thus are there parties of *principle* involved in the very nature of our constitution, which may properly enough be denominated those of *Court* and *Country*.[a] The strength and violence

[a] These words have become of general use, and therefore I shall employ them without intending to express by them a universal blame of the one party or approbation of the other. The Court party may no doubt on some occasions consult best the interest of the country, and the Country party oppose it. In like manner, the Roman parties were denominated *Optimates* and *Populares*; and Cicero, like a true party man, defines the Optimates to be such as in all their public conduct regulated themselves by the sentiments of the best and worthiest Romans; *pro Sextio*. The term of "Country party" may afford a favorable definition or etymology of the same kind; but it would be folly to draw any argument from that head, and I have no regard to it in employing these terms.—Note in Editions A, C, D, N.

of each of these parties will much depend upon the particular administration. An administration may be so bad as to throw a great majority into the opposition, as a good administration will reconcile to the court many of the most passionate lovers of liberty. But however the nation may fluctuate between them, the parties themselves will always subsist so long as we are governed by a limited monarchy.

But besides this difference of *principle* those parties are very much fomented by a difference of *interest*, without which they could scarcely ever be dangerous or violent. The crown will naturally bestow all trust and power upon those whose principles, real or pretended, are most favorable to monarchical government; and this temptation will naturally engage them to go greater lengths than their principles would otherwise carry them. Their antagonists, who are disappointed in their ambitious aims, throw themselves into the party whose sentiments incline them to be most jealous of royal power, and naturally carry those sentiments to a greater height than sound politics will justify. Thus Court and Country, which are the genuine offspring of the British government, are a kind of mixed parties, and are influenced both by principle and by interest. The heads of the factions are commonly most governed by the latter motive, the inferior members of them by the former.[b]

As to ecclesiastical parties, we may observe that, in all ages of the world, priests have been enemies to liberty;[c] and it is certain that this steady conduct of theirs must have been founded on fixed

---

[b] I must be understood to mean this of persons who have any motive for taking party on any side. For, to tell the truth, the greatest part are commonly men who associate themselves they know not why: from example, from passion, from idleness. But still it is requisite there be some source of division, either in principle or interest; otherwise such persons would not find parties to which they could associate themselves.—Editions A, C, D, N.

[c] This proposition is true notwithstanding that, in the early times of the English government, the clergy were the great and principal opposers of the crown; but at that time their possessions were so immensely great that they composed a considerable part of the proprietors of England and in many contests were direct rivals of the crown.—Note in Editions C, D, N.

reasons of interest and ambition. Liberty of thinking and of expressing our thoughts is always fatal to priestly power and to those pious frauds on which it is commonly founded; and, by an infallible connection which prevails among all kinds of liberty, this privilege can never be enjoyed, at least has never yet been enjoyed, but in a free government. Hence it must happen in such a constitution as that of Great Britain that the established clergy, while things are in their natural situation, will always be of the Court party; as on the contrary, dissenters of all kinds will be of the Country party, since they can never hope for that toleration which they stand in need of but by means of our free government. All princes that have aimed at despotic power have known of what importance it was to gain the established clergy; as the clergy, on their part, have shown a great facility in entering into the views of such princes.[d] Gustavius Vasa was, perhaps, the only ambitious monarch that ever depressed the Church at the same time that he discouraged liberty. But the exorbitant power of the bishops in Sweden, who at that time overtopped the crown itself, together with their attachment to a foreign family, was the reason of his embracing such an unusual system of politics.

This observation concerning the propensity of priests to the government of a single person is not true with regard to one sect only. The *Presbyterian* and *Calvinistic* clergy in Holland were professed friends to the family of Orange; as the *Arminians,* who were esteemed heretics, were of the Louvestein faction and zealous for liberty. But if a prince have the choice of both, it is easy to see that he will prefer the Episcopal to the Presbyterian form of government, both because of the greater affinity between mon-

[d] "Judaei sibi ipsi reges imposuere, qui mobilitate vulgi expulsi, resumpta per arma dominatione, fugas civium, urbium eversiones, fratrum, conjugum, parentum neces, aliaque solita regibus ausi, superstitionem fovebant; quia honor sacerdotii firmamentum potentiae, assumebatur." [The Jews appointed their own kings. Through the fickle nature of the mob, the kings were expelled; when they had regained their power by force of arms they exiled citizens, destroyed cities, killed brothers, wives, and parents, committed such other outrageous deeds as kings usually commit, and furthered the cause of superstition, for to strengthen their power they had assumed the priesthood.]—Tacit. *Hist.* lib. v.

archy and episcopacy and because of the facility which he will find, in such a government, of ruling the clergy by means of their ecclesiastical superiors.[e]

If we consider the first rise of parties in England, during the great rebellion, we shall observe that it was conformable to this general theory and that the species of government gave birth to them by a regular and infallible operation. The English constitution, before that period, had lain in a kind of confusion; yet so as that the subjects possessed many noble privileges, which, though not exactly bounded and secured by law, were universally deemed from long possession to belong to them as their birthright. An ambitious, or rather a misguided, prince [2] arose who deemed all these privileges to be concessions of his predecessors, revocable at pleasure; and, in prosecution of this principle, he openly acted in violation of liberty during the course of several years. Necessity at last constrained him to call a Parliament; the spirit of liberty arose and spread itself: the prince, being without any support, was obliged to grant everything required of him, and his enemies, jealous and implacable, set no bounds to their pretensions. Here, then, began those contests in which it was no wonder that men of that age were divided into different parties, since even at this day the impartial are at a loss to decide concerning the justice of the quarrel. The pretensions of the Parliament, if yielded to, broke the balance of the constitution by rendering the government almost entirely republican. If not yielded to, the nation was perhaps still in danger of absolute power from the settled principles and inveterate habits of the king, which had plainly appeared in every concession that he had been constrained to make to his people. In this question, so delicate and uncertain, men naturally fell to the side which was most conformable to their usual principles; and the more passionate favorers of monarchy declared for the king, as the zealous friends of liberty sided with the Parliament. The hopes of success being nearly equal on both

[e] "Populi imperium, juxta libertatem: paucorum dominatio, regiae libidini propior est." [The supremacy of the people is akin to freedom: the rule of a small group is more closely related to the whim of a king.]— Tacit. *Ann.* lib. vi.

sides, *interest* had no general influence in this contest, so that *Roundhead* and *Cavalier* [3] were merely parties of principle, neither of which disowned either monarchy or liberty; but the former party inclined most to the republican part of our government, the latter to the monarchical. In this respect they may be considered as Court and Country party, inflamed into a civil war by an unhappy concurrence of circumstances and by the turbulent spirit of the age. The commonwealth's men and the partisans of absolute power lay concealed in both parties and formed but an inconsiderable part of them.

The clergy had concurred with the king's arbitrary designs and, in return, were allowed to persecute their adversaries, whom they called heretics and schismatics. The established clergy were Episcopal, the nonconformists Presbyterian; so that all things concurred to throw the former, without reserve, into the king's party and the latter into that of the Parliament.[f]

Everyone knows the event of this quarrel—fatal to the king first, to the Parliament afterward. After many confusions and revolutions, the royal family was at last restored and the ancient government re-established. Charles II was not made wiser by the example of his father, but prosecuted the same measures, though, at first, with more secrecy and caution. New parties arose under the appellation of *Whig* and *Tory*, which have continued ever since to confound and distract our government. To determine the nature of these parties is perhaps one of the most difficult problems that can be met with and is a proof that history may con-

[f] The clergy had concurred in a shameless manner with the king's arbitrary designs, according to their usual maxims in such cases, and in return were allowed to persecute their adversaries, whom they called heretics and schismatics. The established clergy were Episcopal, the nonconformists Presbyterians; so that all things concurred to throw the former, without reserve, into the king's party, and the latter into that of the Parliament. The *Cavaliers* being the Court party and the *Roundheads* the Country party, the union was infallible betwixt the former and the established prelacy, and betwixt the latter and Presbyterian nonconformists. This union is so natural, according to the general principles of politics, that it requires some very extraordinary situation of affairs to break it.— Editions A, C, D, N.

tain questions as uncertain as any to be found in the most abstract sciences. We have seen the conduct of the two parties during the course of seventy years in a vast variety of circumstances, possessed of power and deprived of it, during peace and during war; persons who profess themselves of one side or other we meet with every hour, in company, in our pleasures, in our serious occupations; we ourselves are constrained in a manner to take party, and, living in a country of the highest liberty, everyone may openly declare all his sentiments and opinions; yet are we at a loss to tell the nature, pretensions, and principles of the different factions.[g]

When we compare the parties of *Whig* and *Tory* with those of *Roundhead* and *Cavalier,* the most obvious difference that appears between them consists in the principles of *passive obedience* and *indefeasible right,* which were but little heard of among the Cavaliers but became the universal doctrine and were esteemed the true characteristic of a Tory. Were these principles pushed into their most obvious consequences, they imply a formal renunciation of all our liberties and an avowal of absolute monarchy; since nothing can be a greater absurdity than a limited power which must not be resisted, even when it exceeds its limitations. But, as the most rational principles are often but a weak counterpoise to passion, it is no wonder that these absurd principles[h] were found too weak for that effect. The Tories, as men, were enemies to oppression; and also, as Englishmen, they were enemies to arbitrary power. Their zeal for liberty was, perhaps, less fervent than that of their antagonists, but was sufficient to make them forget all their general principles when they saw themselves openly threatened with a subversion of the ancient government. From these sentiments arose the *Revolution,* an event of mighty consequence and the firmest foundation of British

[g] The question is perhaps in itself somewhat difficult, but has been rendered more so by the prejudices and violence of party.—Editions A, C, D, N.

[h] Editions A, C, D, N: "sufficient, according to a justly celebrated author,* to shock the common sense of a Hottentot or Samoiede."

* Dissertation on Parties, [by Lord Bolingbroke,] Letter X.

liberty. The conduct of the Tories during that event and after it will afford us a true insight into the nature of that party.

In the *first* place, they appear to have had the genuine sentiments of Britons in their affection for liberty and in their determined resolution not to sacrifice it to any abstract principle whatsoever or to any imaginary rights of princes. This part of their character might justly have been doubted of before the Revolution, from the obvious tendency of their avowed principles and from their compliances[i] with a court which seemed to make little secret of its arbitrary designs. The Revolution showed them to have been, in this respect, nothing but a genuine Court party, such as might be expected in a British government; that is, *lovers of liberty, but greater lovers of monarchy.* It must, however, be confessed that they carried their monarchical principles further even in practice, but more so in theory, than was in any degree consistent with a limited government.

Secondly, neither their principles nor affections concurred, entirely or heartily, with the settlement made at the Revolution or with that which has since taken place. This part of their character may seem opposite to the former, since any other settlement, in those circumstances of the nation, must probably have been dangerous, if not fatal, to liberty. But the heart of man is made to reconcile contradictions, and this contradiction is not greater than that between *passive obedience* and the *resistance* employed at the Revolution. A *Tory,* therefore, since the Revolution, may be defined, in a few words, to be *a lover of monarchy, though without abandoning liberty, and a partisan of the family of Stuart;* as a *Whig* may be defined to be *a lover of liberty, though without renouncing monarchy, and a friend to the settlement in the Protestant line.*[j]

[i] In Editions A, C, and D, we read *"almost unbounded* compliances."

[j] In Editions A and C, the definitions of Whig and Tory were followed by remarks in the text which are thrown into a note in Editions D and N, and omitted altogether in O. [This note has also been omitted here; cf. Hume's own statement in footnote k on page 92. The last paragraph of the present essay was part of the note which Hume reinstated in Edition O.]

These different views with regard to the settlement of the crown were accidental but natural additions to the principles of the Court and Country parties, which are the genuine divisions in the British government. A passionate lover of monarchy is apt to be displeased at any change of the succession as savoring too much of a commonwealth; a passionate lover of liberty is apt to think that every part of the government ought to be subordinate to the interests of liberty.

Some who will not venture to assert that the *real* difference between Whig and Tory was lost at the Revolution seem inclined to think that the difference is now abolished, and that affairs are so far returned to their natural state that there are at present no other parties among us but Court and Country; that is, men who, by interest or principle, are attached either to monarchy or liberty. The Tories have been so long obliged to talk in the republican style that they seem to have made converts of themselves by their hypocrisy and to have embraced the sentiments as well as language of their adversaries. There are, however, very considerable remains of that party in England, with all their old prejudices; and a proof that Court and Country are not our only parties is that almost all the dissenters side with the court, and the lower clergy, at least of the Church of England, with the Opposition. This may convince us that some bias still hangs upon our constitution, some extrinsic weight which turns from its natural course and causes a confusion in our parties.[k]

k Some of the opinions delivered in these Essays with regard to the public transactions in the last century the author, on more accurate examination, found reason to retract in his *History of Great Britain*. And as he would not enslave himself to the systems of either party, neither would he fetter his judgment by his own preconceived opinions and principles; nor is he ashamed to acknowledge his mistakes. These mistakes were indeed, at that time, almost universal in this kingdom.

XII

OF THE COALITION OF PARTIES

To ABOLISH ALL DISTINCTIONS OF PARTY may not be practicable, perhaps not desirable in a free government. The only dangerous parties are such as entertain opposite views with regard to the essentials of government, the succession of the crown, or the more considerable privileges belonging to the several members of the constitution; where there is no room for any compromise or accommodation, and where the controversy may appear so momentous as to justify even an opposition by arms to the pretensions of antagonists. Of this nature was the animosity continued for above a century past between the parties in England —an animosity which broke out sometimes into civil war, which occasioned violent revolutions, and which continually endangered the peace and tranquillity of the nation. But as there have appeared of late the strongest symptoms of a universal desire to abolish these party distinctions, this tendency to a coalition affords the most agreeable prospect of future happiness and ought to be carefully cherished and promoted by every lover of his country.

There is not a more effectual method of promoting so good an end than to prevent all unreasonable insult and triumph of the one party over the other, to encourage moderate opinions, to find the proper medium in all disputes, to persuade each that its antagonist may possibly be sometimes in the right, and to keep a balance in the praise and blame which we bestow on either side. The two former Essays concerning the *original contract* and *passive obedience*[a] are calculated for this purpose with regard to the *philosophical* and *practical* controversies between the parties, and tend to show that neither side are in these respects so fully supported by reason as they endeavor to flatter themselves. We

a [See pp. 43 ff. and 64 ff.]

shall proceed to exercise the same moderation with regard to the *historical* disputes between the parties by proving that each of them was justified by plausible topics, that there were on both sides wise men who meant well to their country and that the past animosity between the factions had no better foundation than narrow prejudice or interested passion.

The popular party, who afterward acquired the name of Whigs, might justify by very specious arguments that opposition to the crown from which our present free constitution is derived. Though obliged to acknowledge that precedents in favor of prerogative had uniformly taken place during many reigns before Charles the First, they thought that there was no reason for submitting any longer to so dangerous an authority. Such might have been their reasoning: as the rights of mankind are forever to be deemed sacred, no prescription of tyranny or arbitrary power can have authority sufficient to abolish them. Liberty is a blessing so inestimable that wherever there appears any probability of recovering it a nation may willingly run many hazards, and ought not even to repine at the greatest effusion of blood or dissipation of treasure. All human institutions, and none more than government, are in continual fluctuation. Kings are sure to embrace every opportunity of extending their prerogatives; and if favorable incidents be not also laid hold of for extending and securing the privileges of the people, a universal despotism must forever prevail among mankind. The example of all the neighboring nations proves that it is no longer safe to entrust with the crown the same high prerogatives which had formerly been exercised during rude and simple ages. And though the example of many late reigns may be pleaded in favor of a power in the prince somewhat arbitrary, more remote reigns afford instances of stricter limitations imposed on the crown; and those pretensions of the Parliament now branded with the title of innovations are only a recovery of the just rights of the people.

These views, far from being odious, are surely large and generous and noble; to their prevalence and success the kingdom owes its liberty, perhaps its learning, its industry, commerce, and naval power; by them chiefly the English name is distinguished among the society of nations and aspires to a rivalship with that of the freest and most illustrious commonwealths of antiquity. But as all these mighty consequences could not reasonably be foreseen at the time when the contest began, the royalists of that age wanted not specious arguments on their side by which they could justify their defense of the then established prerogatives of the prince. We shall state the question as it might have appeared to them at the assembling of that Parliament which, by its violent encroachments on the crown, began the civil wars.

The only rule of government, they might have said, known and acknowledged among men is use and practice; reason is so uncertain a guide that it will always be exposed to doubt and controversy; could it ever render itself prevalent over the people, men had always retained it as their sole rule of conduct; they had still continued in the primitive unconnected state of nature without submitting to political government, whose sole basis is, not pure reason, but authority and precedent. Dissolve these ties, you break all the bonds of civil society and leave every man at liberty to consult his private interest by those expedients which his appetite, disguised under the appearance of reason, shall dictate to him. The spirit of innovation is in itself pernicious, however favorable its particular object may sometimes appear—a truth so obvious that the popular party themselves are sensible of it and therefore cover their encroachments on the crown by the plausible pretense of their recovering the ancient liberties of the people.

But the present prerogatives of the crown, allowing all the suppositions of that party, have been incontestably established ever since the accession of the house of Tudor, a period which, as it now comprehends a hundred and sixty years, may be allowed sufficient to give stability to any constitution. Would it not have appeared ridiculous in the reign of the Emperor Adrian to have talked of the republican constitution as the rule of government or to have supposed that the former rights of the senate and consuls and tribunes were still subsisting?

But the present claims of the English monarchs are much more favorable than those of the Roman emperors during that age. The authority of Augustus was a plain usurpation grounded only on military violence, and forms such an epoch in the Roman history as is obvious to every reader. But if Henry VII really, as some pretend, enlarged the power of the crown, it was only by insensible acquisitions which escaped the apprehensions of the people and have scarcely been remarked even by historians and politicians. The new government, if it deserves the epithet, is an imperceptible transition from the former, is entirely ingrafted on it, derives its title fully from that root, and is to be considered only as one of those gradual revolutions to which human affairs in every nation will be forever subject.

The house of Tudor, and after them that of Stuart, exercised no prerogatives but what had been claimed and exercised by the Plantagenets.[1] Not a single branch of their authority can be said to be an innovation. The only difference is that perhaps former kings exerted these powers only by intervals and were not able, by reason of the opposition of their barons, to render them so steady a rule of administration.[b] But the sole inference from this fact is that those ancient times were more turbulent and seditious, and that royal authority, the constitution, and the laws have happily of late gained the ascendant.

Under what pretense can the popular party now speak of recovering the ancient constitution? The former control over the kings was not placed in the commons, but in the barons; the people had no authority, and even little or no liberty, till the crown, by suppressing these factious tyrants, enforced the execution of the laws and obliged all the subjects equally to respect each other's rights, privileges, and properties. If we must return to the ancient barbarous and feudal constitution, let those gentlemen who now behave themselves with so much insolence to their sovereign set the first example. Let them make

b The author believes that he was the first writer who advanced that the family of Tudor possessed in general more authority than their immediate predecessors, an opinion which he hopes will be supported by history, but which he proposes with some diffidence. There are strong symptoms of arbitrary power in some former reigns even after signing of the charters. The power of the crown in that age depended less on the constitutions than on the capacity and vigor of the prince who wore it.—Edition N.

court to be admitted as retainers to a neighboring baron and, by submitting to slavery under him, acquire some protection to themselves together with the power of exercising rapine and oppression over their inferior slaves and villains. This was the condition of the commons among their remote ancestors.

But how far back must we go in having recourse to ancient constitutions and governments? There was a constitution still more ancient than that to which these innovators affect so much to appeal. During that period there was no *Magna Charta;* [2] the barons themselves possessed few regular, stated privileges; and the House of Commons probably had not an existence.

It is ridiculous to hear the Commons, while they are assuming, by usurpation, the whole power of government, talk of reviving the ancient institutions. Is it not known that, though representatives received wages from their constituents, to be a member of the Lower House was always considered as a burden and an exemption from it as a privilege? Will they persuade us that power, which of all human acquisitions is the most coveted and in comparison of which even reputation and pleasure and riches are slighted, could ever be regarded as a burden by any man?

The property acquired of late by the Commons, it is said, entitles them to more power than their ancestors enjoyed. But to what is this increase of their property owing but to an increase of their liberty and their security? Let them therefore acknowledge that their ancestors, while the crown was restrained by the seditious barons, really enjoyed less liberty than they themselves have attained after the sovereign acquired the ascendant; and let them enjoy that liberty with moderation and not forfeit it by new exorbitant claims and by rendering it a pretense for endless innovations.

The true rule of government is the present established practice of the age. That has most authority because it is recent; it is also best known, for the same reason. Who has assured those tribunes that the Plantagenets did not exercise as high acts of authority as the Tudors? Historians, they say, do not mention them. But historians are also silent with regard to the chief exertions of prerogative by the Tudors. Where any power or prerogative is fully and undoubtedly established, the exercise of it passes for a thing of course and readily escapes the notice of history and annals. Had we no other monuments of Elizabeth's reign than what are preserved even by Camden, the most copious, judicious, and exact of our historians, we should be entirely ignorant of the most important maxims of her government.

Was not the present monarchical government in its full extent authorized by lawyers, recommended by divines, acknowledged by politicians, acquiesced in—nay, passionately cherished—by the people in general, and all this during a period of at least a hundred and sixty years, and till of late without the smallest murmur or controversy? This general consent surely, during so long a time, must be sufficient to render a constitution legal and valid. If the origin of all power be derived, as is pretended, from the people, here is their consent in the fullest and most ample terms that can be desired or imagined.

But the people must not pretend because they can, by their consent, lay the foundations of government, that therefore they are to be permitted at their pleasure to overthrow and subvert them. There is no end of these seditious and arrogant claims. The power of the crown is now openly struck at; the nobility are also in visible peril; the gentry will soon follow; the popular leaders, who will then assume the name of gentry, will next be exposed to danger; and the people themselves, having become incapable of civil government and lying under the restraint of no authority, must for the sake of peace admit, instead of their legal and mild monarchs, a succession of military and despotic tyrants.

These consequences are the more to be dreaded as the present fury of the people, though glossed over by pretensions to civil liberty, is in reality incited by the fanaticism of religion, a principle the most blind, headstrong, and ungovernable by which human nature can possibly be actuated. Popular rage is dreadful from whatever motive derived, but must be attended with the most pernicious consequences when it arises from a principle which disclaims all control by human law, reason, or authority.

These are the arguments which each party may make use of to justify the conduct of their predecessors during that great crisis. The event, if that can be admitted as a reason, has shown that the arguments of the popular party were better founded; but perhaps, according to the established maxims of lawyers and politicians, the views of the royalists ought beforehand to have appeared more solid, more safe, and more legal. But this is certain, that the greater moderation we now employ in representing past events, the nearer shall we be to produce a full coalition of the parties and an entire acquiescence in our present establishment. Moderation is of advantage to every establishment; nothing but zeal can overturn a settled power, and an overactive zeal in friends is apt to beget a like spirit in antagonists. The transition from a moderate opposition against an establishment to an entire acquiescence in it is easy and insensible.

There are many invincible arguments which should induce the malcontent party to acquiesce entirely in the present settlement of the constitution. They now find that the spirit of civil liberty, though at first connected with religious fanaticism, could purge itself from that pollution and appear under a more genuine and engaged aspect: a friend to toleration, and encourager of all the enlarged and generous sentiments that do honor to human nature. They may observe that the popular claims could stop at a proper period and, after retrenching the high claims of prerogative, could still maintain a due respect to monarchy, the nobility, and to all ancient institutions. Above all, they must be sensible that the very principle which made the strength of their party and from which it derived its chief authority has now deserted them and gone over to their antagonists. The plan of liberty is settled, its happy effects are proved by experience, a long tract of time has given it stability; and whoever would attempt to overturn it and to recall the past government or abdicated family would, besides other more criminal imputations, be exposed in their turn to the reproach of faction and innovation. While they peruse the history of past events, they ought to reflect both that those rights of the crown are long since annihilated and that the tyranny and violence and oppression to which they often give rise are ills from which the established liberty of the constitution has now at last happily protected the people. These reflections will prove a better security to our freedom and privileges than to deny, contrary to the clearest evidence of facts, that such regal powers ever had an existence. There is not a more effectual method of betraying a cause than to lay the stress of the argument on a wrong place and, by disputing an untenable post, inure the adversaries to success and victory.

XIII

OF CIVIL LIBERTY

THOSE WHO EMPLOY THEIR PENS on political subjects, free from party rage and party prejudices, cultivate a science which, of all others, contributes most to public utility, and even to the private satisfaction of those who addict themselves to the study of it. I am apt, however, to entertain a suspicion that the world is still too young to fix many general truths in politics which will remain true to the latest posterity. We have not as yet had experience of three thousand years, so that not only the art of reasoning is still imperfect in this science, as in all others, but we even want sufficient materials upon which we can reason. It is not fully known what degree of refinement, either in virtue or vice, human nature is susceptible of, nor what may be expected of mankind from any great revolution in their education, customs, or principles. Machiavel was certainly a great genius, but, having confined his study to the furious and tyrannical governments of ancient times or to the little disorderly principalities of Italy, his reasonings, especially upon monarchical government, have been found extremely defective; and there scarcely is any maxim in his *Prince* which subsequent experience has not entirely refuted. "A weak prince," says he,

is incapable of receiving good counsel, for, if he consult with several, he will not be able to choose among their different counsels. If he abandon himself to one, that minister may perhaps have capacity, but he will not long be a minister; he will be sure to dispossess his master and place himself and his family upon the throne.

I mention this, among many instances of the errors of that politician, proceeding, in a great measure, from his having lived in too early an age of the world to be a good judge of political truth. Almost all the princes of Europe are at present governed by their minister and have been so for near two centuries, and yet no such event has ever happened or can possibly happen. Sejanus might project dethroning the Caesars; but Fleury,[1] though ever so vicious, could not, while in his senses, entertain the least hopes of dispossessing the Bourbons.

Trade was never esteemed an affair of state till the last century, and there scarcely is any ancient writer on politics who has made mention of it.[a] Even the Italians have kept a profound silence with regard to it, though it has now engaged the chief attention as well of ministers of state as of speculative reasoners. The great opulence, grandeur, and military achievements of the two maritime powers seem first to have instructed mankind in the importance of an extensive commerce.

Having, therefore, intended in this Essay to make a full comparison of civil liberty and absolute government, and to show the great advantages of the former above the latter, I began to entertain a suspicion that no man in this age was sufficiently qualified for such an undertaking, and that whatever anyone should advance on that head would in all probability be refuted by further experience and be rejected by posterity. Such mighty revolutions have happened in human affairs and so many events have arisen contrary to the expectation of the ancients that they are sufficient to beget the suspicion of still further changes.

It had been observed by the ancients that all the arts and sciences arose among free nations, and that the Persians and Egyptians, notwithstanding their ease, opulence, and luxury, made but faint efforts toward a relish in those finer pleasures which were carried to such perfection by the Greeks amidst continual wars, attended with poverty and the greatest simplicity of life and manners. It had also been observed that, when the Greeks lost their liberty, though they increased mightily in riches by means of the conquests of Alexander, yet the arts from that moment declined among them and have never since been able

---

[a] Xenophon mentions it, but with a doubt if it be of any advantage to a state. Εἰ δὲ καὶ ἐμπορία ὠφελεῖ τι πόλιν, etc. [but if trade, too, is beneficial for a state] XEN. HIERO—Plato totally excludes it from his imaginary republic. *De Legibus*, lib. iv.

to raise their head in that climate. Learning was transplanted to Rome, the only free nation at that time in the universe, and, having met with so favorable a soil, it made prodigious shoots for above a century till the decay of liberty produced also the decay of letters and spread a total barbarism over the world. From these two experiments, of which each was double in its kind and showed the fall of learning in absolute governments as well as its rise in popular ones, Longinus thought himself sufficiently justified in asserting that the arts and sciences could never flourish but in a free government. And in this opinion he has been followed by several eminent writers[b] in our own country who either confined their view merely to ancient facts or entertained too great a partiality in favor of that form of government established among us.

But what would these writers have said to the instances of modern Rome and Florence? Of which the former carried to perfection all the finer arts of sculpture, painting, and music, as well as poetry, though it groaned under tyranny and under the tyranny of priests, while the latter made its chief progress in the arts and sciences after it began to lose its liberty by the usurpation of the family of Medici. Ariosto, Tasso, Galileo, no more than Raphael or Michael Angelo,[2] were not born in republics. And though the Lombard school was famous as well as the Roman, yet the Venetians have had the smallest share in its honors and seem rather inferior to the other Italians in their genius for the arts and sciences. Rubens established his school at Antwerp, not at Amsterdam. Dresden, not Hamburg, is the center of politeness in Germany.

But the most eminent instance of the flourishing of learning in absolute governments is that of France, which scarcely ever enjoyed any established liberty and yet has carried the arts and sciences as near perfection as any other nation. The English are, perhaps, greater philosophers, the Italians better painters and musicians, the Romans were greater orators, but the French are the only people, except the Greeks, who have been at once

[b] Mr. Addison and Lord Shaftesbury.

philosophers, poets, orators, historians, painters, architects, sculptors, and musicians. With regard to the stage, they have excelled even the Greeks, who far excelled the English. And, in common life, they have, in a great measure, perfected that art, the most useful and agreeable of any, *l'art de vivre*, the art of society and conversation.

If we consider the state of the sciences and polite arts in our own country, Horace's observation, with regard to the Romans, may in a great measure be applied to the British:

> Sed in longum tamen aevum
> Manserunt, hodieque manent *vestigia ruris*.[3]

The elegance and propriety of style have been very much neglected among us. We have no dictionary of our language and scarcely a tolerable grammar. The first polite prose we have was written by a man who is still alive.[c] As to Sprat, Locke, and even Temple, they knew too little of the rules of art to be esteemed elegant writers. The prose of Bacon, Harrington, and Milton [5] is altogether stiff and pedantic, though their sense be excellent. Men in this country have been so much occupied in the great disputes of *religion, politics,* and *philosophy* that they had no relish for the seemingly minute observations of grammar and criticism. And though this turn of thinking must have considerably improved our sense and our talent of reasoning, it must be confessed that even in those sciences above mentioned we have not any standard book which we can transmit to posterity. And the utmost we have to boast of are a few essays toward a more just philosophy, which indeed promise well but have not as yet reached any degree of perfection.

It has become an established opinion that commerce can never flourish but in a free government, and this opinion seems to be founded on a longer and larger experience than the foregoing, with regard to the arts and sciences. If we trace commerce in its progress through Tyre, Athens, Syracuse, Carthage, Venice, Florence, Genoa, Antwerp, Holland, England, etc., we shall always find it to have fixed its seat in free governments. The

c Dr. Swift.[4]

three greatest trading towns now in Europe are London, Amsterdam, and Hamburg—all free cities and Protestant cities, that is, enjoying a double liberty. It must, however, be observed that the great jealousy entertained of late with regard to the commerce of France seems to prove that this maxim is no more certain and infallible than the foregoing, and that the subjects of an absolute prince may become our rivals in commerce as well as in learning..

Durst I deliver my opinion in an affair of so much uncertainty, I would assert that, notwithstanding the efforts of the French, there is something hurtful to commerce inherent in the very nature of absolute government and inseparable from it, though the reason I should assign for this opinion is somewhat different from that which is commonly insisted on. Private property seems to me almost as secure in a civilized European monarchy as in a republic; nor is danger much apprehended in such a government from the violence of the sovereign more than we commonly dread harm from thunder or earthquakes, or any accident the most unusual and extraordinary. Avarice, the spur of industry, is so obstinate a passion and works its way through so many real dangers and difficulties that it is not likely to be scared by an imaginary danger which is so small that it scarcely admits of calculation. Commerce, therefore, in my opinion, is apt to decay in absolute governments, not because it is there less *secure*, but because it is less *honorable*. A subordination of rank is absolutely necessary to the support of monarchy. Birth, titles, and place must be honored above industry and riches; and while these notions prevail, all the considerable traders will be tempted to throw up their commerce in order to purchase some of those employments to which privileges and honors are annexed.

Since I am upon this head, of the alterations which time has produced or may produce in politics, I must observe that all kinds of government, free and absolute, seem to have undergone in modern times a great change for the better with regard both to foreign and domestic management. The *balance* of power is a secret in politics, fully known only to the present age, and I must add that the internal police of states has also received great improvements within the last century. We are informed by Sallust that Catiline's army was much augmented by the accession of the highwaymen about Rome, though I believe that all of that profession who are at present dispersed over Europe would not amount to a regiment. In Cicero's pleadings for Milo I find this argument, among others, made use of to prove that his client had not assassinated Clodius. Had Milo, said he, intended to have killed Clodius, he had not attacked him in the daytime and at such a distance from the city; he had waylaid him at night near the suburbs, where it might have been pretended that he was killed by robbers, and the frequency of the accident would have favored the deceit. This is a surprising proof of the loose policy of Rome and of the number and force of these robbers, since Clodius [d] was at that time attended by thirty slaves, who were completely armed and sufficiently accustomed to blood and danger in the frequent tumults excited by that seditious tribune.

But though all kinds of government be improved in modern times, yet monarchical government seems to have made the greatest advances toward perfection. It may now be affirmed of civilized monarchies what was formerly said in praise of republics alone, *that they are a government of laws, not of men.* They are found susceptible of order, method, and constancy to a surprising degree. Property is there secure, industry encouraged, the arts flourish, and the prince lives secure among his subjects, like a father among his children. There are, perhaps, and have been for two centuries, near two hundred absolute princes, great and small, in Europe; and allowing twenty years to each reign, we may suppose that there have been in the whole two thousand monarchs, or tyrants, as the Greeks would have called them; yet of these, there has not been one, not even Philip II of Spain, so bad as Tiberius, Caligula, Nero, or Domitian, who were four in twelve among the Roman emperors. It must, however, be confessed that, though monarchical governments have approached nearer to popular ones in gentleness and stability,

d *Vide* Asc. Ped. in *Orat, pro Milone.*

they are still inferior. Our modern education and customs instill more humanity and moderation than the ancient, but have not as yet been able to overcome entirely the disadvantages of that form of government.

But here I must beg leave to advance a conjecture which seems probable but which posterity alone can fully judge of. I am apt to think that in monarchical governments there is a source of improvement, and in popular governments a source of degeneracy, which in time will bring these species of civil polity still nearer an equality. The greatest abuses which arise in France, the most perfect model of pure monarchy, proceed not from the number or weight of the taxes, beyond what are to be met with in free countries, but from the expensive, unequal, arbitrary, and intricate method of levying them, by which the industry of the poor, especially of the peasants and farmers, is in a great measure discouraged, and agriculture rendered a beggarly and slavish employment. But to whose advantage do these abuses tend? If to that of the nobility, they might be esteemed inherent in that form of government, since the nobility are the true supports of monarchy, and it is natural their interest should be more consulted in such a constitution than that of the people. But the nobility are, in reality, the chief losers by this oppression, since it ruins their estates and beggars their tenants. The only gainers by it are the *financiers,* a race of men rather odious to the nobility and the whole kingdom. If a prince or minister, therefore, should arise, endowed with sufficient discernment to know his own and the public interest, and with sufficient force of mind to break through ancient customs, we might expect to see these abuses remedied, in which case the difference between that absolute government and our free one would not appear so considerable as at present.

The source of degeneracy which may be remarked in free governments consists in the practice of contracting debt and mortgaging the public revenues, by which taxes may, in time, become altogether intolerable and all the property of the state be brought into the hands of the public. This practice is of modern date. The Athenians, though governed by a republic, paid near two hundred per cent for those sums of money which any emergency made it necessary for them to borrow, as we learn from Xenophon.ᵉ Among the moderns, the Dutch first introduced the practice of borrowing great sums at low interest, and have well nigh ruined themselves by it. Absolute princes have also contracted debt, but, as an absolute prince may make a bankruptcy when he pleases, his people can never be oppressed by his debts. In popular governments the people, and chiefly those who have the highest offices, being commonly the public creditors, it is difficult for the state to make use of this remedy, which, however it may sometimes be necessary, is always cruel and barbarous. This, therefore, seems to be an inconvenience which nearly threatens all free governments, especially our own at the present juncture of affairs. And what a strong motive is this to increase our frugality of public money, lest, for want of it, we be reduced by the multiplicity of taxes or, what is worse, by our public impotence and inability for defense, to curse our very liberty and wish ourselves in the same state of servitude with all the nations who surround us?

FROM THE HISTORY OF ENGLAND

Sir Robert Philips, one of the "popular leaders," in a speech in Parliament in 1628 spoke on the grievances of the nation:

I can live though another who has no right be put to live along with me; nay, I can live though burdened with imposi-

---

ᵉ Κτῆσιν δὲ ἀπ' οὐδενὸς ἂν οὕτω καλὴν κτήσαιντο ὥσπερ ἀφ' οὗ ἂν προτελέσωσιν εἰς τὴν ἀφορμήν. . . Οἱ δέ γε πλεῖστοι' Ἀθηναίων πλείονα λήψονται κατ' ἐνιαυτὸν ἢ ὅσα ἂν εἰσενέγκωσιν. Οἱ γὰρ μνᾶν προτελέσαντες, ἐγγὺς δυοῖν μναῖν πρόσοδον ἕξουσιν [καὶ ταῦτα ἐν πόλει] ὃ δοκεῖ τῶν ἀνθρωπίνων ἀσφαλέστατόν τε καὶ πολυχρονιώτατον εἶναι. [Nothing would bring in a nicer return than the money advanced by them to form the capital fund. . . . Most Athenians will get a greater return *per annum* than they contributed: those who advance one *mina* will get an income of almost two *minae* (and their security against risk is given by the state) which seems to be the safest and most durable of human institutions.]— ΞΕΝ. ΠΟΡΟΙ.

tions beyond what at present I labor under; but to have my liberty, which is the soul of my life, ravished from me; to have my person pent up in a jail, without relief by law, and to be so adjudged—O, improvident ancestors! O, unwise forefathers! to be so curious in providing for the quiet possession of our lands and the liberties of Parliament, and at the same time to neglect our personal liberty and let us lie in prison, and that during pleasure, without redress or remedy! If this be law, why do we talk of liberties? Why trouble ourselves with disputes about a constitution, franchises, property of goods, and the like? What may any man call his own, if not the liberty of his person? [Vol. V, Ch. LI, p. 35.]

The truth is, the Great Charter and the old Statutes were sufficiently clear in favor of personal liberty. . . . [Vol. V, Ch. LI, p. 41.]

Arbitrary imprisonment is a grievance which, in some degree, has place almost in every government except in that of Great Britain; and our absolute security from it we owe chiefly to the present Parliament [1679], a merit which makes some atonement for the faction and violence into which their prejudices had, in other particulars, betrayed them. The Great Charter had laid the foundation of this valuable part of liberty, the petition of right had renewed and extended it; but some provisions were still wanting to render it complete and prevent all evasion or delay from ministers and judges. The act of habeas corpus which passed this session served these purposes. By this act it was prohibited to send anyone to a prison beyond sea. No judge, under severe penalties, must refuse to any prisoner a writ of habeas corpus, by which the jailer was directed to produce in court the body of the prisoner (whence the writ has its name) and to certify the cause of his detainer and imprisonment. If the jail lie within twenty miles of the judge, the writ must be obeyed in three days; and so proportionably for greater distances. Every prisoner must be indicted the first term after his commitment and brought to trial in the subsequent term. And no man, after being enlarged by order of court, can be recommitted for the same offense. This law seems necessary for the protection of liberty in a mixed monarchy; and as it has not place in any other form of government, this consideration alone may induce us to prefer our present constitution to all others. It must, however, be confessed that there is some difficulty to reconcile with such extreme liberty the full security and the regular police of a state, especially the police of great cities. [Vol. VI, Ch. LXVII, p. 204.]

The convention annexed to this settlement of the crown [1689] a declaration of rights, where all the points which had of late years been disputed between the king and people were finally determined and the powers of royal prerogative were more narrowly circumscribed and more exactly defined than in any former period of the English government. [Vol. VI, Ch. LXXI, p. 362.]

XIV

OF THE RISE AND PROGRESS OF THE ARTS AND SCIENCES

WE MAY THEREFORE CONCLUDE [a] that there is no subject in which we must proceed with more caution than in tracing the history of the arts and sciences, lest we assign causes which never existed and reduce what is merely contingent to stable and universal principles. Those who cultivate the sciences in any state are always few in number, the passion which governs them limited, their taste and judgment delicate and easily perverted, and their application disturbed with the smallest accident. Chance, therefore, or secret and unknown causes must have a great influence on the rise and progress of all the refined arts.

But there is a reason which induces me not to ascribe the matter altogether to chance. Though the persons who cultivate the sciences with such astonishing success as to attract the admiration of posterity be always few in all nations and all ages, it is impossible but a share of the same spirit and genius must be antecedently diffused throughout the people among whom they arise, in order to produce, form, and cultivate from their earliest infancy the taste and judgment of those eminent writers. The mass cannot be altogether insipid from which such refined spirits are extracted. "There is a God within us," says Ovid, "who breathes that divine fire by which we are animated." [b] Poets in all ages have advanced this claim to inspiration. There is not, however, anything supernatural in the case. Their fire is not kindled from heaven. It only runs along the earth, is caught from

---

[a] [The first six paragraphs of this Essay are here omitted.]
[b] "Est Deus in nobis; agitante calescimus illo:
   Impetus hic, sacrae semina mentis habet."—Ovid. *Fast. lib. i.*

one breast to another, and burns brightest where the materials are best prepared and most happily disposed. The question, therefore, concerning the rise and progress of the arts and sciences is not altogether a question concerning the taste, genius, and spirit of a few, but concerning those of a whole people, and may therefore be accounted for, in some measure, by general causes and principles. I grant that a man who should inquire why such a particular poet as Homer, for instance, existed at such a place, in such a time, would throw himself headlong into chimera and could never treat of such a subject without a multitude of false subtleties and refinements. He might as well pretend to give a reason why such particular generals as Fabius and Scipio lived in Rome at such a time and why Fabius came into the world before Scipio. For such incidents as these no other reason can be given than that of Horace:

> Scit genius, natale comes, qui temperat astrum,
> Naturae Deus humanae, mortalis in unum ———
> ——— Quodque caput, vultu mutabilis, albus et ater.[1]

But I am persuaded that in many cases good reasons might be given why such a nation is more polite and learned at a particular time than any of its neighbors. At least this is so curious a subject that it were a pity to abandon it entirely before we have found whether it be susceptible of reasoning and can be reduced to any general principles.

My first observation on this head is: *That it is impossible for the arts and sciences to arise at first among any people unless that people enjoy the blessing of a free government.*

In the first ages of the world, when men are as yet barbarous and ignorant, they seek no further security against mutual violence and injustice than the choice of some rulers, few or many, in whom they place an implicit confidence, without providing any security, by laws or political institutions, against the violence and injustice of these rulers. If the authority be centered in a single person and if the people, either by conquest or by the ordinary course of propagation, increase to a great multitude, the monarch, finding it impossible in his own person to execute every office of sovereignty in every place, must delegate his authority to inferior magistrates, who preserve peace and order in their respective districts. As experience and education have not yet refined the judgments of men to any considerable degree, the prince, who is himself unrestrained, never dreams of restraining his ministers, but delegates his full authority to everyone whom he sets over any portion of the people. All general laws are attended with inconveniences when applied to particular cases, and it requires great penetration and experience both to perceive that these inconveniences are fewer than what result from full discretionary powers in every magistrate and also to discern what general laws are, upon the whole, attended with fewest inconveniences. This is a matter of so great difficulty that men may have made some advances, even in the sublime arts of poetry and eloquence, where a rapidity of genius and imagination assists their progress before they have arrived at any great refinement in their municipal laws, where frequent trials and diligent observation can alone direct their improvements. It is not, therefore, to be supposed that a barbarous monarch, unrestrained and uninstructed, will ever become a legislator or think of restraining his bashaws in every province or even his cadis in every village. We are told that the late Czar, though actuated with a noble genius and smit with the love and admiration of European arts, yet professed an esteem for the Turkish policy in this particular and approved of such summary decisions of causes as are practiced in that barbarous monarchy, where the judges are not restrained by any methods, forms, or laws. He did not perceive how contrary such a practice would have been to all his other endeavors for refining his people. Arbitrary power, in all cases, is somewhat oppressive and debasing; but it is altogether ruinous and intolerable when contracted into a small compass, and becomes still worse when the person who possesses it knows that the time of his authority is limited and uncertain. *Habet subjectos tanquam suos; viles ut alienos.*[c] He

---

[c] [He keeps us in submission as if we were his slaves; he considers us cheap because we belong to someone else.]—Tacit. *Hist.* lib. i.

governs the subjects with full authority, as if they were his own; and with negligence or tyranny, as belonging to another. A people governed after such a manner are slaves in the full and proper sense of the word, and it is impossible they can ever aspire to any refinements of taste or reason. They dare not so much as pretend to enjoy the necessaries of life in plenty or security.

To expect, therefore, that the arts and sciences should take their first rise in a monarchy is to expect a contradiction. Before these refinements have taken place, the monarch is ignorant and uninstructed; and not having knowledge sufficient to make him sensible of the necessity of balancing his government upon general laws, he delegates his full power to all inferior magistrates. This barbarous policy debases the people and forever prevents all improvements. Were it possible that, before science were known in the world, a monarch could possess so much wisdom as to become a legislator and govern his people by law, not by the arbitrary will of their fellow subjects, it might be possible for that species of government to be the first nursery of arts and sciences. But that supposition seems scarcely to be consistent or rational.

It may happen that a republic in its infant state may be supported by as few laws as a barbarous monarchy and may entrust as unlimited an authority to its magistrates or judges. But besides that the frequent elections by the people are a considerable check upon authority, it is impossible but in time the necessity of restraining the magistrates, in order to preserve liberty, must at last appear and give rise to general laws and statutes. The Roman consuls for some time decided all causes without being confined by any positive statutes, till the people, bearing this yoke with impatience, created the *decemvirs,* who promulgated the *Twelve Tables,*[2] a body of laws which, though perhaps they were not equal in bulk to one English act of Parliament, were almost the only written rules which regulated property and punishment for some ages in that famous republic. They were however sufficient, together with the forms of a free government, to secure the lives and properties of the citizens, to exempt one man from the dominion of another, and to protect everyone against the violence or tyranny of his fellow citizens. In such a situation the sciences may raise their heads and flourish, but never can have being amidst such a scene of oppression and slavery as always results from barbarous monarchies, where the people alone are restrained by the authority of the magistrates and the magistrates are not restrained by any law or statute. An unlimited despotism of this nature, while it exists, effectually puts a stop to all improvements and keeps men from attaining that knowledge which is requisite to instruct them in the advantages arising from a better police and more moderate authority.

Here, then, are the advantages of free states: Though a republic should be barbarous, it necessarily, by an infallible operation, gives rise to law, even before mankind have made any considerable advances in the other sciences. From law arises security, from security curiosity, and from curiosity knowledge. The latter steps of this progress may be more accidental, but the former are altogether necessary. A republic without laws can never have any duration. On the contrary, in a monarchical government law arises not necessarily from the forms of government. Monarchy, when absolute, contains even something repugnant to law. Great wisdom and reflection can alone reconcile them. But such a degree of wisdom can never be expected before the greater refinements and improvements of human reason. These refinements require curiosity, security, and law. The first growth, therefore, of the arts and sciences can never be expected in despotic governments.[d]

There are other causes which discourage the rise of the refined arts in despotic governments, though I take the want of

---

[d] According to the necessary progress of things, law must precede science. In republics law may precede science and may arise from the very nature of the government. In monarchies it arises not from the nature of the government and cannot precede science. An absolute prince that is barbarous renders all his ministers and magistrates as absolute as himself, and there needs no more to prevent forever all industry, curiosity, and science.—Editions B, D, and N.

laws and the delegation of full powers to every petty magistrate to be the principal. Eloquence certainly springs up more naturally in popular governments. Emulation, too, in every accomplishment must there be more animated and enlivened, and genius and capacity have a fuller scope and career. All these causes render free governments the only proper *nursery* for the arts and sciences.

The next observation which I shall make on this head is: *That nothing is more favorable to the rise of politeness and learning than a number of neighboring and independent states connected together by commerce and policy.* The emulation which naturally arises among those neighboring states is an obvious source of improvement. But what I would chiefly insist on is the stop which such limited territories give both to *power* and to *authority.*
. . . .

If we consider the face of the globe, Europe, of all the four parts of the world, is the most broken by seas, rivers, and mountains; and Greece of all countries of Europe. Hence these regions were naturally divided into several distinct governments; and hence the sciences arose in Greece, and Europe has been hitherto the most constant habitation of them.

I have sometimes been inclined to think that interruptions in the periods of learning, were they not attended with such a destruction of ancient books and the records of history, would be rather favorable to the arts and sciences by breaking the progress of authority and dethroning the tyrannical usurpers over human reason. In this particular they have the same influence as interruptions in political governments and societies. Consider the blind submission of the ancient philosophers to the several masters in each school, and you will be convinced that little good could be expected from a hundred centuries of such a servile philosophy. Even the Eclectics, who arose about the age of Augustus, notwithstanding their professing to choose freely what pleased them from every different sect, were yet, in the main, as slavish and dependent as any of their brethren; since they sought for truth, not in nature, but in the several schools, where they supposed she must necessarily be found, though not united in a body, yet dispersed in parts. Upon the revival of learning, those sects of Stoics and Epicureans, Platonists and Pythagoreans could never regain any credit or authority; and at the same time, by the example of their fall, kept men from submitting with such blind deference to those new sects which have attempted to gain an ascendant over them.

The third observation which I shall form on this head of the rise and progress of the arts and sciences is: *That though the only proper nursery of these noble plants be a free state, yet may they be transplanted into any government; and that a republic is most favorable to the growth of the sciences, and a civilized monarchy to that of the polite arts.*

To balance a large state or society, whether monarchical or republican, on general laws is a work of so great difficulty that no human genius, however comprehensive, is able by the mere dint of reason and reflection to effect it. The judgments of many must unite in this work; experience must guide their labor; time must bring it to perfection; and the feeling of inconveniences must correct the mistakes which they inevitably fall into in their first trials and experiments. Hence appears the impossibility that this undertaking should be begun and carried on in any monarchy, since such a form of government, ere civilized, knows no other secret or policy than that of entrusting unlimited powers to every governor or magistrate and subdividing the people into so many classes and orders of slavery. From such a situation no improvement can ever be expected in the sciences, in the liberal arts, in laws, and scarcely in the manual arts and manufactures. The same barbarism and ignorance with which the government commences is propagated to all posterity and can never come to a period by the efforts or ingenuity of such unhappy slaves.

But though law, the source of all security and happiness, arises late in any government and is the slow product of order and of liberty, it is not preserved with the same difficulty with which it is produced, but when it has once taken root is a hardy plant which will scarcely ever perish through the ill culture of men or the rigor of the seasons. The arts of luxury, and much more the liberal arts, which depend on a refined taste or sentiment, are easily lost because they are always relished by a few only whose leisure, fortune, and genius fit them for such amusements. But what is profitable to every mortal, and in common life when once discovered, can scarcely fall into oblivion but by the total subversion of society and by such furious inundations of barbarous invaders as obliterate all memory of former arts and civility. Imitation also is apt to transport these coarser and more useful arts from one climate to another and to make them precede the refined arts in their progress, though perhaps they sprang after them in their first rise and propagation. From these causes proceed civilized monarchies, where the arts of government, first invented in free states, are preserved to the mutual advantage and security of sovereign and subject.

However perfect, therefore, the monarchical form may appear to some politicians, it owes all its perfection to the republican; nor is it possible that a pure despotism established among a barbarous people can ever, by its native force and energy, refine and polish itself. It must borrow its laws and methods and institutions, and consequently its stability and order, from free governments. These advantages are the sole growth of republics. The extensive despotism of a barbarous monarchy, by entering into the detail of the government as well as into the principal points of administration, forever prevents all such improvements.

In a civilized monarchy the prince alone is unrestrained in the exercise of his authority and possesses alone a power which is not bounded by anything but custom, example, and the sense of his own interest. Every minister or magistrate, however eminent, must submit to the general laws which govern the whole society and must exert the authority delegated to him after the manner which is prescribed. The people depend on none but their sovereign for the security of their property. He is so far removed from them and is so much exempt from private jealousies or interests that this dependence is scarcely felt. And thus a species of government arises to which, in a high political rant, we may give the name of *tyranny*, but which, by a just and prudent administration, may afford tolerable security to the people and may answer most of the ends of political society.

But though in a civilized monarchy, as well as in a republic, the people have security for the enjoyment of their property, yet in both these forms of government those who possess the supreme authority have the disposal of many honors and advantages which excite the ambition and avarice of mankind. The only difference is that, in a republic, the candidates for office must look downward to gain the suffrages of the people; in a monarchy, they must turn their attention upward to court the good graces and favor of the great. To be successful in the former way it is necessary for a man to make himself *useful* by his industry, capacity, or knowledge; to be prosperous in the latter way it is requisite for him to render himself *agreeable* by his wit, complaisance, or civility. A strong genius succeeds best in republics, a refined taste in monarchies. And consequently the sciences are the more natural growth of the one, and the polite arts of the other.

Not to mention that monarchies, receiving their chief stability from a superstitious reverence to priests and princes, have commonly abridged the liberty of reasoning with regard to religion and politics, and consequently metaphysics and morals. All these form the most considerable branches of science. Mathematics and natural philosophy, which only remain, are not half so valuable.[e]

Among the arts of conversation no one pleases more than mutual deference or civility, which leads us to resign our own inclinations to those of our companion, and to curb and conceal that presumption and arrogance so natural to the human mind. A good-natured man who is well educated practices this

e Immediately after this passage, we find in the early Editions B, D, and N: "There is a very great connection among all the arts that contribute to pleasure, and the same delicacy of taste which enables us to make improvements in one will not allow the others to remain altogether rude and barbarous."

civility to every mortal without premeditation or interest. But in order to render that valuable quality general among any people, it seems necessary to assist the natural disposition by some general motive. Where power rises upward from the people to the great, as in all republics, such refinements of civility are apt to be little practiced, since the whole state is by that means brought near to a level and every member of it is rendered in a great measure independent of another. The people have the advantage by the authority of their suffrages, the great by the superiority of their station. But in a civilized monarchy there is a long train of dependence from the prince to the peasant, which is not great enough to render property precarious or depress the minds of the people, but is sufficient to beget in everyone an inclination to please his superiors and to form himself upon those models which are most acceptable to people of condition and education. Politeness of manners, therefore, arises most naturally in monarchies and courts, and where that flourishes none of the liberal arts will be altogether neglected or despised.

The republics in Europe are at present noted for want of politeness. "The good manners of a Swiss civilized in Holland" [f] is an expression for rusticity among the French. The English, in some degree, fall under the same censure, notwithstanding their learning and genius. And if the Venetians be an exception to the rule, they owe it perhaps to their communication with the other Italians, most of whose governments beget a dependence more than sufficient for civilizing their manners.

. . . .

But to return from this digression, I shall advance it as a fourth observation on this subject, of the rise and progress of the arts and sciences: *That when the arts and sciences come to perfection in any state, from that moment they naturally, or rather necessarily, decline and seldom or never revive in that nation where they formerly flourished.*

[f] "C'est la politesse d'un Suisse
En Hollande civilisé."—ROUSSEAU.

It must be confessed that this maxim, though conformable to experience, may at first sight be esteemed contrary to reason. If the natural genius of mankind be the same in all ages and in almost all countries (as seems to be the truth), it must very much forward and cultivate this genius to be possessed of patterns in every art which may regulate the taste and fix the objects of imitation. The models left us by the ancients gave birth to all the arts about two hundred years ago and have mightily advanced their progress in every country of Europe. Why had they not a like effect during the reign of Trajan and his successors, when they were much more entire and were still admired and studied by the whole world? So late as the Emperor Justinian, the Poet, by way of distinction, was understood among the Greeks to be Homer; among the Romans, Virgil. Such admirations still remained for these divine geniuses, though no poet had appeared for many centuries who could justly pretend to have imitated them.

A man's genius is always, in the beginning of life, as much unknown to himself as to others, and it is only after frequent trials attended with success that he dares think himself equal to those undertakings in which those who have succeeded have fixed the admiration of mankind. If his own nation be already possessed of many models of eloquence, he naturally compares his own juvenile exercises with these and, being sensible of the great disproportion, is discouraged from any further attempts and never aims at a rivalship with those authors whom he so much admires. A noble emulation is the source of every excellence. Admiration and modesty naturally extinguish this emulation, and no one is so liable to an excess of admiration and modesty as a truly great genius.

Next to emulation, the greatest encourager of the noble arts is praise and glory. A writer is animated with new force when he hears the applauses of the world for his former productions; and, being roused by such a motive, he often reaches a pitch of perfection which is equally surprising to himself and to his readers. But when the posts of honor are all occupied, his first attempts are but coldly received by the public, being compared to productions which are both in themselves more excellent and have already the advantage of an established reputation. Were Molière and Corneille to bring upon the stage at present their early productions, which were formerly so well received, it would discourage the young poets to see the indifference and disdain of the public. The ignorance of the age alone could have given admission to the *Prince of Tyre*, but it is to that we owe the *Moor*. Had *Every Man in his Humor* been rejected, we had never seen *Volpone*.[3]

Perhaps it may not be for the advantage of any nation to have the arts imported from their neighbors in too great perfection. This extinguishes emulation and sinks the ardor of the generous youth. So many models of Italian painting brought to England, instead of exciting our artists, is the cause of their small progress in that noble art. The same, perhaps, was the case of Rome when it received the arts from Greece. That multitude of polite productions in the French language, dispersed all over Germany and the North, hinder these nations from cultivating their own language and keep them still dependent on their neighbors for those elegant entertainments.

It is true, the ancients had left us models in every kind of writing which are highly worthy of admiration. But besides that they were written in languages known only to the learned, besides this I say, the comparison is not so perfect or entire between modern wits and those who lived in so remote an age. Had Waller[4] been born in Rome during the reign of Tiberius, his first productions had been despised when compared to the finished odes of Horace. But in this Island, the superiority of the Roman poet diminished nothing from the fame of the English. We esteemed ourselves sufficiently happy that our climate and language could produce but a faint copy of so excellent an original.

In short, the arts and sciences, like some plants, require a fresh soil; and however rich the land may be and however you may recruit it by art or care, it will never, when once exhausted, produce anything that is perfect or finished in the kind.

XV

OF REFINEMENT IN THE ARTS [a]

ANOTHER ADVANTAGE OF INDUSTRY and of refinements in the mechanical arts is that they commonly produce some refinements in the liberal [arts]; nor can one be carried to perfection without being accompanied, in some degree, with the other. The same age which produces great philosophers and politicians, renowned generals and poets, usually abounds with skillful weavers and ship carpenters. We cannot reasonably expect that a piece of woolen cloth will be wrought to perfection in a nation which is ignorant of astronomy or where ethics are neglected. The spirit of the age affects all the arts, and the minds of men being once roused from their lethargy and put into a fermentation turn themselves on all sides and carry improvements into every art and science. Profound ignorance is totally banished, and men enjoy the privilege of rational creatures to think as well as to act, to cultivate the pleasures of the mind as well as those of the body.

The more these refined arts advance, the more sociable men become; nor is it possible that, when enriched with science and possessed of a fund of conversation, they should be contented to remain in solitude or live with their fellow citizens in that distant manner which is peculiar to ignorant and barbarous nations. They flock into cities; love to receive and communicate knowledge, to show their wit or their breeding, their taste in conversation or living, in clothes or furniture. Curiosity allures the wise, vanity the foolish, and pleasure both. Particular clubs and societies are everywhere formed; both sexes meet in an easy and sociable manner; and the tempers of men, as well as their

[a] In Editions F, G, H, this Essay is entitled "Of Luxury." [The first three paragraphs are here omitted.]

behavior, refine apace. So that, beside the improvements which they receive from knowledge and the liberal arts, it is impossible but they must feel an increase of humanity from the very habit of conversing together and contributing to each other's pleasure and entertainment. Thus *industry, knowledge,* and *humanity* are linked together by an indissoluble chain, and are found, from experience as well as reason, to be peculiar to the more polished and what are commonly denominated the more luxurious ages.

Nor are these advantages attended with disadvantages that bear any proportion to them. The more men refine upon pleasure, the less will they indulge in excesses of any kind, because nothing is more destructive to true pleasure than such excesses. One may safely affirm that the Tartars are oftener guilty of beastly gluttony when they feast on their dead horses than European courtiers with all their refinement of cookery. And if libertine love, or even infidelity to the marriage bed, be more frequent in polite ages, when it is often regarded only as a piece of gallantry, drunkenness, on the other hand, is much less common—a vice more odious and more pernicious, both to mind and body. And in this matter I would appeal, not only to an Ovid or a Petronius, but to a Seneca or a Cato. We know that Caesar, during Catiline's conspiracy, being necessitated to put into Cato's hands a *billet-doux* which discovered an intrigue with Servilla, Cato's own sister, that stern philosopher threw it back to him with indignation and, in the bitterness of his wrath, gave him the appellation of drunkard, as a term more opprobrious than that with which he could more justly have reproached him.

But industry, knowledge, and humanity are not advantageous in private life alone; they diffuse their beneficial influence on the *public,* and render the government as great and flourishing as they make individuals happy and prosperous. The increase and consumption of all the commodities which serve to the ornament and pleasure of life are advantages to society, because at the same time that they multiply those innocent gratifications to individuals they are a kind of *storehouse* of labor, which, in the exigencies of state, may be turned to the public service. In a nation where there is no demand for such superfluities men sink into indolence, lose all enjoyment of life, and are useless to the public, which cannot maintain or support its fleets and armies from the industry of such slothful members.

The bounds of all the European kingdoms are at present nearly the same they were two hundred years ago. But what a difference is there in the power and grandeur of those kingdoms which can be ascribed to nothing but the increase of art and industry? When Charles VIII of France invaded Italy, he carried with him about 20,000 men; yet this armament so exhausted the nation, as we learn from Guicciardin,[1] that for some years it was not able to make so great an effort. The late King of France, in time of war, kept in pay above 400,000 men,[b] though from Mazarine's[2] death to his own he was engaged in a course of wars that lasted near thirty years.

This industry is much promoted by the knowledge inseparable from ages of art and refinement; as, on the other hand, this knowledge enables the public to make the best advantage of the industry of its subjects. Laws, order, police, discipline— these can never be carried to any degree of perfection before human reason has refined itself by exercise and by an application to the more vulgar arts, at least of commerce and manufacture. Can we expect that a government will be well modeled by a people who know not how to make a spinning wheel or to employ a loom to advantage? Not to mention that all ignorant ages are infested with superstition, which throws the government off its bias and disturbs men in the pursuit of their interest and happiness. Knowledge in the arts of government begets mildness and moderation by instructing men in the advantages of human maxims above rigor and severity, which drive subjects into rebellion and make the return to submission impracticable, by cutting off all hopes of pardon. When the tempers of men are softened, as well as their knowledge improved, this humanity appears still more conspicuous and is the chief characteristic which distinguishes a civilized age from times of

b The inscription on the Place de Vendôme says 440,000.

barbarity and ignorance. Factions are then less inveterate, revolutions less tragical, authority less severe, and seditions less frequent. Even foreign wars abate of their cruelty; and after the field of battle, where honor and interest steel men against compassion as well as fear, the combatants divest themselves of the brute and resume the man.

Nor need we fear that men, by losing their ferocity, will lose their martial spirit or become less undaunted and vigorous in defense of their country or their liberty. The arts have no such effect in enervating either the mind or body. On the contrary, industry, their inseparable attendant, adds new force to both. And if anger, which is said to be the whetstone of courage, loses somewhat of its asperity by politeness and refinement, a sense of honor, which is a stronger, more constant, and more governable principle, acquires fresh vigor by that elevation of genius which arises from knowledge and a good education. Add to this that courage can neither have any duration nor be of any use when not accompanied with discipline and martial skill, which are seldom found among a barbarous people. The ancients remarked that Datames was the only barbarian that ever knew the art of war. And Pyrrhus, seeing the Romans marshal their army with some art and skill, said with surprise, "These barbarians have nothing barbarous in their discipline!" It is observable that as the old Romans, by applying themselves solely to war, were almost the only uncivilized people that ever possessed military discipline, so the modern Italians are the only civilized people, among Europeans, that ever wanted courage and a martial spirit. Those who would ascribe this effeminacy of the Italians to their luxury or politeness or application to the arts need but consider the French and English, whose bravery is as incontestable as their love for the arts and their assiduity in commerce. The Italian historians give us a more satisfactory reason for the degeneracy of their countrymen. They show us how the sword was dropped at once by all the Italian sovereigns; while the Venetian aristocracy was jealous of its subjects, the Florentine democracy applied itself entirely to commerce; Rome was governed by priests, and Naples by women. War then became the business of soldiers of fortune, who spared one another and, to the astonishment of the world, could engage a whole day in what they called a battle and return at night to their camp without the least bloodshed.

What has chiefly induced severe moralists to declaim against refinement in the arts is the example of ancient Rome, which, joining to its poverty and rusticity virtue and public spirit, rose to such a surprising height of grandeur and liberty; but having learned from its conquered provinces the Asiatic luxury fell into every kind of corruption, whence arose sedition and civil wars, attended at last with the total loss of liberty. All the Latin classics, whom we peruse in our infancy, are full of these sentiments and universally ascribe the ruin of their state to the arts and riches imported from the East, insomuch that Sallust[3] represents a taste for painting as a vice no less than lewdness and drinking. And so popular were these sentiments during the latter ages of the republic that this author abounds in praises of the old rigid Roman virtue, though himself the most egregious instance of modern luxury and corruption; speaks contemptuously of the Grecian eloquence, though the most elegant writer in the world; nay, employs preposterous digressions and declamations to this purpose, though a model of taste and correctness.

But it would be easy to prove that these writers mistook the cause of the disorders in the Roman state and ascribed to luxury and the arts what really proceeded from an ill-modeled government and the unlimited extent of conquests. Refinement on the pleasures and conveniences of life has no natural tendency to beget venality and corruption. The value which all men put upon any particular pleasure depends on comparison and experience; nor is a porter less greedy of money which he spends on bacon and brandy than a courtier who purchases champagne and ortolans. Riches are valuable at all times and to all men because they always purchase pleasures such as men are accustomed to and desire; nor can anything restrain or regulate the love of money but a sense of honor and virtue, which, if it be not nearly equal at all times, will naturally abound most in ages of knowledge and refinement.

Of all European kingdoms Poland seems the most defective in the arts of war as well as peace, mechanical as well as liberal; yet it is there that venality and corruption do most prevail. The nobles seem to have preserved their crown elective for no other purpose than regularly to sell it to the highest bidder. This is almost the only species of commerce with which that people are acquainted.

The liberties of England, so far from decaying since the improvements in the arts, have never flourished so much as during that period. And though corruption may seem to increase of late years, this is chiefly to be ascribed to our established liberty, when our princes have found the impossibility of governing without parliaments or of terrifying parliaments by the phantom of prerogative. Not to mention that this corruption or venality prevails much more among the electors than the elected, and therefore cannot justly be ascribed to any refinements in luxury.

If we consider the matter in a proper light, we shall find that a progress in the arts is rather favorable to liberty and has a natural tendency to preserve, if not produce, a free government. In rude, unpolished nations, where the arts are neglected, all labor is bestowed on the cultivation of the ground, and the whole society is divided into two classes, proprietors of land and their vassals or tenants. The latter are necessarily dependent and fitted for slavery and subjection, especially where they possess no riches and are not valued for their knowledge in agriculture, as must always be the case where the arts are neglected. The former naturally erect themselves into petty tyrants and must either submit to an absolute master for the sake of peace and order; or, if they will preserve their independence like the ancient barons, they must fall into feuds and contests among themselves and throw the whole society into such confusion as is perhaps worse than the most despotic government. But where luxury nourishes commerce and industry, the peasants, by a proper cultivation of the land, become rich and independent; while the tradesmen and merchants acquire a share of the property and draw authority and consideration to that middling rank of men who are the best and firmest basis of public liberty.

These submit not to slavery, like the peasants, from poverty and meanness of spirit; and having no hopes of tyrannizing over others, like the barons, they are not tempted for the sake of that gratification to submit to the tyranny of their sovereign. They covet equal laws, which may secure their property and preserve them from monarchical as well as aristocratical tyranny.

The lower house is the support of our popular government, and all the world acknowledges that it owed its chief influence and consideration to the increase of commerce, which threw such a balance of property into the hands of the Commons. How inconsistent, then, is it to blame so violently a refinement in the arts, and to represent it as the bane of liberty and public spirit!

. . . .

XVI

OF COMMERCE

THE GREATNESS OF A STATE[a] and the happiness of its subjects, how independent soever they may be supposed in some respects, are commonly allowed to be inseparable with regard to commerce; and as private men receive greater security in the possession of their trade and riches from the power of the public, so the public becomes powerful in proportion to the opulence and extensive commerce of private men. This maxim is true in general, though I cannot forbear thinking that it may possibly admit of exceptions, and that we often establish it with too little reserve and limitation. There may be some circumstances where the commerce and riches and luxury of individuals, instead of adding strength to the public, will serve only to thin its armies and diminish its authority among the neighboring nations. Man is a very variable being and susceptible of many different opinions, principles, and rules of conduct. What may be true while he adheres to one way of thinking will be found false when he has embraced an opposite set of manners and opinions.

The bulk of every state may be divided into *husbandmen* and *manufacturers*. The former are employed in the culture of the land; the latter works up the materials furnished by the former into all the commodities which are necessary or ornamental to human life. As soon as men quit their savage state, where they live chiefly by hunting and fishing, they must fall into these two classes, though the arts of agriculture employ, *at first*, the most numerous part of the society.[b] Time and experience im-

---

a [The first three paragraphs of this Essay are here omitted.]

b Mons. Melon, in his political Essay on Commerce, asserts that even at present, if you divide France into twenty parts, sixteen are laborers or peasants; two only artisans; one belonging to the law, church, and military; and one merchants, financiers, and bourgeois. This calculation is cer-

prove so much these arts that the land may easily maintain a much greater number of men than those who are immediately employed in its culture or who furnish the more necessary manufactures to such as are so employed.

If these superfluous hands apply themselves to the finer arts, which are commonly denominated the arts of *luxury*, they add to the happiness of the state, since they afford to many the opportunity of receiving enjoyments with which they would otherwise have been unacquainted. But may not another scheme be proposed for the employment of these superfluous hands? May not the sovereign lay claim to them and employ them in fleets and armies, to increase the dominions of the state abroad and spread its fame over distant nations? It is certain that the fewer desires and wants are found in the proprietors and laborers of land, the fewer hands do they employ; and consequently the superfluities of the land, instead of maintaining tradesmen and manufacturers, may support fleets and armies to a much greater extent than where a great many arts are required to minister to the luxury of particular persons. Here, therefore, seems to be a kind of opposition between the greatness of the state and the happiness of the subject. A state is never greater than when all its superfluous hands are employed in the service of the public. The ease and convenience of private persons require that these hands should be employed in their service. The one can never be satisfied but at the expense of the other. As the ambition of the sovereign must entrench on the luxury of individuals, so the luxury of individuals must diminish the force and check the ambition of the sovereign.

Nor is this reasoning merely chimerical, but is founded on history and experience. The republic of Sparta was certainly more powerful than any state now in the world consisting of an equal number of people, and this was owing entirely to the want of commerce and luxury. The Helotes were the laborers,

---

tainly very erroneous. In France, England, and indeed most parts of Europe, half of the inhabitants live in cities; and even of those who live in the country, a great number are artisans, perhaps above a third.

the Spartans were the soldiers or gentlemen. It is evident that the labor of the Helotes could not have maintained so great a number of Spartans had these latter lived in ease and delicacy, and given employment to a great variety of trades and manufactures. The like policy may be remarked in Rome. And, indeed, throughout all ancient history it is observable that the smallest republics raised and maintained greater armies than states consisting of triple the number of inhabitants are able to support at present. It is computed that, in all European nations, the proportion between soldiers and people does not exceed one to a hundred. But we read that the city of Rome alone, with its small territory, raised and maintained in early times ten legions against the Latins. Athens, the whole of whose dominions was not larger than Yorkshire, sent to the expedition against Sicily near forty thousand men.[c] Dionysius the elder, it is said, maintained a standing army of a hundred thousand foot and ten thousand horse, besides a large fleet of four hundred sail,[d] though his territories extended no further than the city of Syracuse—about a third of the island of Sicily, and some seaport towns and garrisons on the coast of Italy and Illyricum. It is true the ancient armies, in time of war, subsisted much upon plunder; but did not the enemy plunder in their turn?—which was a more ruinous way of levying a tax than any other that could be devised. In short, no probable reason can be assigned for the great power of the more ancient states above the modern but their want of commerce and luxury. Few artisans were maintained by the labor of the farmers, and therefore more soldiers might live upon it. Livy says that Rome, in his time, would find it difficult to raise as large an army as that which, in her early days, she sent out against the Gauls and Latins.[e]

[c] Thucydides, lib. vii.

[d] Diod. Sic. lib. vii. This account, I own, is somewhat suspicious, not to say worse, chiefly because this army was not composed of citizens but of mercenary forces.

[e] Titi Livii, lib. vii. cap. 24. "Adeo in quae laboramus," says he, "sola crevimus, devitias luxuriemque." [Our growth has been confined only to the things for which we strive: wealth and luxury.]

Instead of those soldiers who fought for liberty and empire in Camillus' time, there were in Augustus' days musicians, painters, cooks, players, and tailors; and if the land was equally cultivated at both periods, it could certainly maintain equal numbers in the one profession as in the other. They added nothing to the mere necessaries of life in the latter period more than in the former.

It is natural on this occasion to ask whether sovereigns may not return to the maxims of ancient policy and consult their own interest in this respect more than the happiness of their subjects? I answer that it appears to me almost impossible, and that because ancient policy was violent and contrary to the more natural and usual course of things. It is well known with what peculiar laws Sparta was governed and what a prodigy that republic is justly esteemed by everyone who has considered human nature as it has displayed itself in other nations and other ages. Were the testimony of history less positive and circumstantial, such a government would appear a mere philosophical whim or fiction and impossible ever to be reduced to practice. And though the Roman and other ancient republics were supported on principles somewhat more natural, yet was there an extraordinary concurrence of circumstances to make them submit to such grievous burdens. They were free states; they were small ones; and the age being martial, all their neighbors were continually in arms. Freedom naturally begets public spirit, especially in small states, and this public spirit, this *amor patriae*, must increase when the public is almost in continual alarm and men are obliged every moment to expose themselves to the greatest dangers for its defense. A continual succession of wars makes every citizen a soldier; he takes the field in his turn, and during his service he is chiefly maintained by himself. This service is indeed equivalent to a heavy tax, yet is it less felt by a people addicted to arms who fight for honor and revenge more than pay, and are unacquainted with gain and industry as well as pleasure.[f]

---

[f] The more ancient Romans lived in perpetual war with all their neighbors, and in old Latin the term *hostis* expressed both a stranger and an enemy. This is remarked by Cicero, but by him is ascribed to the humanity of his ancestors, who softened as much as possible the denomination of

Not to mention the great equality of fortunes among the inhabitants of the ancient republics, where every field belonging to a different proprietor was able to maintain a family and rendered the numbers of citizens very considerable, even without trade and manufactures.

But though the want of trade and manufactures among a free and very martial people may sometimes have no other effect than to render the public more powerful, it is certain that in the common course of human affairs it will have a quite contrary tendency. Sovereigns must take mankind as they find them, and cannot pretend to introduce any violent change in their principles and ways of thinking. A long course of time with a variety of accidents and circumstances are requisite to produce those great revolutions which so much diversify the face of human affairs. And the less natural any set of principles are which support a particular society, the more difficulty will a legislator meet with in raising and cultivating them. It is his best policy to comply with the common bent of mankind and give it all the improvements of which it is susceptible. Now according to the most natural course of things, industry and arts and trade increase the power of the sovereign as well as the happiness of the subjects, and that policy is violent which aggrandizes the public by the poverty of individuals. This will easily appear from a few considerations which will present to us the consequences of sloth and barbarity.

Where manufactures and mechanic arts are not cultivated, the bulk of the people must apply themselves to agriculture; and if

---

an enemy by calling him by the same appellation which signified a stranger. De Off. lib. ii. It is however much more probable, from the manners of the times, that the ferocity of those people was so great as to make them regard all strangers as enemies and call them by the same name. It is not, besides, consistent with the most common maxims of policy or of nature that any state should regard its public enemies with a friendly eye or preserve any such sentiments for them as the Roman orator would ascribe to his ancestors. Not to mention that the early Romans really exercised piracy, as we learn from their first treaties with Carthage, preserved by Polybius, lib. iii, and consequently, like the Sallee and Algerine rovers, were actually at war with most nations, and a stranger and an enemy were with them almost synonymous.

their skill and industry increase, there must arise a great superfluity from their labor beyond what suffices to maintain them.
They have no temptation, therefore, to increase their skill and
industry, since they cannot exchange that superfluity for any commodities which may serve either to their pleasure or vanity. A
habit of indolence naturally prevails. The greater part of the land
lies uncultivated. What is cultivated yields not its utmost, for
want of skill and assiduity in the farmers. If at any time the
public exigencies require that great numbers should be employed
in the public service, the labor of the people furnishes now no
superfluities by which these numbers can be maintained. The
laborers cannot increase their skill and industry on a sudden.
Lands uncultivated cannot be brought into tillage for some years.
The armies, meanwhile, must either make sudden and violent
conquests or disband for want of subsistence. A regular attack
or defense, therefore, is not to be expected from such a people,
and their soldiers must be as ignorant and unskillful as their
farmers and manufacturers.

Everything in the world is purchased by labor, and our passions are the only causes of labor. When a nation abounds in
manufactures and mechanic arts, the proprietors of land, as well
as the farmers, study agriculture as a science and redouble their
industry and attention. The superfluity which arises from their
labor is not lost, but is exchanged with manufactures for those
commodities which men's luxury now makes them covet. By this
means, land furnishes a great deal more of the necessaries of life
than what suffices for those who cultivate it. In times of peace
and tranquillity, this superfluity goes to the maintenance of
manufacturers and the improvers of liberal arts. But it is easy for
the public to convert many of these manufacturers into soldiers
and maintain them by that superfluity which arises from the labor
of the farmers. Accordingly we find that this is the case in all
civilized governments. When the sovereign raises an army, what
is the consequence? He imposes a tax. This tax obliges all the
people to retrench what is least necessary to their subsistence.
Those who labor in such commodities must either enlist in the
troops or turn themselves to agriculture, and thereby oblige some
laborers to enlist for want of business. And to consider the matter

abstractly, manufactures increase the power of the state only as they store up so much labor, and that of a kind to which the public may lay claim without depriving anyone of the necessaries of life. The more labor, therefore, that is employed beyond mere necessaries, the more powerful is any state; since the persons engaged in that labor may easily be converted to the public service. In a state without manufactures, there may be the same number of hands; but there is not the same quantity of labor nor of the same kind. All the labor is there bestowed upon necessaries, which can admit of little or no abatement.

Thus the greatness of the sovereign and the happiness of the state are in a great measure united with regard to trade and manufactures. It is a violent method, and in most cases impracticable, to oblige the laborer to toil in order to raise from the land more than what subsists himself and family. Furnish him with manufactures and commodities, and he will do it of himself; afterward you will find it easy to seize some part of his superfluous labor and employ it in the public service without giving him his wonted return. Being accustomed to industry, he will think this less grievous than if at once you obliged him to an augmentation of labor without any reward. The case is the same with regard to the other members of the state. The greater is the stock of labor of all kinds, the greater quantity may be taken from the heap without making any sensible alteration in it.

A public granary of corn, a storehouse of cloth, a magazine of arms—all these must be allowed real riches and strength in any state. Trade and industry are really nothing but a stock of labor which, in times of peace and tranquillity, is employed for the ease and satisfaction of individuals, but in the exigencies of state may in part be turned to public advantage. Could we convert a city into a kind of fortified camp and infuse into each breast so martial a genius and such a passion for public good as to make everyone willing to undergo the greatest hardships for the sake of the public, these affections might now, as in ancient times, prove alone a sufficient spur to industry and support the community. It would then be advantageous, as in camps, to banish all arts and luxury, and by restrictions on equipage and tables make the provisions and forage last longer than if the army were loaded with a number of superfluous retainers. But as these principles are too disinterested and too difficult to support, it is requisite to govern men by other passions and animate them with a spirit of avarice and industry, art and luxury. The camp is, in this case, loaded with a superfluous retinue, but the provisions flow in proportionately larger. The harmony of the whole is still supported, and the natural bent of the mind being more complied with, individuals as well as the public find their account in the observance of those maxims.

The same method of reasoning will let us see the advantage of *foreign* commerce in augmenting the power of the state as well as the riches and happiness of the subject. It increases the stock of labor in the nation, and the sovereign may convert what share of it he finds necessary to the service of the public. Foreign trade by its imports furnishes materials for new manufactures, and by its exports it produces labor in particular commodities which could not be consumed at home. In short, a kingdom that has a large import and export must abound more with industry, and that employed upon delicacies and luxuries, than a kingdom which rests contented with its native commodities. It is therefore more powerful, as well as richer and happier. The individuals reap the benefit of these commodities so far as they gratify the senses and appetites; and the public is also a gainer, while a greater stock of labor is by this means stored up against any public exigency; that is, a greater number of laborious men are maintained who may be diverted to the public service without robbing anyone of the necessaries or even the chief conveniences of life.

If we consult history we shall find that, in most nations, foreign trade has preceded any refinement in home manufactures and given birth to domestic luxury. The temptation is stronger to make use of foreign commodities which are ready for use and which are entirely new to us than to make improvements on any domestic commodity, which always advance by slow degrees and never affect us by their novelty. The profit is also very great in exporting what is superfluous at home and what bears no price to foreign nations whose soil or climate is not favorable to that commodity. Thus men become acquainted with the *pleasures* of luxury and the *profits* of commerce, and their *delicacy* and *industry* being once awakened carry them on to further improvements in every branch of domestic as well as foreign trade; and this perhaps is the chief advantage which arises from a commerce with strangers. It arouses men from their indolence and, presenting the gayer and more opulent part of the nation with objects of luxury which they never before dreamed of, raises in them a desire of a more splendid way of life than what their ancestors enjoyed. And at the same time, the few merchants who possessed the secret of this importation and exportation make great profits and, becoming rivals in wealth to the ancient nobility, tempt other adventurers to become their rivals in commerce. Imitation soon diffuses all those arts, while domestic manufacturers emulate the foreign in their improvements and work up every home commodity to the utmost perfection of which it is susceptible. Their own steel and iron, in such laborious hands, become equal to the gold and rubies of the Indies.

When the affairs of the society are once brought to this situation, a nation may lose most of its foreign trade and yet continue a great and powerful people. If strangers will not take any particular commodity of ours, we must cease to labor in it. The same hands will turn themselves toward some refinement in other commodities which may be wanted at home; and there must always be materials for them to work upon, till every person in the state who possesses riches enjoys as great plenty of home commodities, and those in as great perfection as he desires, which can never possibly happen. China is represented as one of the most flourishing empires in the world, though it has very little commerce beyond its own territories.

It will not, I hope, be considered as a superfluous digression if I here observe that as the multitude of mechanical arts is advantageous, so is the great number of persons to whose share the productions of these arts fall. A too great disproportion among the citizens weakens any state. Every person, if possible, ought to enjoy the fruits of his labor in a full possession of all the necessaries and many of the conveniences of life. No one can doubt but such an equality is most suitable to human nature and diminishes much less from the *happiness* of the rich than it adds to that of the poor. It also augments the *power of the state* and makes any extraordinary taxes or impositions be paid with more cheerfulness. Where the riches are engrossed by a few, these must contribute very largely to the supplying of the public necessities; but when the riches are dispersed among multitudes, the burden feels light on every shoulder, and the taxes make not a very sensible difference on anyone's way of living.

Add to this that, where the riches are in few hands, these must enjoy all the power and will readily conspire to lay the whole burden on the poor and oppress them still further, to the discouragement of all industry.

In this circumstance consists the great advantage of England above any nation at present in the world or that appears in the records of any story. It is true the English feel some disadvantages in foreign trade by the high price of labor, which is in part the effect of the riches of their artisans as well as of the plenty of money. But as foreign trade is not the most material circumstance, it is not to be put in competition with the happiness of so many millions; and if there were no more to endear to them that free government under which they live, this alone were sufficient. The poverty of the common people is a natural if not an infallible effect of absolute monarchy; though I doubt whether it be always true, on the other hand, that their riches are an infallible result of liberty. Liberty must be attended with particular accidents and a certain turn of thinking in order to produce that effect. Lord Bacon, accounting for the great advantages obtained by the English in their wars with France, ascribes them chiefly to the superior ease and plenty of the common people among the former; yet the government of the two kingdoms was at that time pretty much alike. Where the laborers and artisans are accustomed to work for low wages and to retain but a small part of the fruits of their labor, it is difficult for them, even in a free government, to better their condition or conspire among themselves to heighten their wages; but even where they are accustomed to a more plentiful way of life, it is easy for the rich, in an arbitrary government, to conspire against *them* and throw the whole burden of the taxes on their shoulders.

It may seem an odd position that the poverty of the common people in France, Italy, and Spain is, in some measure, owing to the superior riches of the soil and happiness of climate; yet there want no reasons to justify this paradox. In such a fine mold or soil as that of those more southern regions, agriculture is an easy art; and one man with a couple of sorry horses will be able, in a season, to cultivate as much land as will pay a pretty considerable rent to the proprietor. All the art which the farmer knows is to leave his ground fallow for a year as soon as it is exhausted, and the warmth of the sun alone and temperature of the climate enrich it and restore its fertility. Such poor peasants, therefore, require only a simple maintenance for their labor. They have no stock or riches which claim more; and at the same time they are forever dependent on the landlord, who gives no leases nor fears that his land will be spoiled by the ill methods of cultivation. In England, the land is rich but coarse, must be cultivated at a great expense, and produces slender crops when not carefully managed and by a method which gives not the full profit but in a course of several years. A farmer, therefore, in England must have a considerable stock and a long lease, which beget proportional profits. The vineyards of Champagne and Burgundy that often yield to the landlord about five pounds per acre are cultivated by peasants who have scarcely bread; the reason is that peasants need no stock but their own limbs with instruments of husbandry which they can buy for twenty shillings. The farmers are commonly in some better circumstances in those countries. But the graziers are most at their ease of all those who cultivate the land. The reason is still the same. Men must have profits proportionable to their expense and hazard. Where so considerable a number of the laboring poor, as the peasants and farmers, are in very low circumstances, all the rest must partake of their poverty, whether the government of that nation be monarchical or republican.

We may form a similar remark with regard to the general history of mankind. What is the reason why no people living between the tropics could ever yet attain to any part of civility or reach even any police in their government and any military discipline, while few nations in the temperate climates have been altogether deprived of these advantages? It is probable that one cause of this phenomenon is the warmth and equality of weather in the torrid zone, which render clothes and houses less requisite for the inhabitants and thereby remove, in part, that necessity which is the great spur to industry and invention. *Curis acuens mortalia corda.*[1] Not to mention that the fewer goods or possessions of this kind any people enjoy, the fewer quarrels are likely to arise amongst them, and the less necessity will there be for a settled police or regular authority to protect and defend them from foreign enemies or from each other.

XVII

OF THE BALANCE OF POWER

IT IS A QUESTION whether the *idea* of the balance of power be owing entirely to modern policy, or whether the *phrase* only has been invented in these later ages? It is certain that Xenophon, in his *Institution of Cyrus*,[a] represents the combination of the Asiatic powers to have arisen from a jealousy of the increasing force of the Medes and Persians; and though that elegant composition should be supposed altogether a romance, this sentiment, ascribed by the author to the Eastern princes, is at least a proof of the prevailing notion of ancient times.

. . . .

In short, the maxim of preserving the balance of power is founded so much on common sense and obvious reasoning that it is impossible it could altogether have escaped antiquity, where we find in other particulars so many marks of deep penetration and discernment. If it was not so generally known and acknowledged as at present, it had at least an influence on all the wiser and more experienced princes and politicians. And indeed, even at present, however generally known and acknowledged among speculative reasoners, it has not in practice an authority much more extensive among those who govern the world.

After the fall of the Roman Empire, the form of government established by the northern conquerors incapacitated them, in a great measure, for further conquests and long maintained each state in its proper boundaries. But when vassalage and the feudal militia were abolished, mankind were anew alarmed by the danger of universal monarchy from the union of so many kingdoms and principalities in the person of the Emperor Charles.[1] But the power of the house of Austria, founded on extensive but divided

a Lib. i.

dominions, and their riches, derived chiefly from mines of gold and silver, were more likely to decay of themselves from internal defects than to overthrow all the bulwarks raised against them. In less than a century, the force of that violent and haughty race was shattered, their opulence dissipated, their splendor eclipsed. A new power succeeded more formidable to the liberties of Europe, possessing all the advantages of the former and laboring under none of its defects, except a share of that spirit of bigotry and persecution with which the house of Austria was so long, and still is, so much infatuated.[b]

In the general wars maintained against this ambitious power, Great Britain has stood foremost, and she still maintains her station. Beside her advantages of riches and situation, her people are animated with such a national spirit and are so fully sensible of the blessings of their government that we may hope their vigor never will languish in so necessary and so just a cause. On the contrary, if we may judge by the past, their passionate ardor seems rather to require some moderation, and they have oftener erred from a laudable excess than from a blamable deficiency.

In the *first* place, we seem to have been more possessed with the ancient Greek spirit of jealous emulation than actuated by the prudent views of modern politics. Our wars with France have been begun with justice, and even perhaps from necessity, but have always been too far pushed, from obstinancy and passion.

---

[b] Europe has now for above a century remained on the defensive against the greatest force that ever perhaps was formed by the civil or political combination of mankind. And such is the influence of the maxim here treated of that, though that ambitious nation in the five last general wars have been victorious in four [*] and unsuccessful only in one,[†] they have not much enlarged their dominions nor acquired a total ascendant over Europe. On the contrary, there remains still hope of maintaining the resistance so long that the natural revolutions of human affairs, together with unforeseen events and accidents, may guard us against universal monarchy and preserve the world from so great an evil.—Editions F, G, H, N.

[*] Those concluded by the peace of the Pyrenees, Nimeguen, Ryswick, and Aix-la-Chapelle.
[†] That concluded by the peace of Utrecht.

The same peace which was afterward made at Ryswick in 1697 was offered so early as the year ninety-two; that concluded at Utrecht in 1712 might have been finished on as good conditions at Gertruytenberg in the year eight; and we might have given at Frankfort in 1743 the same terms which we were glad to accept of at Aix-la-Chapelle in the year forty-eight. Here, then, we see that above half of our wars with France and all our public debts are owing more to our own imprudent vehemence than to the ambition of our neighbors.

In the *second* place, we are so declared in our opposition to French power and so alert in defense of our allies that they always reckon upon our forces as upon their own and, expecting to carry on war at our expense, refuse all reasonable terms of accommodation. *Habent subjectos tanquam suos; viles ut alienos.*[b] All the world knows that the factious vote of the House of Commons in the beginning of the last Parliament, with the professed humor of the nation, made the Queen of Hungary inflexible in her terms and prevented that agreement with Prussia which would immediately have restored the general tranquillity of Europe.

In the *third* place, we are such true combatants that, when once engaged, we lose all concern for ourselves and our posterity and consider only how we may best annoy the enemy. To mortgage our revenues at so deep a rate in wars where we are only accessories was surely the most fatal delusion that a nation which had any pretension to politics and prudence has ever yet been guilty of. That remedy of funding, if it be a remedy and not rather a poison, ought, in all reason, to be reserved to the last extremity; and no evil but the greatest and most urgent should ever induce us to embrace so dangerous an expedient.

These excesses to which we have been carried are prejudicial and may perhaps in time become still more prejudicial another way, by begetting, as is usual, the opposite extreme and rendering us totally careless and supine with regard to the fate of Europe.

. . . .

b [They keep us in submission as if we were their slaves; they consider us cheap because we belong to someone else.—Tacitus. *Hist.* lib. i. See p. 113.]

XVIII

IDEA OF A PERFECT COMMONWEALTH [a]

It is not with forms of government as with other artificial contrivances, where an old engine may be rejected if we can discover another more accurate and commodious or where trials may safely be made even though the success be doubtful. An established government has an infinite advantage by that very circumstance of its being established, the bulk of mankind being governed by authority, not reason, and never attributing authority to anything that has not the recommendation of antiquity.

To tamper, therefore, in this affair or try experiments merely upon the credit of supposed argument and philosophy can never be the part of a wise magistrate, who will bear a reverence to what carries the marks of age; and though he may attempt some improvements for the public good, yet will he adjust his innovations as much as possible to the ancient fabric and preserve entire the chief pillars and supports of the constitution.

The mathematicians in Europe have been much divided concerning that figure of a ship which is the most commodious for sailing; and Huygens,[1] who at last determined the controversy, is justly thought to have obliged the learned as well as commercial world, though Columbus had sailed to America and Sir Francis Drake[2] made the tour of the world without any such discovery. As one form of government must be allowed more perfect than another, independent of the manners and humors of particular men, why may we not inquire what is the most perfect of all, though the common botched and inaccurate governments seem to

[a] "Of all mankind, there are none so pernicious as political projectors if they have power, nor so ridiculous if they want it; as, on the other hand, a wise politician is the most beneficial character in nature if accompanied with authority, and the most innocent and not altogether useless even if deprived of it."—Editions F, G, H. N.

serve the purposes of society and though it be not so easy to establish a new system of government as to build a vessel upon a new construction? The subject is surely the most worthy of curiosity of any the wit of man can possibly devise. And who knows, if this controversy were fixed by the universal consent of the wise and learned, but, in some future age, an opportunity might be afforded of reducing the theory to practice, either by a dissolution of some old government or by the combination of men to form a new one in some distant part of the world? In all cases it must be advantageous to know what is the most perfect in the kind, that we may be able to bring any real constitution or form of government as near it as possible by such gentle alterations and innovations as may not give too great disturbance to society.

All I pretend to in the present Essay is to revive this subject of speculation, and therefore I shall deliver my sentiments in as few words as possible. A long dissertation on that head would not, I apprehend, be very acceptable to the public, who will be apt to regard such disquisitions both as useless and chimerical.

All plans of government which suppose great reformation in the manners of mankind are plainly imaginary. Of this nature are the *Republic* of Plato and the *Utopia* of Sir Thomas More. The *Oceana*[3] is the only valuable model of a commonwealth that has yet been offered to the public.

The chief defects of the *Oceana* seem to be these: *first,* its rotation is inconvenient, by throwing men, of whatever abilities, by intervals, out of public employment. *Secondly,* its *Agrarian* is impracticable. Men will soon learn the art which was practiced in ancient Rome, of concealing their possessions under other people's names, till at last the abuse will become so common that they will throw off even the appearance of restraint. *Thirdly,* the *Oceana* provides not a sufficient security for liberty or the redress of grievances. The senate must propose and the people consent, by which means the senate have not only a negative upon the people but, what is of much greater consequence, their negative goes before the votes of the people. Were the king's negative of the same nature in the English constitution and could he prevent any bill from coming into Parliament, he would be an absolute monarch. As his negative follows the votes of the houses, it is of little consequence; such a difference is there in the manner of placing the same thing. When a popular bill has been debated in Parliament, is brought to maturity, all its conveniences and inconveniences weighed and balanced, if afterward it be presented for the royal assent few princes will venture to reject the unanimous desire of the people. But could the king crush a disagreeable bill in embryo—as was the case for some time in the Scottish Parliament, by means of the Lords of the Articles—the British government would have no balance, nor would grievances ever be redressed; and it is certain that exorbitant power proceeds not in any government from new laws so much as from neglecting to remedy the abuses which frequently rise from the old ones. A government, says Machiavel, must often be brought back to its original principles. It appears, then, that in the *Oceana* the whole legislature may be said to rest in the senate, which Harrington would own to be an inconvenient form of government, especially after the *Agrarian* is abolished.

Here is a form of government to which I cannot, in theory, discover any considerable objection.

Let Great Britain and Ireland, or any territory of equal extent, be divided into one hundred counties, and each county into one hundred parishes, making in all ten thousand. If the country proposed to be erected into a commonwealth be of more narrow extent, we may diminish the number of counties, but never bring them below thirty. If it be of greater extent, it were better to enlarge the parishes or throw more parishes into a county than increase the number of counties.

Let all the freeholders of twenty pounds a year in the county and all the householders worth five hundred pounds in the town parishes meet annually in the parish church and choose by ballot some freeholder of the county for their member, whom we shall call the *county representative*.

Let the one hundred county representatives, two days after their election, meet in the county town and choose by ballot, from their own body, ten county *magistrates* and one senator. There are, therefore, in the whole commonwealth one hundred senators, one thousand and one hundred county magistrates, and ten thousand county representatives, for we shall bestow on all senators the authority of county magistrates and on all county magistrates the authority of county representatives.

Let the senators meet in the capital and be endowed with the whole executive power of the commonwealth: the power of peace and war, of giving orders to generals, admirals, and ambassadors, and, in short, all the prerogatives of a British king except his negative.

Let the county representatives meet in their particular counties and possess the whole legislative power of the commonwealth, the greater number of counties deciding the question; and where these are equal, let the senate have the casting vote.

Every new law must first be debated in the senate; and though rejected by it, if ten senators insist and protest, it must be sent down to the counties. The senate, if they please, may join to the copy of the law their reasons for receiving or rejecting it.

Because it would be troublesome to assemble all the county representatives for every trivial law that may be requisite, the senate have their choice of sending down the law either to the county magistrates or county representatives.

The magistrates, though the law be referred to them, may, if they please, call the representatives and submit the affair to their determination.

Whether the law be referred by the senate to the county magistrates or representatives, a copy of it and of the senate's reasons must be sent to every representative eight days before the day appointed for the assembling, in order to deliberate concerning it. And though the determination be, by the senate, referred to the magistrates, if five representatives of the county order the magistrates to assemble the whole court of representatives and submit the affair to their determination, they must obey.

Either the county magistrates or representatives may give to the senator of the county the copy of a law to be proposed to the senate; and if five counties concur in the same order, the law, though refused by the senate, must come either to the county magistrates or representatives, as is contained in the order of the five counties.

Any twenty counties, by a vote either of their magistrates or representatives, may throw any man out of all public offices for a year, thirty counties for three years.

The senate has a power of throwing out any member or number of members of its own body, not to be re-elected for that year. The senate cannot throw out twice in a year the senator of the same county.

The power of the old senate continues for three weeks after the annual election of the county representatives. Then all the new senators are shut up in a conclave like the cardinals, and by an intricate ballot, such as that of Venice or Malta, they choose the following magistrates: a protector, who represents the dignity of the commonwealth and presides in the senate; two secretaries of state; these six councils—a council of state, a council of religion and learning, a council of trade, a council of laws, a council of war, a council of the admiralty—each council consisting of five persons; together with six commissioners of the treasury and a first commissioner. All these must be senators. The senate also names all the ambassadors to foreign courts, who may either be senators or not.

The senate may continue any or all of these, but must re-elect them every year.

The protector and two secretaries have session and suffrage in the council of state. The business of that council is all foreign politics. The council of state has session and suffrage in all the other councils.

The council of religion and learning inspects the universities and clergy. That of trade inspects everything that may affect commerce. That of laws inspects all the abuses of law by the inferior magistrates and examines what improvements may be made of the municipal law. That of war inspects the militia and its discipline, magazines, stores, etc.; and when the republic is in war, examines into the proper orders for generals. The council of admiralty has the same power with regard to the navy, together with the nomination of the captains and all inferior officers.

None of these councils can give orders themselves, except where they receive such powers from the senate. In other cases, they must communicate everything to the senate.

When the senate is under adjournment, any of the councils may assemble it before the day appointed for its meeting.

Besides these councils or courts, there is another called the *court of competitors,* which is thus constituted. If any candidates for the office of senator have more votes than a third of the representatives, that candidate who has most votes, next to the senator elected, becomes incapable for one year of all public offices, even of being a magistrate or representative; but he takes his seat in the court of competitors. Here then is a court which may sometimes consist of a hundred members, sometimes have no members at all, and by that means be for a year abolished.

The court of competitors has no power in the commonwealth. It has only the inspection of public accounts and the accusing of any man before the senate. If the senate acquit him, the court of competitors may if they please appeal to the people, either magistrates or representatives. Upon that appeal, the magistrates or representatives meet on the day appointed by the court of competitors and choose in each county three persons, from which number every senator is excluded. These, to the number of three hundred, meet in the capital and bring the person accused to a new trial.

The court of competitors may propose any law to the senate, and if refused may appeal to the people, that is, to the magistrates or representatives, who examine it in their counties. Every senator who is thrown out of the senate by a vote of the court takes his seat in the court of competitors.

The senate possesses all the judicative authority of the House of Lords, that is, all the appeals from the inferior courts. It likewise appoints the Lord Chancellor and all the officers of the law.

Every county is a kind of republic within itself, and the representatives may make bylaws, which have no authority till three months after they are voted. A copy of the law is sent to the senate and to every other county. The senate or any single county may at any time annul any bylaw of another county.

The representatives have all the authority of the British justices of the peace in trials, commitments, etc.

The magistrates have the appointment of all the officers of the revenue in each county. All causes with regard to the revenue are carried ultimately by appeal before the magistrates. They pass the accounts of all the officers, but must have their own accounts examined and passed at the end of the year by the representatives.

The magistrates name rectors or ministers to all the parishes.

The Presbyterian government is established, and the highest ecclesiastical court is an assembly or synod of all the presbyters of the county. The magistrates may take any cause from this court and determine it themselves.

The magistrates may try and depose or suspend any presbyter.

The militia is established in imitation of that of Switzerland, which, being well known, we shall not insist upon it. It will only be proper to make this addition that an army of twenty thousand men be annually drawn out by rotation, paid and encamped during six weeks in summer, that the duty of a camp may not be altogether unknown.

The magistrates appoint all the colonels and downward, the senate all upward. During war the general appoints the colonel and downward, and his commission is good for a twelvemonth, but after that it must be confirmed by the magistrates of the county to which the regiment belongs. The magistrates may break any officer in the county regiment, and the senate may do the same to any officer in the service. If the magistrates do not think proper to confirm the general's choice, they may appoint another officer in the place of him they reject.

All crimes are tried within the county by the magistrates and a jury, but the senate can stop any trial and bring it before themselves.

Any county may indict any man before the senate for any crime.

The protector, the two secretaries, the council of state, with any five or more that the senate appoints, are possessed on extraordinary emergencies of *dictatorial* power for six months.

The protector may pardon any person condemned by the inferior courts.

In time of war no officer of the army that is in the field can have any civil office in the commonwealth.

The capital, which we shall call London, may be allowed four members in the senate. It may therefore be divided into four counties. The representatives of each of these choose one senator and ten magistrates. There are therefore in the city four senators, forty-four magistrates, and four hundred representatives. The magistrates have the same authority as in the counties. The representatives also have the same authority, but they never meet in one general court; they give their votes in their particular county or division of hundreds.

When they enact any bylaw, the greater number of counties or divisions determines the matter. And where these are equal, the magistrates have the casting vote.

The magistrates choose the mayor, sheriff, recorder, and other officers of the city.

In the commonwealth, no representative, magistrate, or senator, as such, has any salary. The protector, secretaries, councils, and ambassadors have salaries.

The first year in every century is set apart for correcting all inequalities which time may have produced in the representative. This must be done by the legislature.

The following political aphorisms may explain the reason of these orders.

The lower sort of people and small proprietors are good enough judges of one not very distant from them in rank or habitation, and therefore, in their parochial meetings, will probably choose the best or nearly the best representative. But they are wholly unfit for county meetings and for electing into the higher offices of the republic. Their ignorance gives the grandees an opportunity of deceiving them.

Ten thousand, even though they were not annually elected, are a basis large enough for any free government. It is true, the nobles in Poland are more than ten thousand, and yet these oppress the people. But as power always continues there in the same persons and families, this makes them in a manner a different nation from the people. Besides, the nobles are there united under a few heads of families.

All free governments must consist of two councils, a lesser and greater, or, in other words, of a senate and people. The people, as Harrington observes, would want wisdom without the senate; the senate, without the people, would want honesty.

A large assembly of one thousand, for instance, to represent the people, if allowed to debate, would fall into disorder. If not allowed to debate, the senate has a negative upon them and the worst kind of negative, that before resolution.

Here, therefore, is an inconvenience which no government has yet fully remedied but which is the easiest to be remedied in the world. If the people debate, all is confusion. If they do not debate, they can only resolve, and then the senate carves for them. Divide the people into many separate bodies, and then they may debate with safety and every inconvenience seems to be prevented.

Cardinal de Retz [4] says that all numerous assemblies, however composed, are mere mob, and swayed in their debates by the least motive. This we find confirmed by daily experience. When an absurdity strikes a member, he conveys it to his neighbor, and so on till the whole be infected. Separate this great body, and though every member be only of middling sense, it is not probable that anything but reason can prevail over the whole. Influence and example being removed, good sense will always get the better of bad among a number of people.[b]

There are two things to be guarded against in every senate: its combination and its division. Its combination is most dangerous; and against this inconvenience we have provided the following remedies: (1) The great dependence of the senators on the people by annual elections, and that not by an undistinguished rabble, like the English electors, but by men of fortune and education. (2) The small power they are allowed. They have few offices to dispose of; almost all are given by the magistrates in the counties. (3) The court of competitors, which, being composed of men that are their rivals next to them in interest and uneasy in their present situation, will be sure to take all advantages against them.

The division of the senate is prevented: (1) By the smallness of their number. (2) As faction supposes a combination in a separate interest, it is prevented by their dependence on the

[b] "Good sense is one thing, but follies are numberless; and every man has a different one. The only way of making a people wise is to keep them from uniting into large assemblies."

people. (3) They have a power of expelling any factious member. It is true, when another member of the same spirit comes from the county, they have no power of expelling him; nor is it fit they should, for that shows the humor to be in the people, and may possibly arise from some ill conduct in public affairs. (4) Almost any man, in a senate so regularly chosen by the people, may be supposed fit for any civil office. It would be proper, therefore, for the senate to form some *general* resolutions with regard to the disposing of offices among the members, which resolutions would not confine them in critical times, when extraordinary parts on the one hand or extraordinary stupidity on the other appears in any senator; but they would be sufficient to prevent intrigue and faction by making the disposal of the offices a thing of course. For instance, let it be a resolution that no man shall enjoy any office till he has sat four years in the senate; that, except ambassadors, no man shall be in office two years following; that no man shall attain the higher offices but through the lower; that no man shall be protector twice, etc. The senate of Venice govern themselves by such resolutions.

In foreign politics the interest of the senate can scarcely ever be divided from that of the people, and therefore it is fit to make the senate absolute with regard to them; otherwise there could be no secrecy or refined policy. Besides, without money no alliance can be executed, and the senate is still sufficiently dependent. Not to mention that the legislative power, being always superior to the executive, the magistrates or representatives may interpose whenever they think proper.

The chief support of the British government is the opposition of interest, but that, though in the main serviceable, breeds endless factions. In the foregoing plan, it does all the good without any of the harm. The *competitors* have no power of controlling the senate; they have only the power of accusing and appealing to the people.

It is necessary, likewise, to prevent both combination and division in the thousand magistrates. This is done sufficiently by the separation of places and interests.

But, lest that should not be sufficient, their dependence on the ten thousand for their elections serves to the same purpose.

Nor is that all; for the ten thousand may resume the power whenever they please, and not only when they all please, but when any five of a hundred please, which will happen upon the very first suspicion of a separate interest.

The ten thousand are too large a body either to unite or divide, except when they meet in one place and fall under the guidance of ambitious leaders. Not to mention their annual election by the whole body of the people that are of any consideration.

A small commonwealth is the happiest government in the world within itself, because everything lies under the eye of the rulers. But it may be subdued by great force from without. This scheme seems to have all the advantages both of a great and a little commonwealth.

Every county law may be annulled either by the senate or another county, because that shows an opposition of interest, in which case no part ought to decide for itself. The matter must be referred to the whole, which will best determine what agrees with general interest.

As to the clergy and militia, the reasons of these orders are obvious. Without the dependence of the clergy on the civil magistrates, and without a militia, it is in vain to think that any free government will ever have security or stability.

In many governments, the inferior magistrates have no rewards but what arise from their ambition, vanity, or public spirit. The salaries of the French judges amount not to the interest of the sums they pay for their offices. The Dutch burgomasters have little more immediate profit than the English justices of peace or the members of the House of Commons formerly. But lest any should suspect that this would beget negligence in the administration (which is little to be feared, considering the natural ambition of mankind), let the magistrates have competent salaries. The senators have access to so many honorable and lucrative offices that their attendance needs not be bought. There is little attendance required of the representatives.

That the foregoing plan of government is practicable no one can doubt who considers the resemblance that it bears to the commonwealth of the United Provinces, a wise and renowned government. The alterations in the present scheme seem all evidently for the better. (1) The representation is more equal. (2) The unlimited power of the burgomasters in the towns, which forms a perfect aristocracy in the Dutch commonwealth, is corrected by a well-tempered democracy, in giving to the people the annual election of the county representatives. (3) The negative, which every province and town has upon the whole body of the Dutch Republic with regard to alliances, peace and war, and the imposition of taxes, is here removed. (4) The counties, in the present plan, are not so independent of each other; nor do they form separate bodies so much as the seven provinces, where the jealousy and envy of the smaller provinces and towns against the greater, particularly Holland and Amsterdam, have frequently disturbed the government. (5) Larger powers, though of the safest kind, are intrusted to the senate than the States-General possess, by which means the former may become more expeditious and secret in their resolutions than it is possible for the latter.

The chief alterations that could be made on the British government, in order to bring it to the most perfect model of limited monarchy, seem to be the following. *First,* the plan of Cromwell's Parliament ought to be restored, by making the representation equal, and by allowing none to vote in the county elections who possess not a property of two-hundred-pound value. *Secondly,* as such a House of Commons would be too weighty for a frail House of Lords like the present, the bishops and Scotch peers ought to be removed. The number of the upper house ought to be raised to three or four hundred, the seats not hereditary but during life. They ought to have the election of their own members, and no commoner should be allowed to refuse a seat that was offered him. By this means the House of Lords would consist entirely of the men of chief credit, abilities, and interest in the nation; and every turbulent leader in the House of Commons might be taken off and connected by interest with the House of Peers. Such an aristocracy would be an excellent barrier both to the monarchy and against it. At present, the balance of our government depends in some measure on the abilities and behavior of the sovereign, which are variable and uncertain circumstances.

This plan of limited monarchy, however corrected, seems still liable to three great inconveniences. *First*, it removes not entirely, though it may soften, the parties of *Court* and *Country*. *Secondly*, the king's personal character must still have great influence on the government. *Thirdly*, the sword is in the hands of a single person, who will always neglect to discipline the militia in order to have a pretense for keeping up a standing army.

We shall conclude this subject with observing the falsehood of the common opinion that no large state such as France or Great Britain could ever be modeled into a commonwealth, but that such a form of government can only take place in a city or small territory. The contrary seems probable. Though it is more difficult to form a republican government in an extensive country than in a city, there is more facility, when once it is formed, of preserving it steady and uniform without tumult and faction. It is not easy for the distant parts of a large state to combine in any plan of free government; but they easily conspire in the esteem and reverence for a single person who, by means of this popular favor, may seize the power and, forcing the more obstinate to submit, may establish a monarchical government. On the other hand, a city readily concurs in the same notions of government, the natural equality of property favors liberty, and the nearness of habitation enables the citizens mutually to assist each other. Even under absolute princes, the subordinate government of cities is commonly republican, while that of counties and provinces is monarchical. But these same circumstances which facilitate the erection of commonwealths in cities render their constitution more frail and uncertain. Democracies are turbulent. For however the people may be separated or divided into small parties, either in their votes or elections, their near habitation in a city will always make the force of popular tides and currents very sensible. Aristocracies are better adapted for peace and order, and accordingly were most admired by ancient writers; but they are jealous and oppressive. In a large government which is modeled with masterly skill, there is compass and room enough to refine the democracy, from the lower people who may be admitted into the first elections or first concoction of the commonwealth to the higher magistrates who direct all the movements. At the same time, the parts are so distant and remote that it is very difficult, either by intrigue, prejudice, or passion, to hurry them into any measures against the public interest.

It is needless to inquire whether such a government would be immortal. I allow the justness of the poet's exclamation on the endless projects of human race, "Man and forever!" The world itself probably is not immortal. Such consuming plagues may arise as would leave even a perfect government a weak prey to its neighbors. We know not to what length enthusiasm or other extraordinary movements of the human mind may transport men to the neglect of all order and public good. Where difference of interest is removed, whimsical, unaccountable factions often arise from personal favor or enmity. Perhaps rust may grow to the springs of the most accurate political machine and disorder its motions. Lastly, extensive conquests, when pursued, must be the ruin of every free government, and of the more perfect governments sooner than of the imperfect because of the very advantages which the former possess above the latter. And though such a state ought to establish a fundamental law against conquests, yet republics have ambition as well as individuals, and present interest makes men forgetful of their posterity. It is a sufficient incitement to human endeavors that such a government would flourish for many ages, without pretending to bestow on any work of man that immortality which the Almighty seems to have refused to his own productions.

NOTES

INTRODUCTION

1. Edmund Jennings Randolph (1753–1813), former aide-de-camp to General Washington, was a prominent Virginian who served Virginia as Attorney General, as member of the Continental Congress, and later as Governor. As delegate to the Constitutional Convention in 1787, Randolph proposed the famous "Virginia plan," upon which our federal government was subsequently modeled. The plan provided for three separate branches of government—the legislature to consist of two houses with proportional representation in each, a single executive, and a national judiciary to be chosen by the legislature. Randolph refused to sign the Constitution on the ground that it was not sufficiently republican in character, but nevertheless urged Virginia to ratify it. He later served as Attorney General for the Federal Government and as Secretary of State. In 1795 he resumed the practice of law in Virginia, and in 1807 was chief counsel for Aaron Burr when the latter was tried for treason.

2. Elbridge Gerry (1744–1814) was one of the signers of the Declaration of Independence and of the Articles of Confederation and later was elected Congressman from Massachusetts. He was a member of the famous XYZ mission to France in 1797–1798. As Governor of Massachusetts in 1810–1811, Gerry's name became associated with a plan to redistrict the state in such a way as to continue Republican control, giving rise to the famous term "gerrymander." Gerry was elected Vice-President of the United States in 1813 and died the following year.

3. George Mason (1725–1792), wealthy Virginia planter and Revolutionary statesman, was a member of the Virginia Constitutional Convention of 1776. He prepared the Declaration of Rights and wrote most of the constitution for Virginia, and later proposed the plan whereby Virginia agreed to relinquish her claims to land in the undeveloped West in favor of national ownership. As a member of the Federal Constitutional Convention, Mason refused to sign the Constitution and actively opposed Virginia's ratification. Though elected, he also declined to serve as first United States Senator from his state.

4. Gouveneur Morris (1752–1816), a New York lawyer who worked tirelessly for the colonial cause, was one of the signers

159

of the Articles of Confederation and the Constitution, and a member of the Continental Congress. As United States Minister to France from 1792 to 1794, Morris kept a diary which later was published as *A Diary of the French Revolution 1789–1893* and is regarded as an important sourcebook on that historic event.

I. OF THE LIBERTY OF THE PRESS

1. François Marie Arouet (1694–1778), known as "Voltaire." *La Henriade* (printed secretly, 1723) is an epic poem against intolerance, with special reference to Henry IV of France. The translation of the passage which Hume quotes reads as follows: "And he made the untamed English like his yoke, Who can neither serve nor live in liberty."

2. By "the republican part of the government" Hume is referring to the English House of Commons.

3. The Court of the Star Chamber (created by Henry VII) was a high civil and criminal court which decided its cases without juries. It had almost unlimited powers of prosecution and became an instrument of persecution. It consisted of members of the king's Privy Council and two judges appointed by the king. It was finally abolished by the "Long Parliament" in 1641.

II. THAT POLITICS MAY BE REDUCED TO A SCIENCE

1. Henry III (r. 1574–89) was the last king of the House of Valois. He was involved in the plotting of the Massacre of St. Bartholomew (1572). His reign was marked by persecution of the Huguenots. Henry IV (r. 1589–1610) was brought up as a Calvinist but renounced Protestantism in 1593. He issued the Edict of Nantes in 1598, guaranteeing the Huguenots freedom of religious exercise.

2. Elsewhere Hume mentions "the spirit of tyranny, of which nations are as susceptible as individuals," in reference to the treatment of Ireland by England. (*History of England,* Vol. VI, Ch. LXIV, p. 71.)

3. The three Punic Wars, between Rome and Carthage, covered a period of over one hundred years, dating: 264–241 B.C., 218–201 B.C., and 149–146 B.C., respectively.

4. The First Triumvirate consisted of Pompey, Julius Caesar, and Marcus Licinius Crassus, who took over the government of

Rome in 60 B.C. The Second Triumvirate, which governed Rome from 43 to 31 B.C., was composed of Octavius, Mark Antony, and Lepidus.

5. The reference throughout this passage is to Sir Robert Walpole (1676–1745), prime minister from 1715 to 1717 and again from 1721 to 1742. A controversial but powerful figure, it was he who unified cabinet government in the person of the prime minister and managed to transfer power from the House of Lords to the House of Commons.

6. The reference is to the "Glorious Revolution" of 1688 and the subsequent accession of William and Mary. William III ruled jointly with Mary from 1689 until her death in 1694 and then as sole sovereign until 1702.

7. Reference here is to Marcus Porcius Cato (234–149 B.C.), "Cato the Elder," and to Marcus Junius Brutus (85?–42 B.C.), called "patriots" because they opposed the dictatorship of the First Triumvirate (see note 4 above).

8. The Court party was a popular name for the royalists who supported the Stuarts. The Country party was formed to defend the rights of the people against the renewed encroachments of the Stuarts on Parliament. The Court party later became the Tories and the Country party, the Whigs. Cf. Hume's own essay, "Of the Parties of Great Britain," p. 85. See also Note XI, 3.

III. OF THE FIRST PRINCIPLES OF GOVERNMENT

1. Hume is referring here to Locke's *Second Treatise of Government* (1690). Cf. Chapter IX, "Of the Ends of Political Society and Government."

2. Reference is here to William III. See Note II, 6.

VI. OF THE ORIGINAL CONTRACT

1. The divine-rights theory, which was revived subsequent to the formation of the nation-state, became the major argument to justify absolute power of the monarch. His right to govern was traced to God's command. Consequently, he could do no wrong, nor forfeit his right to the obedience of the people. In England, the foremost representative of this theory was James I (r. 1603–1625), who took an active part in the controversy. His most important work is *The True Law of Free Monarchies* (1589).

2. "The other party" are the defenders of the natural rights of

the individual, a theory designed to limit royal power and enhance the concept of self-government. The interpretation of natural right as a right of the individual to political equality entered political thought in England through the arguments of the Levellers and later found its most effective formulation in Locke's *Second Treatise of Government.* Cf. also the Introduction, p. xlvi.

3. Cf. Locke's *Second Treatise of Government,* especially §§ 4, 22, 61, 95, and 123.

4. "Republican writers" were the political theorists who favored the sovereignty of Parliament. They were not necessarily anti-monarchical. The foremost representatives of this group were, among others, Milton, Harrington, Algernon Sidney, Halifax, and Locke.

5. The Revolution of 1688.

6. Hume refers here to the fact that William and Mary were invited to rule, not by popular vote, but by a majority of the members of Parliament.

7. Henry IV (r. 1399–1413) was formally declared king by Parliament after he invaded England and defeated Richard II. Henry VII (r. 1485–1509) was acknowledged as king after he had invaded England and defeated Richard III.

8. Henry VIII (r. 1509–47) proclaimed, with the approval of Parliament, the Act of Supremacy (1534), which separated the Catholic Church in England from the Roman Catholic Church, constituted an independent Anglican Church, and appointed the king the supreme head of the Church and its clergy.

9. Charles I (r. 1625–49) dissolved three Parliaments in four years for non-compliance and ruled for eleven years without Parliament, causing the Civil War of 1642–45. He was later condemned as a tyrant and enemy of the nation by a court constituted by the House of Commons and was beheaded in 1649.

10. Reference here is to the rivalry between the houses of York and Lancaster for the throne of England. This rivalry brought on the Wars of the Roses, so called because the emblem of the House of York was a white rose and that of Lancaster a red rose.

11. Hume refers here to Edward III of England (r. 1327–77) and his claim to the throne of France. The war with Philip of France (r. 1328–50) precipitated the Hundred Years' War (1337–1453).

12. "In the midst of these events Gordian Caesar was acclaimed by the army. He was declared 'imperator,' because there was no other 'imperator' at the moment."

13. On Tories and Whigs, see "Of the Parties of Great Britain," pp. 85 ff. Cf. Introduction, p. xlii.

VII. OF PASSIVE OBEDIENCE

1. For Charles I, see Note VI, 9. James II (r. 1685–88) was overthrown and forced to flee the country, in the Revolution of 1688.

IX. WHETHER THE BRITISH GOVERNMENT INCLINES MORE TO ABSOLUTE MONARCHY OR TO A REPUBLIC

1. Cf. James Harrington (1611–77): *The Commonwealth of Oceana* (1656) and his "Aphorisms" on government.

X. OF PARTIES IN GENERAL

1. The Guelfs and the Ghibellines were the primary rival parties in Italy from the twelfth to the fifteenth centuries, the former being partisans of the Pope and the latter supporting the authority of the German emperors in Italy.

XI. OF THE PARTIES OF GREAT BRITAIN

1. I. e., the House of Commons. See also Note I, 2.

2. Reference here is to Charles I. See Note VI, 9.

3. During the reign of Charles I, "Roundhead" and "Cavalier" were popular names for the Country party and the Court party respectively. The former were so called because they cut their hair short. See also Note II, 8.

XII. OF THE COALITION OF PARTIES

1. Plantagenet was the English royal house which occupied the throne of England continuously from 1154 to 1399 as the House of Anjou, and then through its descendents, the warring houses of York and Lancaster (see Note VI, 10), until 1485.

The Tudors occupied the throne from 1485 until 1603; and the Stuarts from 1603 to 1688 (except for the period of the Commonwealth from 1649–60).

2. The Magna Charta was signed by John I on June 15, 1215. Although it guaranteed freedom and a voice in the affairs of state solely to the barons of the realm, it is generally considered the basic document in the progress of the British people toward individual liberty. The terms of the Magna Charta were often violated by subsequent rulers, and the time from 1215 to 1688 is marked by an almost uninterrupted struggle of the people not only to enforce the basic principles of the Magna Charta, but also to broaden their application by extending the guarantees to the commons and by assigning the major voice in the affairs of state to Parliament. The Revolution of 1688 decided this contest in favor of Parliament.

XIII. OF CIVIL LIBERTY

1. Lucius Aelius Sejanus (died 31 A.D.) attempted, unsuccessfully, to usurp the throne of Emperor Tiberius. André Hercule de Fleury (1653–1743), a French Cardinal and statesman, had great influence over Louis XV and became in effect, but not in title, prime minister of France (1726–43).

2. The family of Medici was the ruling house of Florence from the fourteenth to the sixteenth century. Lodovico Ariosto (1474–1533) and Torquato Tasso (1544–95) were Italian poets; Galileo (1564–1642), Italian astronomer and physicist; Raphael (1483–1520), Italian painter; Michelangelo (1475–1564), Italian painter, sculptor, and poet.

3. "Traces of our rustic provenience have nevertheless survived for a long time and still survive today."

4. Jonathan Swift (1667–1745) was an English writer and satirist. His best known works are *Gulliver's Travels* (1726), *A Tale of a Tub*, and *The Battle of the Books* (both, 1704).

5. Thomas Sprat (1635–1713), English prelate, writer, and poet; John Locke (1632–1704), English philosopher and political theorist (see Note VI, 2); Sir William Temple (1628–99), English statesman, essayist, and diplomat; Francis Bacon (1561–1626), English philosopher; James Harrington (1611–77), English political theorist; and John Milton (1608–74), English poet and political writer advocating the sovereignty of Parliament.

XIV. OF THE RISE AND PROGRESS OF THE ARTS AND SCIENCES

1. "The Genius knows, the companion who rules the star of our birth, the God of the nature of man, although he is mortal for each individual, and although his face changes, being white or black."

2. Decemvirs: In 451 B.C. a commission of patrician decemvirs was given temporary dictatorship to codify and make public the law, which hitherto had been subject to arbitrary interpretation by the (patrician) magistrates. The commission prepared ten tables which, together with two tables drawn up by a new commission of decemvirs appointed in the following year, formed the celebrated Law of the Twelve Tables. However, these laws favored the patricians and thus laid the legal ground for the century-long struggle of the plebeians to gain political equality. The second commission tried to perpetuate itself in office but was forced by a threatening revolt of the plebeians to resign.

3. Hume is referring here to the plays, *Pericles, Prince of Tyre* (1608?), and *Othello, the Moor of Venice* (1604), both by Shakespeare, and to *Every Man in His Humor* (1598) and *Volpone, or the Fox* (1607), by Ben Jonson.

4. Edmund Waller (1606–87), English poet and political writer defending the royalist cause.

XV. OF REFINEMENT IN THE ARTS

1. Charles VIII (r. 1483–98) attempted to reinstate the House of Anjou in Naples and entered Naples in 1495. He was driven out later in the same year by the forces of Ferdinand II of Naples. Francesco Guicciardini (1483–1540), Italian statesman, was the author of *Storia d'Italia* (16 books published in 1561; 4 books, 1564), the major historical work of his time.

2. Jules Mazarin (1602–61), French Cardinal and statesman, succeeded Richelieu as prime minister (1642). The "late king" mentioned by Hume was Louis XIV (r. 1643–1715).

3. Sallust (86–34 B.C.), Roman historian and author of *History of the Jugurthine War, Conspiracy of Catiline,* and *History of the Roman Republic.*

XVI. OF COMMERCE

1. "Exciting mortal hearts with cares."

XVII. OF THE BALANCE OF POWER

1. Reference is here to the Holy Roman Emperor Charles V (r. 1519–56), of whom it was said that the sun never set on his realm, which extended over three continents and was the largest known until that time.

XVIII. IDEA OF A PERFECT COMMONWEALTH

1. Christian Huygens (1629–95), Dutch astronomer and mathematician.

2. Sir Francis Drake (1545?–96), English navigator and the first man known to have sailed around the world (1577–80).

3. *The Commonwealth of Oceana* by the English political theorist, James Harrington (1611–77).

4. Cardinal de Retz (1614–79), French politician. His *Memoires* give a picture of contemporary court life.